A Jungian and Psychoanalytic Approach to Biblical Myth and Religion

This book describes some of the major psychological processes that underpin various biblical stories and some of the theological speculation to which they have given rise. Psychological biblical criticism, as described here, is suggested as an alternative or supplement to historical-cultural, textual, philological, literary, and other types of biblical criticism.

Using a combination of Jungian and psychoanalytic theory, Corbett shows how some biblical material arises from human psychodynamics, while some originates in the archetypal level of the psyche and is further elaborated as it passes through the human level of the psyche. The author addresses some of the traditional anxieties about psychological approaches to biblical stories. He views Jung's approach as an evolving mythology of the sacred that offers an alternative to purely theological approaches to the Bible and to the traditions that emerged from it.

This book will be of value to practicing psychotherapists and analysts, particularly those who treat patients with a religious background, as well as trainees, clergy, and graduate students in this area.

Lionel Corbett is a psychiatrist and Jungian analyst. He is the author of seven books and co-author of four volumes of collected papers. His primary interest is in Jung's concept of the religious function of the psyche.

A Jungian and Psychoanalytic Approach to Biblical Myth and Religion

Lionel Corbett

Routledge
Taylor & Francis Group
LONDON AND NEW YORK

Designed cover image: © Getty

First published 2025
by Routledge
4 Park Square, Milton Park, Abingdon, Oxon OX14 4RN

and by Routledge
605 Third Avenue, New York, NY 10158

Routledge is an imprint of the Taylor & Francis Group, an informa business

© 2025 Lionel Corbett

The right of Lionel Corbett to be identified as author of this work has been asserted in accordance with sections 77 and 78 of the Copyright, Designs and Patents Act 1988.

All rights reserved. No part of this book may be reprinted or reproduced or utilised in any form or by any electronic, mechanical, or other means, now known or hereafter invented, including photocopying and recording, or in any information storage or retrieval system, without permission in writing from the publishers.

Trademark notice: Product or corporate names may be trademarks or registered trademarks, and are used only for identification and explanation without intent to infringe.

British Library Cataloguing-in-Publication Data
A catalogue record for this book is available from the British Library

ISBN: 978-1-032-88278-9 (hbk)
ISBN: 978-1-032-88276-5 (pbk)
ISBN: 978-1-003-53700-7 (ebk)

DOI: 10.4324/9781003537007

Typeset in Times New Roman
by SPi Technologies India Pvt Ltd (Straive)

Contents

	Introduction: Psyche as the source of religious imagery and religious experience	1
1	The psychological approach to religion and the Bible	6
2	Religions as expressions of the psyche	24
3	The psyche expresses itself in the Bible	38
4	The Bible as a mythic text	50
5	Psychopathology in religious traditions and texts	69
6	Religious narcissism and power dynamics in religion	125
7	Mental illness in biblical characters	140
8	The psychodynamics of religions' emphasis on sin	153
9	The biblical portrayal of Jesus	163
	References	*189*
	Index	*199*

Introduction
Psyche as the source of religious imagery and religious experience

This book describes some of the psychological processes that are relevant to religious beliefs, to biblical stories, and to the doctrines and dogmas to which these stories have given rise. The book is based on Jung's ideas that "religious statements are psychic confessions" (CW 11, para. 555) and "statements made in the Holy Scriptures are also utterances of the soul" (ibid., para. 557). In his model, religion and the Bible reveal the psyche unfolded. Some biblical and theological material arises from human psychodynamics, while some originates in the archetypal level of the psyche and is given color and texture as it passes through the psyche's human levels.

For Jung, because religious experiences are products of the psyche, they do not need to be seen as emanating from a metaphysical deity in a heavenly realm. The experience of transcendent reality reported by characters in biblical stories is the result of their contact with non-ego, archetypal, or transpersonal levels of the psyche. The theological structures and metaphysical beliefs built upon these experiences are also products of the psyche.

Theological interpretations of biblical stories are not necessary for Jung's approach to religion. The psychologist can approach the Bible, religious ideas, and religious experiences using psychological interpretive methods. Theologians are sometimes concerned that such a purely psychological approach reduces religion and religious experience to "nothing but" psychological processes rather than acknowledging religion's transcendent source. These theologians do not believe that their metaphysical categories can be fully explained in terms of psychology. The attempt to do so is referred to as "psychologism."[1] The concern is that to view religion psychologically seems to make doctrinal ideas and notions of divinity less meaningful or less real. Psychology seems to ignore the element of mystery in religious experiences, or it risks violating their sacred nature. Consequently, theologians are often concerned to differentiate their interpretations of the Bible and religious experience from psychological approaches, as if only theology is competent to deal with religious realities such as the experience of the sacred or divinity's self-disclosure. Theologians believe that such experience should not be (or cannot legitimately be) subject to psychological scrutiny alone, without benefit of doctrine and dogma.

However, Jung believes that because both religious experience and the resulting metaphysical speculation arise from the archetypal level of the psyche and from the Self, which he terms the "God within us" (CW 7, para. 399), a psychological approach to spiritual experience is based on the real presence of the sacred as it manifests itself psychologically. For Jung, the numinous quality of such experience is sufficient to recognize its transpersonal quality, whether or not its content fits within a preexisting theological framework (Corbett, 2020). The ultimate mystery and sacredness of numinous material are not reduced by seeing it as a product of the psyche.

Whether they are found in the Bible or in a dream, religious symbols and imagery always convey a depth of meaning far beyond their surface manifestations. This meaning is often impossible to capture in the net of conceptual thought and can be expressed only in mythic imagery. Our understanding of this material cannot be limited to its traditional doctrinal and dogmatic interpretations, which would limit our appreciation of it. The interpretation of religious experiences and biblical material does do not need to be confined within the limits of a preexisting religious system such as Christianity or Judaism. These experiences can be amplified using psychological interpretive approaches. Jung's approach therefore offers an alternative to traditional theological understanding of the religious function of the psyche and the human religious impulse.

The theologian's interpretations of sacred texts such as the Bible are often biased in terms of the theologian's own tradition. Analogously, psychological approaches to sacred texts are a function of the psychologist's favorite theory. In this book, I have largely used a combination of Jungian psychology and psychoanalytic self-psychology to discuss the archetypal underpinnings and the personal psychodynamics found in biblical stories and their theological elaboration. Like all mythic imagery, biblical material has many levels of meaning, so that different psychological theories may be necessary to illumine any given Bible story.

For the psychological approach to the Bible to be relevant, we have to assume that some of the psychological dynamics that we recognize today were also operating in the minds of the biblical authors and that these dynamics will be reflected in their texts. That is, the psychologist assumes there are some fundamental aspects of the archetypal psyche, and of human nature and human psychology, that have remained constant over time in spite of profound cultural changes. By acknowledging the importance of the unconscious, depth psychology casts light on hitherto unexamined or neglected aspects of the biblical text while acknowledging the importance of historical, cultural, and other hermeneutic approaches to the Bible. Even for those who believe that the Bible is divinely inspired, this inspiration has to be refracted through the prism of the psyche of the writer, including not only the writer's religious and social concerns but also his complexes, defenses, prejudices, and other mental mechanisms.

I adopt the view that much biblical material is legendary, folkloric, or mythic and not necessarily historically based. However, on the mistaken assumption that the Bible's mythic stories are literal history, theologians have built an enormous superstructure of doctrine and dogma onto them. The resulting interpretation of biblical stories has been the subject of a great deal of controversy and speculation since the founding of the biblical traditions. These theological interpretations of the Bible can themselves be analyzed psychologically. Just as we see archetypal and personal psychodynamic elements in the text, we also see them in the doctrine and dogma to which the text has given rise. This material is colored by the psychology of its authors and by factors such as the need of religious hierarchies to maintain control of their congregations' beliefs. Some biblical theology was based on its authors' need to cope with and explain existential threats such as famine or plague. Theological speculation was used to explain successes and defeats in battle, while some arose from purely narcissistic motivations such as the need to be special to God or to feel superior to other traditions. Some of these personality dynamics are unconscious. The idea that the God-image of one's own tradition is superior to that of all the others, or that only adherents to one's own tradition are chosen or saved, is also colored by the human narcissistic need to be special. Our contemporary understanding of narcissism is therefore relevant to the study of the Bible and the religions that emerged from it.

Some of the biblical authors' theology was based on their attempts to articulate and understand their experience of the Self and the archetypal levels of the psyche, which they projectively attributed to an external deity who lived in a heavenly realm. Not only their direct experience of the sacred but also human level psychodynamics colored the resulting image of God.

Doctrines and dogmas have symbolic, archetypal as well as theological meanings. The clarification of their psychological underpinnings, rather than being a challenge to the traditions, may even allow them to become relevant again, at a time when some religious teachings clash either with our experience or with science. Doctrine and dogma often seem to be irrelevant to daily life because their original meaning is lost in the unconscious. That is why, speaking of metaphysical ideas, Jung wanted to "take these thought-forms that have become historically fixed [and] try to melt them down again and pour them into molds of immediate experience" (CW 11, para. 148). This potential for the renewal of traditional doctrines that have become rigid is accomplished in part by reinterpreting them symbolically.

One of the ways the psychological approach is useful is that it reveals the projection onto divinity of human psychological traits. For example, the Bible is replete with violence that is assumed to be an attribute of the divine. Isaiah 34: 5–6 says: "The Lord has a sword: it is sated with blood." In an act of divine vengeance against Yhwh's enemies, "the sword shall devour and be sated, and drink its fill of their blood" (Jeremiah, 46: 10). This kind of language appalls and repulses the modern reader. Such blood lust, made manifest in the idea that God requires blood sacrifices or commands the massacre of the inhabitants of conquered cities, results from the projection of human violence onto divinity. Theological ideas about the nature of divinity are often based on such characteristics of human psychology, which can be understood in psychodynamic terms.

Throughout the book, I use male pronouns to talk about the biblical God, in order to correspond with the biblical usage, purely out of custom and convenience. Biblical quotations are based on the New Revised Version of the Bible unless otherwise stated.

Why this book arose

This book emerged in part because during many years of working with religious people in psychotherapy and Jungian analysis, I have often discovered a relationship between important intrapsychic dynamics and the individual's religious beliefs. Unconscious residues from childhood religious indoctrination may still affect adult behavior. I then have to understand the individual's religious background in order to understand some of his or her psychological constitution. Conversely, understanding the individual's psychological structures would help me understand why he or she was drawn to particular theological beliefs. The individual's psychology and theology seem to mutually interpenetrate.

While teaching analytic trainees and graduate students in depth psychology and psychotherapy, I find that many have little or no interest in religion and only a limited idea of the basic tenets of Christianity and Judaism. Many contemporary students and psychotherapists grew up with no acquaintance with the Bible or with religious language. Words such as "grace" or "covenant" have little meaning or importance to many students, so they may not grasp how these ideas affect their clients' thinking and feeling. I have therefore summarized some of the major theological concepts and biblical stories that are central to the theistic traditions as I try to show their psychological roots.

I confess to some distress when I find that even trainees in Jungian training programs do not pay much attention to Jung's ideas about religion. I hope this book will show how these ideas are central to his psychology. Just as Jung (CW 11, para. 559) wrote that his work on the biblical Job was not the work of a biblical scholar but that of a "layman and a physician," I offer this text in the same spirit.

Note

1 Raymond Hostie's (1957) critique is typical. He believes that Jung went beyond the field of psychology into areas that belong to theology alone. He sees Jung's approach as in danger of losing the transcendent mystery of religion and even of losing the need for faith. Martin Buber's (1952) critique is similar, with an additional concern that if the soul is producing religious imagery, an intrapsychic image of God is really the soul experiencing itself, so there is no distinction between the subject and object

of religious experience. Then, there is no real relationship between God and the soul. Joseph Goldbrunner (1964) interprets Jung's religious work as "psychologism," meaning that Jung levels down supra-psychic realities to the level of purely psychological reality. This type of criticism ignores Jung's insistence on the reality of the psyche and fails to grasp his understanding of the irreducible depths of the psyche and its innate religious function, which produces sacred imagery. Dominican scholar Victor White (1960) realized that the soul cannot be distinguished from the psyche, so that theology and psychology must overlap, at the same time as this common ground sometimes produces a "battlefield" (p. 11). White was particularly concerned with Jung's critique of the Christian approach to evil and his notion of the dark side of the Self. White believed that Jung did not sufficiently distinguish between the intrapsychic image of God and the reality of the metaphysical God, which White believed transcends representation. White thought that to allow that a psychological experience could be the divine itself "would for us be idolatry" (p. 51). For Jung, however, the reality of the intrapsychic image of God is undeniable, and we cannot know whether it is related to a metaphysical divinity, which could express itself only by means of the psyche. As I have noted elsewhere (Corbett, 2021), the range of Self symbols that Jung describes is often incompatible with Judeo-Christian images of God, and his notion of the dark side of God is incompatible with much Christian God-imagery. Nevertheless, some theologians have given Jung a sympathetic reading. Swiss theologian Hans Schaer (1950) was hopeful about collaboration between Jung's psychology and Christian theology. Schaer believed that Jung tries to strip the Protestant Church from "the last vestiges of ecclesiasticism" and make the individual the bearer of new religious experiences (p. 193).

Chapter 1

The psychological approach to religion and the Bible

The Bible and religion from a Jungian perspective

The Bible and the religions that arose from it express both the human levels of the psyche and its archetypal processes, which, according to Jung, produce our experience of the holy or the sacred. As he puts it: "in God we honor the energy of the archetype" (CW 5, para. 135). This is a very different approach to divinity than one based on doctrine, dogma, and the authority of a sacred text. The psychological approach is not based on the fantasy of a supernatural being who exists in an external, metaphysical realm, an idea that presents so many philosophical difficulties and controversies. In Jung's approach, religious experiences can be approached purely psychologically, without recourse to doctrinal or dogmatic interpretations of them. Furthermore, biblical stories do not need to be understood in terms of literal history; from a psychological viewpoint, they are symbolic, mythic, and metaphorical statements, sometimes of profound spiritual significance. I therefore see Jung's approach as an emerging perspective on the Bible and on religious experience that compensates for the waning influence of the theistic traditions. The psychological approach to religious imagery and to the Bible is an alternative to the kind of theological approach that asserts the truth of its doctrines based on the opinions of Christian Church councils and hierarchies.

The Bible is the original and often the major source of evidence for Jewish and Christian theism. However, the events described in the Bible have been transmitted through a very long sequence of retelling and editing by multiple authors, so that the historical authority of scripture has been called into question by different types of biblical criticism. One of these is a psychological approach to the text, which reveals features within it that are visible only if the unconscious is considered.

Rather than see psychology and theology as being at odds with each other, some authors believe that today the two disciplines can be seen to be complementary. J. Harold Ellens (1997, p. 5) has argued that the relationship between psychology and theology should be "an interface of mutual illumination" rather than one of integration of the two disciplines, which he sees as disparate and alien to each other. In his view, the biblical text itself and the psychological approach to it describe two different ontological realms: the supernatural and the natural. For a combination of different perspectives to be helpful, each discipline has to be seen to bring legitimate value to the enterprise. Ellens acknowledges that for many evangelicals the truth value of the psychological approach has lesser valence than that of theology and the literal interpretation of the biblical message. However, from a depth psychological point of view, theological perspectives on the Bible are not necessarily the most basic. They are often products of preexisting doctrine and dogma, which themselves are amenable to psychological analysis that offers an entirely different perspective on the texts on which they are founded. The psychologist claims that these ideas and texts are analyzable in terms of their origins within the psyche, although the theologian would protest that the transcendent realities they describe are irreducible to psychological terms. One advantage of Jung's approach is that, unlike Ellens, Jung does not depend on the notion of disparate ontologies; the human and archetypal dimensions are both part of the psyche.

Based on the biblical text and a series of decisions by Church councils, theologians have derived models of incarnation, resurrection, atonement, sin, and a range of other dogmas, truths decreed by the church to be divinely revealed. Theologians have also derived doctrines, church teachings declared to be authoritative. However, depth psychologists resist the literal or absolute truth claims of these theological derivatives, partly because they themselves can be analyzed psychologically. The biblical texts on which doctrine and dogma are based can be shown to be colored by a combination of archetypal processes, personalistic psychodynamics, historically transmitted opinions, and the consensus of the faithful. Accordingly, there are some major incompatibilities between theological and psychological approaches to religious material. For example, when Jesus spoke of his "Kingdom," from a symbolic point of view he was speaking not of a physical realm to be expected at some future time but of a state of consciousness, or of a spiritual reality, which is why he said it cannot be observed (Lk 17: 20–21). Much biblical material seems to have been written with a mythopoetic sensibility and was not necessarily intended by its authors to be understood as literal history, which is how the tradition often insists on interpreting it (Tacey, 2015). When the Pope proclaimed the dogma of the physical assumption of the Virgin Mary in 1950, it was understood by the Roman Catholic Church to mean that she was literally taken bodily into heaven. In contrast, Jung saw this as an important symbolic statement, a psychological or mythic truth that restores the importance of the much-neglected feminine aspect of the divine.

The transpersonal and the human levels of the psyche are intimately associated and interpenetrate. Because of the presence of the archetypal level of the psyche and the Self, an intrapsychic expression of the divine, Jung believes that the psyche contains within itself "the faculty of relationship to God" (CW 12, para. 11). The psyche does not need a religious hierarchy, a sacred text, or a priesthood for this purpose. In Jung's approach, the divine is not wholly other to human consciousness as it is in traditional theism, where God is entirely self-sufficient. For Jung (CW 11, para. 100), it is only "a systematic blindness" that sees God as outside humanity, discontinuous from human consciousness. Humanity's further development requires that we stop projecting divinity into an external realm and recognize its manifestations within the psyche (CW 11, para. 141).

Numinous imagery that arises from the archetypal level of the psyche is distinguished by its powerful emotional quality, which Rudolph Otto described as mysterious, tremendous, and fascinating. Important to the psychologist is that the content of the experience may have little or no connection to preexisting theological notions of how divinity should appear or to the ways it manifests itself within traditional sacred texts. One of the reasons that the Roman Catholic Church does not approve of Jung's approach to spirituality[1] is that he focuses on intrapsychic manifestations of the numinosum, with no recourse to external sources of authority, whether biblical or ecclesiastical. Accordingly, Jung's approach is (correctly in some ways) seen as a psychological form of Gnosticism. The Church objects to Jung's symbolic approach to its doctrine and dogma, and to biblical stories, because the Church wants to see them as literal and historical facts rather than psychological or mythic truths.

The value and limitations of interpretations of the Bible

The Bible is one of the sources of Western culture, but it is often unintelligible to modern eyes without some kind of interpretive lens. However, it is impossible to read or interpret the Bible with an attitude of neutrality. All readers bring preexisting commitments to their understanding of the text. Theologians impose their own ideological framework on the biblical stories, and historians, psychologists, literary, and linguistic experts use their own lenses. An interdisciplinary approach is essential. However, there is often conflict between these different viewpoints, such as the tension between critical approaches and theological interpretations of the Bible among theologians and pastors who want to take it literally. Nonetheless, even a literal reading of the Bible involves a degree of interpretation because of controversies about the meaning of important words or the possibility that their meaning has changed since the text was written. Interpretations and translations are typically made from a specific vantage point, with an agenda in mind. Traditionally, important interpretations of biblical texts were decided by committees or significant figures in the history of the tradition, people whose personal psychology and cultural background inevitably influenced their opinions. In recent decades, after many years of resistance by theologians, psychological approaches to the Bible have increasingly gained acceptance. These approaches try to discern the conscious and unconscious psychological factors that color the biblical text. Considerable strides have been made in this direction (Edinger, 1972, Kluger, 1974, Kille, 2001, Ellens & Rollins, 2004, Rollins & Kille, 2007).

The biblical texts have many authors and have undergone multiple editing, redaction,[2] and theological emendations over a long historical period. Nevertheless, theologians have derived important theological inferences from biblical stories, in spite of the multiply determined origins of these texts. It is often believed that because the text has been much edited, psychological diagnosis of a biblical personality cannot be definitive. That practice has been roundly criticized. However, the psychologist can discuss the picture of the individual as presented in the text, making in effect a "literary" diagnosis of the personalities in biblical stories as long as we remember that we are analyzing textual accounts of their behavior rather than the analysis of actual people. The theologian draws metaphysical inferences from the behavior of the person in the text, just as the psychologist makes psychodynamic inferences. It is true that we do not know the extent to which contemporary psychological theory is applicable to people who lived at a very different time in a very different culture. The cultural and historical divide must be considered. What looks pathological to our eyes may have been culturally acceptable when the text was written. However, as Rollins (1999) points out, the psychological approach assumes that the emotions, mental mechanisms, and psychodynamics that we experience today, such as projection and the need to maintain the stability and cohesion of the personality, were also important to the subjects of biblical stories and their authors. We also assume that archetypal processes were operating in whatever ways the culture allowed their expression. The unconscious affected the behavior of the biblical authors, what they wrote, and what they believed. The contemporary psychologist may reasonably assume that at least some essential aspects of human nature have not changed since biblical times, in spite of many cultural changes.

A common objection to the psychological approach is that a text is not the same as a person with a mind, and there is no person present with whom one can check the validity of psychological interpretation. There is also concern that a preoccupation with the personal psychology of the protagonist or even the author of a biblical text obscures the underlying spiritual message. In spite of these potential difficulties, we have no choice but to interpret the text with the tools at our disposal. We may never be sure about the authors' original intentions or whether we correctly understand the behavior of the protagonists, but we can discover the meaning of the text for our own time if it is to be at all relevant.

Just as theologians see the biblical text through the lens of preconceived dogmatic and doctrinal ideas, it is likely that psychologists find only what their favorite theory and their personal prejudices tell them is present. The psychologist may have a transference to the text, based on his or her religious background. Personality traits such as the psychologist's typology or his or her attitude to authority are other possible distorting factors. It is therefore possible that, like the theological interpreter, the psychologist is projecting his personal prejudices and preferences onto the text, creating a biographical image of its characters or a psychodynamic profile that largely exists in the mind of the psychologist. We do not know how reliably the received or canonical text describes the psychology of the personalities it portrays. Some of these descriptions may be, and often are, the result of later redaction, hagiography, and textual manipulation. Given these caveats, we cannot be sure that psychological interpretation of a biblical text accurately reveals the author's unconscious dynamics, or his intention in writing the text, or the meaning of the text to the author. However, using a psychological approach to the text, we can point out the possible conscious and unconscious influences on its author. We can detect personality factors and psychodynamic factors in the protagonists depicted in the text, and we can detect psychopathology. We can discuss the meaning of the text to contemporary readers, which may be different than the authors intended. We can discuss the effect the text has on us and try to understand the reasons it has remained psychologically important over a long period of time. At times, we can identify the harmful or beneficial effects of the text.

When we study biblical stories psychologically, one of our difficulties is knowing what a particular situation may have meant to the original protagonists within their own cultural milieu. The psychologist has to rely on other specialists to clarify the linguistic, historical, and literary aspects of the text. As Andrew Kille (2001) points out, an interdisciplinary approach to the Bible guards against the danger of reducing everything to nothing but psychological categories. I would add that one has to avoid reducing everything to theological categories as if the biblical authors were not also moved by psychological factors.

Theological critics of the psychological approach are sometimes concerned that it undermines or reduces the metaphysical reality of religious entities such as God. Religious believers insist that we cannot reduce a biblical text to nothing but depictions of mental mechanisms, since the text deals with transcendent realities that are beyond the scope of psychology. Jung would respond that statements about metaphysical realities are themselves products of the psyche. (His approach to metaphysical statements is discussed in Corbett, 2023.) In response to theological criticisms of psychological approaches to the Bible, the psychologist might point out that the theologian usually begins his theological speculation and interpretations using the words of the biblical text as they have been transmitted, allowing for translation problems, using the text as he understands it to justify his theology. Theologians do not assume that the words of the biblical characters are merely textual material not based on what actually happened. They see the text as historically meaningful. For example, they try to understand Jesus' message by interpreting the Gospel text as it is written but also in terms of preexisting doctrinal and dogmatic commitments. The psychologist looks at the same text and understands it in terms of psychological theory without relying on preconceived metaphysical presuppositions.

Jung claims that the numinous experiences and descriptions of contact with divinity described in the Bible arise from the transpersonal or archetypal levels of the psyche, not from a metaphysical realm. As soon as these realities become conscious human experiences, they become subjects of psychological study. The theological interpretations of these realities are not independent of the interpreter's psychology, and they are often based on preexisting commitments that are a matter of faith. Many theological interpretations of the Bible are based on nothing more than preexisting creedal assertions developed by Church councils and hierarchies. Jung points out (CW 14, para. 781) that the resulting statements about apparently metaphysical realities "are so boundlessly varied that with the best of intentions we cannot know who is right."

I assume the authors of the Bible wanted to express the importance of their beliefs and experiences, and they wanted to have an effect on the reader. Some of their motivations for writing the text were political, social, and theological. Claims of the superiority or uniqueness of the authors' image of God or claims of being particularly chosen by their God sound as if they were driven by narcissistic needs. At times, these may have been the most fundamental factors. Psychological theory helps us discern some of this agenda, which is usually unconscious. Such a psychological study of the biblical texts neither confirms nor denies their authors' theological beliefs, but it may help us understand why they held them.

Wayne Rollins (1999, pp. 77–78) suggested that the "psychological-critical" approach to the Bible examines it in terms of the structures and dynamics of the psyche, and this is the approach I adopt. I use Jungian theory to discuss the Bible's archetypal imagery and psychoanalytic self-psychology to understand the relevant personal material. From a Jungian point of view, biblical stories can be treated symbolically in the same way we work with dreams, myths, and folklore, revealing psychological themes at the personal and archetypal levels. Jung's work is complemented by the work of authors such as Heinz Kohut (1978), who describe the importance of the personal self, its development, and its fragilities—in other words, the dynamics of the empirical personality, which the Jungian literature abbreviates as the ego. Kohut's personalistic approach to the psyche casts an important light on Bible stories that cannot be captured by an appeal to their archetypal underpinnings alone. From a self-psychological point of view, at least some aspects of the behavior of biblical characters were narcissistically motivated, a way of enhancing self-esteem or a way of protecting a vulnerable sense of self. Kohut casts light on developmental factors that lead to toxic grandiosity, which may lead to abhorrent behavior that is easily disguised by claiming that one is carrying out the will of God, in which case everything, including gratuitous violence, is allowed.

Kille (2001) makes use of Ricoeur's distinction between the historical and cultural world "behind the text," the world in which the text was shaped, in contrast to the world "of the text," its language and narratives, and the world "in front" of the text, its meaning to the reader, which is where a psychological approach is particularly useful. Reader-response criticism of the Bible emphasizes its effect on the reader and what he or she brings to the text. The psychological approach is of value when cultural, linguistic, and historical forms of biblical exegesis are insufficient to explain the psychological importance of biblical stories. Historical criticism[3] tried to discover what the Bible's authors meant when they wrote and how the original readers would have understood the text. This was a valuable approach, but the Bible may mean very different things to modern readers. Today, there is an additional range of approaches to the Bible, from recent perspectives such as ecology, gay liberation, Black, and Asian theology. There is no universal perspective. The psychological approach has the benefit of considering the unconscious, which surely played a part in the writing of the Bible. A depth psychological perspective opens up a range of interpretations that lie below the surface level of the text. Using contemporary psychodynamic understanding of personality combined with an archetypal interpretation of symbol and metaphor, the psychological approach takes us far beyond a literal understanding of the Bible.

Contrasts between psychological and theological approaches to the Bible

Psychological approaches to the Bible suggest that biblical stories and myths contain intrinsic psychological meanings and spiritual truths, but these are not necessarily the meanings that have been insisted upon by traditional religious authorities. Depth psychology allows us to look at these stories from a new perspective. The well-known risk of this approach is that we may overlay a framework of psychological theory to fill in missing details or to make the story fit the theory. Psychological approaches to the Bible are often accused of proof-texting, taking lines out of context to find a meaning that was not intended, in order to prove a point. Apologists for the Bible see it as a mistake to focus on isolated biblical verses; even when they are incomprehensible or reprehensible by modern standards, they are assumed to be somehow related to the Bible's overall message. Traditional believers' need to focus on the overall revelation allows them to gloss over the obviously problematic aspects of the text. When faced with objectionable material, such as the Bible's violence and misogyny, apologists fall back on the importance of taking the book and its message as a whole. In contrast, psychological approaches are not burdened by the need to find a particular message or to gloss over its inconsistencies or overt instances of psychopathology. The clearly pathological material in the Bible and its demonizing of other faiths can be understood in terms of the psychology of its authors, even though this behavior is usually projected and understood to be a divine commandment. Miracle stories can be seen symbolically or metaphorically rather than as contraventions of the laws of nature.

Theologians and psychologists read the Bible with different intentions. Traditional religions understand the Bible's message in terms of their doctrine and dogma. It is the task of these theologians to show how any part of the Bible is related to the whole and to the teaching of their Church. It is also their task to show how theological ideas such as the trinity, a concept that is not clearly found in the Bible, can be justified using biblical statements and how contradictory statements in different parts of the text can be unified or accommodated with each other. These are very different than the tasks of the psychologist, who looks at specific stories without theological preconceptions and so has no need to justify the behavior of the protagonists in the story in terms of a larger ideological agenda or in terms of speculation about the divine purpose. For example, the psychologist has no need to reconcile the Bible's accounts of mass murder, gratuitous cruelty, and other horrific imagery with notions of a benevolent image of God. The psychologist acknowledges this material as the projection of human pathology onto the divine, or, from Jung's point of view, it can be attributed to the dark side of our God-image. Psychological interpretations of the Bible open the reader to meanings that may have nothing to do with theology. Thus, an experience or behavior that the biblical authors believed to be prompted by God, such as the massacre of civilians, may actually have been the result of an autonomous complex or blood lust within the protagonists that they attributed to their God because it seemed to possess them.

Like any literature, biblical stories have their own life and contain implications that may point beyond what their authors intended or realized. At times, we can understand something of the psychology of a biblical author in terms of his or her writing, using a combination of empathy and theory. The fact that biblical stories and characters have captivated so many people for so long, and are still accepted by many as inspired, requires a psychological explanation. I suggest that the Bible has a powerful emotional appeal to many people in part because it resonates with and catalyzes important psychological structures within the reader. The Bible tells mythic stories that are psychologically powerful even if they are not historically true. Social and family pressures to believe these stories are also important.

Traditional theistic religions assume that they convey the divine will through their understanding of sacred texts and their elaboration of divine revelation described in these texts. They also believe that the human religious impulse can be satisfied by a combination of faith, adherence to religious doctrine, dogma, established ritual practices, and belief in an external divinity. Theologians often want to restrict their idea about how the divine reveals itself to its traditional manifestations. For Jung, none of this is necessary. He has shown that the psyche may produce experiences of the Self, the "God within," that are completely novel, with no connection to traditional doctrine and dogma. (Jung's approach is reviewed in Corbett, 2020, 2021.)

Is the Bible authoritative?

Within Judaism and Christianity, the authority of the Bible is axiomatic. The Bible is believed to describe the authors' experience of divine revelation and the interventions of divinity within human history. The New Testament describes the experience of the early followers of Christ. Traditional believers assume that the Bible is divinely inspired or that the writing was guided by God. Christians believe that the Bible reveals what is necessary for their salvation, although exactly how that is achieved is much debated by different denominations.

Some of the Bible's authority arises for purely historical reasons. It has accumulated considerable prestige and cultural allegiance. However, because of its coloring by human psychology, the Bible has also been used to justify all manner of racism, misogyny, homophobia, and violence, so its moral value and its authority are often questioned today. The Bible has also been seen as a source of oppression, particularly of women and people of color. For skeptics, therefore, the Bible is not simply God-given; it is highly conditioned by the cultures in which it arose and by the psychology of its authors, editors, and translators.

The authority of the Bible is taken for granted in fundamentalist circles, where it is seen as internally self-authenticating. Fundamentalists find biblical support for their views, and they tend to mold the meaning of the Bible's stories to support their theology. Theologians derive a set of "timeless truths" from the text, which they incorporate into their creedal statements, but the churches have split into multiple versions of this truth, all insisting that their interpretation is correct. Usually, they focus on biblical themes and passages that support their preferences and ignore or rationalize those that do not. When biblical passages contradict each other, the problem for those who believe the Bible is inerrant becomes finding a deeper understanding that reconciles incompatible statements. Alternatively, believers live with the tension and trust the that the truth will eventually be revealed. Needless to say, the meaning of the word "inerrant" is subject to interpretation.

Contemporary scholars believe that the Hebrew Bible was written over a period of about a thousand years in a cumulative fashion, by multiple authors, copyists, and redactors who gradually added new material and new interpretations of older material, often ignoring the ensuing contradictions. The many different elements of the text were held together by constantly asserting that all the expressions of divinity it describes are manifestations of the same God.

The theistic traditions rely heavily on the written word. Rabbinic authority is based on the interpretation of texts. Orthodox Jews believe that God can be approached through studying the Hebrew Bible, the Torah, and its subsequent Talmudic interpretations, which tradition teaches were handed down at Mt. Sinai as an oral tradition. The authority of the word took hold early among Christian theologians, who have endlessly argued about the meaning of the Bible, leading to religious warfare. Belief and faith in the correct understanding of the Bible became paramount within Christianity. Theology perpetuates itself as a discipline by continuously interpreting and reinterpreting the Bible. Some of this interpretation is quite abstract, based on debates about the meaning of ideas that began as the opinions of Church councils, such as thinking of Jesus as of the same substance as God. These decisions were eventually transmitted as if they were facts rather than opinions. The Bible's mythic imagery, such as the virgin birth, is often treated as if it were a literal, historical, and unique event, acting as the ground onto which a theological superstructure is built.

Liberal theologians and pastors have been faced with a dilemma; they profess to be committed to truth and to acknowledge the value of science, but they are also committed to defend material in the Bible that is impossible by modern standards, such as stories of illness said to be caused by demonic possession (Mark 6: 13). Liberal theologians concede that the Bible contains this kind of error, but they deal with such passages by re-interpreting them, by assuming they are interpolations by the later Church, or by dismissing them as cultural artefacts that are no longer relevant to message of the Gospels. In contrast, many traditional religionists are willing to assert that based on the Bible they know God's wishes for humanity, and pastors often insist on telling their congregants what to believe. Their rhetoric assumes that they know God's plan for humanity because of their interpretation of the Bible.

Some of the biblical text contains archetypal material, but much of it derives from the human level of the psyche, so that its final composition is a composite of mythological imagery that is literalized and interpreted according to human needs, fears, and hopes. Biblical stories depicting encounters with the numinosum, such as Ezekiel's vision or Job's experience of Yhwh speaking to him from a whirlwind, are subsequently interpreted in terms of theological preconceptions. They can now be reinterpreted psychologically. As von Franz (1980) noted, when a new religious attitude appears, such as Jung's approach to numinous experience, previous images of divinity are seen to be mythic rather than literal. Images of God are also seen to be colored by the projection of human psychological material.

In biblical stories, we see divinity described in mythic and anthropomorphic terms because these are the metaphors that were best suited to describe the authors' experience. In the early years of the biblical traditions, it was straightforward to imagine God as a superior personality and to explain the vicissitudes of history in terms of God's actions, as if "he" were a kind of supernatural, celestial person. Needless to say, "his" psychological makeup and preferences often reflected human psychological structures writ large. Anthropomorphic imagery pervades the Bible, but it is no longer a useful way to talk about divinity. Anthropomorphic God-images are a product of the human imagination, the result of the projection onto divinity of human psychological processes such as anger, the need for revenge and punishment, the need for praise, the need to be exclusive, and so on. The early Jews and Christians harshly attacked the worship of idols made of wood and stone. They did not seem to realize that words, concepts, and anthropomorphic metaphors also produce images of divinity. Some religious images, such as the trinity, are archetypal products of the unconscious. At other times, unless they are grounded in direct numinous experience, religious ideas tend to be a product of human needs and preferences.

Historically, many people have seen the Bible and the Church as authoritative guides for their lives. However, our relationship to authority has changed over time. We are heirs to the postmodern doubt about all such overarching belief systems. We are now interested in how religious knowledge claims were obtained, how they serve the powerful, how they foster and maintain social structures, and so on. We no longer automatically trust religious institutions and their traditional texts. We may pay lip service to the Bible, but when we are in difficulty, the process of secularization in the West has led to our seeking help from science rather than the Bible.

Theological illusions and impositions onto the biblical text

Historian and theologian Uta Ranke-Heinemann (1994) describes some of the fallacious or illusory interpretations of the Bible that she believes underpin much Church doctrine and dogma. She points out several tall tales and mythological images that have been asserted to be literal, historical facts that the Church believes cannot be questioned despite their unlikely reality. Examples are the story of the Annunciation to Mary and the angelic reassurance to Joseph that Mary's baby was the Son of God, which are incompatible with the Gospel story that Jesus' parents did not understand his references to his heavenly Father (Luke 2: 41–49). Another such instance is the assertion that Jesus' mother was a virgin before and after his birth[4] and that Jesus did not have any siblings. To maintain the historical illusion of the virgin birth, Jesus' siblings gradually became transformed into stepsiblings or cousins, and the fact of Mary's illegitimate pregnancy was camouflaged.

In the demythologizing tradition of Rudolf Bultmann, using the principles of historical source criticism, Ranke-Heinemann points out many other internal contradictions, discrepancies, and historical inaccuracies within the New Testament. She notes its falsifications in the service of clerical interests and the Church's penchant for taking miraculous stories as if they were literally true. She shows that many stories about Jesus are deliberately modelled after accounts in the Hebrew Bible. She contends that Christianity's "inhumane theology of the cross" has effectively eclipsed Jesus' teachings of love and forgiveness, which she believes were his true message. She believes that this theology has helped to promote inhumanity because of its emphasis on the value of suffering. Ranke-Heinemann points out that the Church has maintained its authority in part by threatening people with hell, which "serves the holy purpose of cradle-to-grave intimidation" (1994, p. 228). Her work was criticized on the grounds that by debunking the Bible's mythic imagery she tries to make religion too rational and that removing the New Testament's miraculous material would diminish its appeal.

In spite of such modern critical approaches to the Bible, which have a much more rigorous standard of truth than claims to faith, the traditional understanding of the Bible inherited from the pre-critical era is still deeply embedded in much Christian thinking. This is especially true among fundamentalists who see the Bible as inerrant. More liberal scholars increasingly question the literal understanding of major doctrines such as the trinity and the incarnation.

The attempts to enforce Church doctrines

Today, in the face of science and critical inquiry, the burden of proof of the Church's assertions rests upon its adherents. In the past, however, the Church has often used brutal methods to suppress arguments and kill opponents (Ellerbe, 1995). Clergy have used threats of eternal damnation to frighten people and promote Church ideology, ostensibly to save souls. To the psychologist, this history suggests an attempt to suppress the Church's doubt about its doctrines and dogmas, except when the use of power for its own sake was simply a way of enhancing the self-esteem and social status of clergy.

The psychologist notes with interest that, for a religion whose teacher emphasized peace, the tradition has been riddled with violent power struggles since its beginning. The Gospels were written and edited to satisfy the agendas of several first-century Christian groups. The groups whose ideas did not gain acceptance in the resulting competition for authority were labelled as heretics and ruthlessly attacked. After the Roman Emperor Constantine's sponsorship of Christianity, fourth-century Christian authorities were able to dictate correct belief and were able to use the Roman legal system to persecute pagans and groups such as the Gnostics. The political power of the Roman Church made disagreement dangerous. Because of this power, a particular line of thought became official doctrine and was gradually elaborated by Church councils. Only certain books were regarded as canonical and inspired by God; the others were declared to be either heretical or apocryphal. The idea persists that there is one set of correct Christian beliefs, but there is no agreement about which are correct. Partly because they can no longer be enforced, ideas such as the incarnation and accounts of Jesus' miracles and resurrection are increasingly called into question or even ignored. Since they contravene our scientific knowledge, these ideas now require faith or a splitting defense in which religious beliefs are hermetically sealed off from the individual's scientific knowledge of the world.

The projection of human psychology onto images of God

A psychological complement to the work of Feuerbach

My emphasis on the intrapsychic origin of biblical material is relevant to the work of German philosopher Ludwig Feuerbach (1804–1872). His *The Essence of Christianity* (first published in 1841) suggests that "theology is anthropology," meaning that our ideas about God are based on the projection of human values and psychological qualities onto an imaginary deity. For Feuerbach, what we call "God" is entirely a product of our own minds. Feuerbach was relatively neglected in his own day, or his work was treated with defensive hostility, but it became an important challenge for later theologians. Without agreeing with Feuerbach's atheism, which I think is mistaken, we can acknowledge and widen his idea of the importance of human projections onto God. We do so by adding to it our contemporary knowledge of the objective psyche, human psychodynamics, and the way these psychological factors influenced the authors of the Bible and the theology derived from it.

According to Feuerbach, religions derive their idea of God in a way that exaggerates or compensates for human characteristics. Thus, because human beings are mortal, we invent a God who is immortal. Because humans are finite and vulnerable, God is infinite and omnipotent. Human knowledge is limited but God is omniscient. That is, according to Feuerbach, whatever is asserted about God is really an assertion about some aspect of human psychology exaggerated to an infinite degree and treated as if it belonged to a metaphysical being. When we talk of attributes of God such as love or will, we are talking about some aspect of human nature or human psychology projected onto an idealized image of divinity. Human belief in God is really belief in human nature writ large; we make our gods in our own image in the form of a superhuman being who has no limitations. Religion is really the relationship of humanity to itself, or to its own essence, because what we imagine to be the divine essence is essentially an idea of the human personality freed from human limitations, made objective, and worshipped. For Feuerbach, therefore, theology is an illusion and God is nothing more than a myth that fulfills our wish that there would be such a being. This idea accounts for the anthropomorphic nature of many God-images, and for the mixture of positive and negative traits seen in the biblical God-image, who is both loving and violent, like human nature. Accordingly, according to Feuerbach: "Consciousness of God is self-consciousness, knowledge of God is self-knowledge. By his God, thou knowest the man, and by the man, his God; the two are identical" (Feuerbach, 2008, p. 10).

For Feuerbach, the notion of the transcendence of God represents the projection of our desire to be released from the limits of human existence. Whatever a given society holds in the highest esteem, or society's most important moral values, are attributed to its image of God. That is, our moral values determine our image of God, rather than morality being dictated by God. Essentially, for Feuerbach, God exists only in terms of the properties we attribute to him. Belief in God is an attempt to avoid taking full responsibility for human vulnerability. The human dependence on God is a substitute for our dependence on each other. Human wholeness is projected onto God. Religion is a way to mythologize human nature. For Feuerbach, the idea of God is therefore an illusory product of projection and wishful thinking, an idea that Freud was later to elaborate in his own theory of the origin of religion.

Feuerbach describes the attribution to divinity of human psychological traits such as narcissism, the need for power and revenge, and the capacity for both compassion and murderous violence. The reason the God of the Hebrew

Bible is so warlike, jealous, and capricious is that human psychology has those attributes, which are projected onto the Bible's image of God. As Feuerbach has it, "theology is nothing else than an unconscious, esoteric pathology, anthropology, and psychology...nothing more than an imaginary psychology and anthropology" (p. 75). Theology is therefore a kind of mythology. For example: "The resurrection of Christ is therefore the satisfied desire of man for an immediate certainty of his personal existence after death" (p. 113). Feuerbach points out that the existence of the gods of Olympus was once considered to be factual. Religious scholars once believed that Balaam's ass[5] really spoke, and they believed in witches, just as they believed in the incarnation and other miracles. Feuerbach believed that once the individual realized he had created his image of God, he would give up the religious life.

Freud continued in the vein of Feuerbach by suggesting that the idea of God is only the illusory projection of an exalted father onto a nonexistent supreme being. However, Feuerbach and Freud made the same mistake, which is to suggest that the detection of these projective mechanisms means there is no God. Rather, these mechanisms mean that what we say about God is colored by human psychology, relational needs, and human personality traits, allowing a radical critique of absolute truth claims about divinity. Feuerbach sees theology as a form of anthropology, but one could equally well say that theology is grounded in psychology since the psyche is the ultimate source of these projections.

In a later work (1872) titled *Lectures on the Essence of Religion*, Feuerbach sounds remarkably contemporary (even proto-Jungian) when he says that

> The ultimate secret of religion is the relationship between the conscious and unconscious...Man with his ego or consciousness stands at the brink of a bottomless abyss: that abyss is his own unconscious being, which seems alien to him...But what part of me is I and what part is not-I?
>
> (p. 310 ff)

Feuerbach believed that even positive projections onto God are harmful in that they do not allow human beings to sufficiently appreciate these qualities within our own nature, so that we do not realize our potential. God is thereby enhanced at the expense of the diminishment of human beings. In a further proto-Jungian mode, Feuerbach suggested that the human task is to take back these projections and reclaim these qualities as parts of ourselves. The crucial piece that Jung adds to this picture is that the Self manifests itself within the psyche, and the resulting images are often novel and relatively free from projected personal material.

Non-realist approaches to religion

Between 1980 and 1998, post-modern philosopher-theologian Don Cupitt denied that there is any objective, metaphysical God outside humanity and independent of human language and representation. Reminiscent of Feuerbach's work, for Cupitt gods are human constructions that embody cultural values and ideals. Cupitt believed that religion is a purely human creation, although he did not think this meant the end of religion or a religious attitude to life. Much influenced by Buddhism, which also holds that the world is not underpinned by a metaphysical deity, Cupitt (2001) tried to develop a purely humanist or naturalistic approach to religion based on innate feelings, created by people themselves but without worshipping an outside power. He objected to the traditional notion of an authoritarian, oppressive, divine being, which he labelled "cosmic terrorism," but he acknowledges the need for religion. For this purpose, he wanted to develop a humanitarian, ethical system of the kind that Jesus taught. Cupitt's approach ignores the psychological importance of the non-rational, mythopoetic, numinous imagery spontaneously produced by the archetypal level of the psyche. This material, which is foundational to religion, is not a product of the conscious personality.

Some philosophers believe that religion is nothing more than a linguistic construction and that religious language does not refer to anything that exists objectively; God exists only within a framework of beliefs, and one has to be part of a religious community to understand the real meaning of their language. Contemporary philosopher Jon Mills (2017) exemplifies such a skeptical attitude to religious material. He sees the idea of God as pathological, "an expression of our suffering" (p. 95). For him, from a psychoanalytic viewpoint, God is nothing more than an intrapsychic idea, an internal object, in part a "compromise formation" resulting from the battle with unconscious drives and fantasies. The need for an ideal object to gratify an infantile wish struggles with resistance against the gratification of this wish, because biblical strictures generate anxiety, ego restrictions, and prohibitions. For Mills, God exists only as an idea born of illusion, desire, and social ideology that conditions belief, combined with an appeal to authority and custom. However, while one may in this way debate the reality of particular ideas about God, philosophical approaches such as those of Mills and Cupitt do not consider the fact that the objective psyche spontaneously produces numinous experiences. According to Jung, one cannot abolish the psyche's innate religious function, which is responsible for the archetypal material described within the Bible. This numinous imagery continues to arise within the individual psyche. It has a powerful effect and feels indisputably real. For Jung, religion is inevitable because of the presence of the Self, an *a priori* image of divinity within the psyche.

Jung on the intrapsychic divine in contrast to the God-image of theology

For Jung, the metaphysical divinity of the theistic traditions results from the projection of the inner divine, the Self or the "God within" (CW 7, para. 399) onto whatever is the local name for God. The Self is experienced in the form of numinous encounters such as those described in the Bible in the story of Moses at the burning bush. Jung believes that the Self continues to express itself in the life of modern individuals, who may experience its numinous manifestations in dreams and synchronistic events in completely novel ways. Numinous experiences are recognizable by their powerful emotional qualities, even when they do not have a traditional content (Corbett, 2020). The transpersonal level of the psyche from which these events emerge interpenetrates and is continuous with the human level, so in Jung's model the divine and human are not radically separate; they are in a mutual process. Divinity is not in an inaccessible realm remote from the human personality. To identify transcendence only with an external God may prevent people from experiencing the transcendent depths within the human personality.

If we confine our notion of God to the descriptions within theistic religious traditions, we do not acknowledge the ongoing intrapsychic manifestations of divinity. The theistic traditions are largely dependent on biblical revelation and received teachings for their knowledge of God, but Jung's model of the Self sees its wide range of manifestations as a form of continuing revelation based on direct experience by means of the psyche. A range of symbols of the Self is described by Corbett (2021). Most of them would not be accepted as images of divinity by traditional theists, partly because their content may actually contradict traditional doctrines. Many theists do not believe that revelation is continuing in this way. However, the numinosity of these Self-symbols suggests their sacredness.

The Self is also the guiding spirit of the individuation process. The Self provides the individual with a set of archetypal endowments that act as a spiritual blueprint for the development of the personality. These endowments embody themselves gradually during the course of the individual's life, so there is an archetypal background to the individual personality.[6]

Jung (CW 11, para. 749, note 2) acknowledges that every attempt to discuss religion psychologically is "immediately suspected of psychologism," reducing divinity to "nothing but" an intrapsychic image. The concern is that to describe the way the divine manifests itself within the psyche somehow makes divinity less objectively real. This critique ignores Jung's insistence on the reality of the psyche. For Jung (CW 14, para. 667), the psyche is a domain in its own right, not reducible to the workings of the brain, so intrapsychic images of the Self are real. Nevertheless, theologians have long objected to the idea that what they consider to be metaphysical entities are manifestations of the psyche. As von Franz (1980) points out, theologians are reluctant to accept the idea that the objects of their worship are the projections of psychological contents. Theologians insist on the metaphysical reality of these objects, as if they originate beyond the psyche. Jung believes that metaphysical speculation itself originates within the psyche, an idea that produces great resistance among traditional religious believers.

One of the advantages of Jung's notion of the Self is that it avoids some of the philosophical problems that trouble traditional theistic notions of God.

Because the Self is directly experienced, Jung bypasses discussions about whether God exists in the metaphysical sense that the theistic traditions describe, with traditional attributes of omniscience, omnipotence, omnibenevolence, and so on. Self symbols may have none of these qualities. Furthermore, because Jung points out that the Self has a dark side, this concept avoids problems such as the difficulty explaining why an omnipotent, entirely loving divine being also permits suffering and evil and is often experienced as absent. Jung focuses only on the intrapsychic manifestations of the Self, whose existence in symbolic form can be demonstrated empirically (Corbett, 2021). Jung's experiential approach makes belief in theological doctrine and dogma unnecessary and avoids the question of whether religious beliefs are rational and based on sufficient evidence. It is not necessary to argue about whether God exists if one has had a numinous experience of the Self. These experiences are so powerful that they are psychologically impossible to deny. They do not require faith in the sense of acquiescence to doctrine and dogma, nor do they require belief in the literal rather than symbolic understanding of stories such as the virgin birth.

Numinous experiences are subject to the criticism that they may have an explanation other than contact with the sacred. Skeptics argue that there may be purely naturalistic explanations for such experiences, in which case the subject is misattributing the experience to an experience of divinity (Taves, 2011). However, not only Jungians but several Freudians have sensed that psychological growth and healing often seem to come from something beyond the ego or the personal self (e.g., Bollas, 1999, Milner, 1969).

For psychotherapists treating religious people, it is important to understand the individual's belief system, since it may consciously or unconsciously affect the person's psychological life. Without some grasp of the individual's religious background, it may be difficult to understand the psychological importance of religious ideas and their hold on the person, which begin to be implanted in childhood. The therapist cannot assume she knows what words such as "God" mean to the individual. These beliefs can be explored for their psychological importance without concern for their truth or verifiability.

Religions and sacred texts reveal how both the dark and light side of both human nature and the archetypal dimensions of the psyche may unfold. We now turn to a description of the ways in which religions express these psychological processes.

Notes

1 The Church's objections to Jung's overall approach are seen in a Vatican publication titled "Jesus Christ: The bearer of the water of life: A Christian reflection on the 'New Age.'" This can be found at: https://www.vatican.va/roman_curia/pontifical_councils/interelg/documents/rc_pc_interelg_doc_20030203_new-age_en.html Retrieved 3/2/2024.
2 Redaction here refers to the ways in which different segments of the text have been edited and assembled into its final shape in order to emphasize particular theological points.

3 During the nineteenth century, the Bible was increasingly seen as a product of human history and culture, because of conflicting vocabularies and writing styles, repetitions, obvious editing, the use of various names for God, and internal contradictions. It was seen to have been formed in particular social contexts with particular religious agendas. Miracle stories were seen as human embellishments of natural phenomena, and the words of God were seen to be the words of early editors. It also became clear that the Bible had been influenced by the religions of surrounding nations. Much of the Hebrew Bible was written not at the time of Moses but by a priestly class after the Babylonian Exile in 586 BCE. Later material was written back into the earlier text to give it more authority. Historical criticism saw the Gospels not as reports of historical events but as expressions of faith of the early Christian community, literary devices made to conform to prophecies in the Hebrew Bible, designed to convince people of Jesus' status. The Gospel of John was seen as a spiritual interpretation of the life of Jesus that put mystical statements into his mouth to express the tradition's evolving image of him.
4 Mary was given the title of ever-virgin at the Council of Chalcedon in 451 CE.
5 In Numbers chapter 22, Balaam's ass refused to move because it saw an angel blocking its path that Balaam could not see. When Balaam struck the ass, it was able to speak.
6 There is a great deal of controversy about the notion of the archetype. Jung's late view was that the archetypes are spiritual principles within the psyche. In a letter, he refers to them as "organs (tools) of God" (Jung, 1976, p. 130).

Chapter 2

Religions as expressions of the psyche

Jung on religion

Jung writes that religion is not only a sociological and historical phenomenon but also "one of the earliest and most universal expressions of the human mind" (CW 11, para 1). He speaks of religions as "psychotherapeutic systems in the truest sense of the word" that "express the whole range of the psychic problem in mighty images; they are…the revelation of the soul's nature" (CW 10, para. 367).[1] Religious ideas and sacred texts display the psyche unfolded, both its archetypal and its human levels. Jung believed that religious statements are "psychic confessions" based on unconscious process (CW 11, para. 555) and that statements in scripture are "utterances of the soul" (CW 11, para. 557). That is, stories and characters in sacred texts, and often their theological exposition and elaboration, express the structures and dynamics of the psyche.

Theistic religions and sacred texts project the experience of the archetypal levels of the psyche onto an external divinity living in a metaphysical realm. Thus, seen through a psychological lens, biblical characters who had numinous experiences, such as Job or Ezekiel, actually experienced archetypal levels of the psyche that the tradition assumed to have emerged from a heavenly dimension. Religions, their sacred texts, and the theological concepts that emerge from them, including their myths, rituals, and metaphysical assertions, all depict psychological processes. Some of the resulting archetypal imagery, such as the idea of the trinity, is found in several religious traditions. These archetypal motifs are elaborated conceptually in order to fit preconceived theological ideology. Some of these archetypal themes seem primitive to modern eyes, as we see in biblical accounts of the temple sacrifices of animals and the associated purity rituals. Other mythic motifs, such as the story of a future paradise, are comforting, while some, such as belief in hell or in witchcraft, have caused considerable suffering.

Much of the Bible's archetypal or mythic imagery, such as the virgin birth (Matt. 1: 18: Lk 1: 26–38), had emerged in several traditions prior to Christianity[2] (Kuhn, 1940; Harpur, 2004). Flood myths are found in several cultures, including Greek and Mesopotamian mythology. The biblical Noah is reminiscent of ancient Akkadian and Babylonian flood stories, written at least a thousand years earlier than the biblical story. However, for over two thousand years, this kind of material has been interpreted as if it were a unique historical event by traditional proponents of Christianity and Judaism. Onto the Bible's mythic substrate, for which there is often little or no historical evidence, a huge theological superstructure has been built by subsequent Christian Church councils and rabbinical authorities. The only justification for belief in the truth of this superstructure comes from the Bible itself and from the authority that religious hierarchies and the councils arrogate to themselves.

Religion as a mirror of human psychodynamics

The projection of human characteristics onto divinity

As well as expressing archetypal imagery, religions also reveal the projected manifestations of human levels of the psyche onto divinity. Examples are the power-drenched, grandiose, violent image of God in the Hebrew Bible, or Yhwh's need to be constantly mirrored and praised, which is characteristics of human potentates. Let us assume for a moment the real existence of biblical characters such as Moses, who, according to the text, believed that God ordered genocidal violence. Men such as Joshua carried out atrocities when they conquered cities. These men attributed their violence to the promptings of what they believed was an external divinity. They believed they were killing in the name of their God. From a psychological standpoint, they were acting under the influence of very human shadow dynamics such as aggression, territoriality, tribalism, greed, hatred, fear, the projection of their negative traits onto other groups, and the narcissistic need to prove the superiority of their God and their nation. In spite of the Bible's teachings of peace, charity, and forgiveness, there is also an inordinate amount of violence and cruelty in the Hebrew Bible. The death penalty is warranted for a wide range of crimes, slavery is allowed, corporal punishment of children is recommended, and many other reprehensible acts are reported to be commanded or sanctioned by God. The psychological approach to this material sees it as typical human attributes projected onto divinity.

In other words, superimposed on the Bible's archetypal imagery and mingled with it are human levels of the psyche, producing not only a tradition of benevolence but also shadow material such as the need for power and dominion, the fear and oppression of women, the need to be superior to other nations, and similar displays emerging from human narcissism. As a result of this combination, religious history becomes not only a matter of divine revelation via the objective psyche but also a vivid demonstration of the enactment of human psychological processes projected as if they were divine commandments.

The ancient Israelites assumed that their successes and failures in war were divinely caused. They unconsciously adopted a simplistic reward–punishment, father–child psychology, believing that misfortune of any kind meant that God was angry with them for some transgression. Their interpretations of the actions of their God were colored not only by theological, cultural, and historical factors but also by their need to feel special and to have a uniquely powerful God. This need is best understood in terms of psychoanalytic self-psychology. There is good evidence in biblical stories for the type of narcissistic structures and processes that Kohut described (Kohut & Wolf, 1978), such as the need for prestige and power to enhance self-esteem and bolster the cohesion of the sense of self. These fundamental features of human psychology seem to have remained constant, and judging from the biblical text, it is clear that they motivated people in traditional societies as much as they do in our society.

Abusive aspects of human psychology projected onto divinity

Several stories within the Hebrew Bible describe the military victories of early Israelite kings. According to these texts, cities were routinely destroyed, and their citizens mercilessly killed, often including non-combatants, women, children, and animals, all at the behest of God. God was said to have commanded the complete destruction of every living being at Ai, Jericho, and other places (Numbers 21: 1–3; Deut. 2: 30–35; Joshua 6: 17–21; 7–8). In a manifest rationalization, the spoils of war were routinely consecrated to Yhwh. One of the ways this behavior has been justified is by suggesting that, rather than being acts of personal hatred and vengeance, these massacres were ritual sacrifices dedicated to God, or the victims were evil and deserved harsh punishment (Lüdeman, 1996). However, this barbarism looks more like human violence rationalized by projecting it onto God, as if God told the people to commit these war crimes.

The need for violent revenge is often due to a narcissistic injury, a blow to one's sense of self or to one's self-esteem or national pride. The resulting narcissistic rage is often a way to maintain self-esteem in the face of an insult, or it seeks to avenge an injury such as the unprovoked attacks by the Amalekites when the Israelites left Egypt (Exod. 17: 8). In an obvious projection, the Amalekites are then said to be cursed by God. This kind of revenge seems to be the motive when the prophet Samuel tells King Saul that God says, "I will punish what Amalek did to Israel," so Saul is commanded to "utterly destroy all that they have…kill both man and woman, infant and suckling, ox and sheep, camel and ass" (1 Sam. 15: 1–3). Because Saul kept the best of the animals rather than destroying all of them, he was rejected by God.

It is noteworthy that the fifth commandment, "Thou shall not kill" (Deut. 5: 17), is followed soon after (Deut. 7: 1) by the commandment to exterminate, "utterly destroy," a range of local Canaanite tribes, the Hittites, the Gir'gashites, the Amorites, the Per-izzites, the Hivites, and the Jeb'usites. This was ordered because these people might turn the Israelites against Yhwh, so to maintain his primacy he forbids intermarriage and also demands the destruction of their altars and monuments. The conquest of the promised land required the slaughter of large numbers of people and animals (e.g., Joshua 6: 21), and Yhwh promised to "blot them out" (Exod. 23: 23). This bloodshed is justified because God promised his own people the land "for an everlasting possession" (Gen. 17: 8). The political ramifications of this mythic promise are continuing. It seems that the commandment not to kill applies only to Yhwh's own people. Not only is this mythology an example of ethnic and religious intolerance, but it also demonstrates the religious justification for violence. Yet the text is regarded as sacred, and the tradition shows little embarrassment about the behavior of people like Joshua.

Penchansky (1999) describes many instances of the biblical God behaving in a vindictive, abusive, and morally questionable manner. Blumenthal (1993) also does so, and he insists that the tradition must not censor this aspect of the biblical God-image. However, the destructiveness of the biblical image of God can in fact be rationalized and excused in various ways. Brueggemann (1997, p. 275) realizes that God's harmful behavior is "endlessly problematic for theology," but he tries to turn God's negative aspects into something positive by suggesting that the power of God is always used righteously, for the sake of his people. Eichrodt (1967) also believes that God's anger is never used maliciously or capriciously; it simply expresses his displeasure, for reasons that human beings cannot conceptualize. Apologists for Yhwh's behavior also suggest that stories of divine ruthlessness and cruelty are residues of an earlier, more primitive God-image that may have been incorporated from neighboring societies.[3] God's positive attributes such as his goodness, righteousness, love, and faithfulness are said to represent a historically later, more sophisticated God-image, but the earlier violent images are still regarded as part of the sacred text. Among the Hebrew prophets, Yhwh's loving characteristics gradually became more prominent than his ruthlessness, although even in the prophetic texts he remains potentially threatening if he is disobeyed. These negative portrayals of Yhwh are problematic for people who believe that the entire text is an authoritative revelation, in which case God's abusive behavior is impossible to reconcile with depictions of him as compassionate and just. "The dark side of God's behavior raises the question of whether the text could really have been given or inspired by a God who is said to provide an absolute moral standard" (Corbett, 2021, p. 218). The dark side of the image of God in the Hebrew Bible is obvious. Perhaps the later Christian insistence on an all-good, loving image of God is a defense against the obvious presence of enormous evil in the world. The eventual invention of the Devil as a source of evil was a tacit acknowledgement that everything was not under control.

When powerful intrapsychic forces such as hatred and revenge are activated, the individual is essentially taken over by a complex and may have little control over the resulting intense emotion. Retaliatory violence is a way to cope with the kind of humiliation and shame experienced in defeat, which produces a threat to the self-esteem of the entire nation. It is easy to defend the resulting vengeful, vindictive behavior under the banner of God's commandment, calling it a "holy war," thus disavowing personal responsibility. In the process, the individual's sadism is released and justified. The unforgiving need for vengeance following a narcissistic injury (Kohut, 1972) is a very human dynamic, and the resulting murders are morally justified by attributing them to a divine commandment: "in the cities of those peoples that the Lord your God gives you for an inheritance, you shall save alive nothing that breathes, /but you shall utterly destroy them" (Deut. 20: 16–17). These kinds of biblical verses are usually ignored or somehow rationalized by contemporary clergy, such as by saying that exhortations to kill all living things were not meant literally but are hyperbolic descriptions of total victory using the vocabulary of the times. Or more simply, God judged the people who were killed to be evil, so they deserved to die. The human shadow is ignored in these explanations.

The triumphalism enjoyed by the victors of biblical battles is a form of narcissistic enhancement produced by the stimulation of infantile grandiosity, the inflation of the victors' sense of self, and the boost in national pride that victory produces. This human pleasure in military victory is easily projected onto God, such as in the Song of Miriam: "Sing to the Lord, for he has triumphed gloriously" (Exod. 15: 20). The "triumph" here refers to the large-scale drowning of men and horses in the Red Sea. The human lust for power and glory in order to bolster national self-esteem is easily projected onto the glory of God. Thus, in order to show his strength, Yhwh hardened Pharaoh's heart so that he would resist Moses' order to let the people of Israel go. This allowed Yhwh to demonstrate his power, which he expressed in a series of plagues culminating in the deaths of Egyptian first-born children. Presumably, Yhwh could have softened Pharoah's heart to avoid this bloodshed, but a display of power was necessary as a demonstration. The biblical image of Yhwh is therefore that of a mass murderer, as we also see in his command to kill the inhabitants of conquered cities. Yhwh is willing to kill thousands of people for the sins of one individual, seen when an Israelite married a Midianite woman, whereupon Yhwh's response was to send a plague that killed 24,000 people (Num. 25: 8), illustrating the type of vengeful rage characteristic of human autocrats. This kind of vindictive behavior was also shown in the story of Uzzah, a man who tried to steady the ark of the covenant when the oxen carrying it stumbled (2 Sam. 6: 3–8). For merely touching it, he was killed, again demonstrating a sensitivity characteristic of a narcissistically vulnerable human despot. Commentators are forced to assume that Uzzah must have been guilty of some other sin for this to have happened because they cannot acknowledge the way the event reveals Yhwh's power shadow. Even children were not exempt from Yhwh's outbursts; when children mocked Elisha, Yhwh avenged the insult by sending two bears to kill them (2 Kings 2: 23–25). Yhwh is so sensitive to slights that he demands the death penalty for insulting his name (Lev. 24: 16), and if necessary, he "will take delight in bringing ruin" upon such people. The enjoyment of inflicting pain is characteristic of human sadists. These examples are all instances of the projection of human psychopathology onto the biblical image of God.

The murderous behavior described in the Bible is attributable to cultural factors as well as to human psychological dynamics. Perhaps the mass murder of conquered populations was common practice, acceptable to the people of the time. However, this is a weak defense; cultural conditions can only release and provide an outlet for human psychological propensities such as sadism, violence, and hatred. Even if the victors were mistaken in their belief that God ordered the deliberate slaughter of non-combatants, they show no reluctance to carry out the order and they seem to revel in the killing. Why this material is regarded as a sacred text is puzzling.

Violence in Christian scriptures

The New Testament is not immune from violent rhetoric. Jesus recommends death to those who do not honor their parents (Matt. 15: 4–7; Mark 7: 9–10, quoting from Leviticus 20: 9). Jesus also says he has come to turn family members against one another (Matt. 10: 35–37), and he promises salvation to those who abandon their families for him (Mark 10: 29–30; Luke 18: 29–30). At the Second Coming, cities that do not accept Jesus will suffer greatly (Matt. 10: 14–15). He threatens eternal punishment (Matt. 25: 46), and at the End Times, evil doers will be cast into a fiery furnace or an unquenchable fire (Matt. 13: 42: Luke, 3–17). Luke 19: 27 has Jesus say: "But as for these enemies of mine, who did not want me to reign over them, bring them here and slay them before me." According to Matthew 23: 33, Jesus says: "You serpents, you brood of vipers, how are you to escape being sentenced to hell?" These and similar sayings seem inordinately cruel and unforgiving. They seem so vindictive and out of character that they may have been later additions unless they simply reveal shadow traits in Jesus.

Similar punitive themes are found in other sections of the New Testament. The Gospel of John teaches that people who do not believe that Jesus is their savior are damned. According to the book of Revelation, in order to destroy unbelievers, at the End Times a quarter of the earth will be destroyed by sword, famine, plague, and wild beasts. Avenging angels will wreak a series of other misfortunes, and there will be death by earthquakes and hailstones. Before being killed, unbelievers will be tortured in a range of sadistic ways. The projection of the author's cruelty and hatred onto divinity is obvious in these verses, and so is a primitive splitting defense into all good and all bad.

On the whole, Christians try to maintain an idealized, loving image of God at all costs, although some acknowledge the dark side of the biblical God-image, with no attempt to justify it theologically (Crenshaw, 1984). Such writers realize that this aspect of divinity is difficult for believers, but they point out that it is not unpleasant enough for them to abandon their God. Metzger

(2009) acknowledges that some theologians over-idealize their God-image. He points out various instances in the New Testament that are unsavory, such as the level of rage expressed in Revelation, Jesus' insistence that there will be no mercy at the Last Judgment, and similar threats of the wrath of God upon those who do not obey Jesus (Matt: 25: 41–46; 13: 41–42; Jn. 3: 36). By and large, Christians have ignored Jesus' admonition about non-violent resistance to evil (Matt. 5: 38–42). They prefer the notion of just war. With some exceptions, they tend to declare any war that the government feels is necessary to be a just war.

Christian fundamentalists are attached to the notion of the apocalypse, the idea that at the End Times there will be catastrophic violence followed by a rebirth. This mythology includes the notion of a cosmic conflict between God and the Devil or between God and the Antichrist. The psychological origins of this fantasy are complex, involving the sense that the world is hopelessly corrupt, and God has no choice but to end it. Other factors that contribute to belief in this myth are deferred hope in Jesus' return, the need to utterly destroy evil, and the need for restitution and revenge at a time in which one's own faith will be validated, and unbelievers will be destroyed (Strozier, 1994). J. Harold Ellens's (2007) study of religious violence shows that it is often motivated by such apocalyptic fantasies.

All traditions have fundamentalists who are prone to violence or who are drawn to violent mythology. They see their own sacred text as the only valid one, and they believe that force may be necessary to impose its values. There are many examples within the history of Christianity of the human proclivity to violence projected onto God, such as the Inquisition, the Crusades, and the persecution of heretics (Ellerbe, 1995). In the Hebrew Bible, the priest Phineas was ordered by God to kill an Israelite man consorting with a Midianite woman. Christian white supremacists, calling themselves Phineas priests, follow this example by attacking any form of multiculturalism (Bushart et al., 1998).

Religion often provides ideological, moral, and spiritual justification for violence (Juergensmeyer, 2001). It is difficult to know whether the violence described in sacred texts kindles violence in religious believers that otherwise would not occur. Some violent religionists are characterologically prone to violence and use their sacred text to support or justify their behavior, which they see as sanctioned by God. Religious violence often has mythic roots such as apocalyptic fantasies. Juergensmeyer (2001) notes that the Christian Identity[4] scenario of cosmic war and its attendant social struggles can be traced back to the ancient mythic conflict between Lucifer and God.

The widespread use of violence among some religionists occurs in spite of the fact that most religions profess to promote peace. Although they do so by admonishing their adherents to behave well, by giving good spiritual advice, and by examining conscience, these ego-level strictures seem to have no effect on deep-seated shadow material or on violently toned, unconscious complexes.

In the mind of the violent Christian, the fact that Jesus taught the love of one's enemies (Mt. 5: 44) is balanced by his statement that he had come to bring not peace but a sword (Mt. 10: 34). His violent overthrow of the tables of the money changers in the Jerusalem temple (Mat. 21: 12–17) seems to offer another justification for necessary aggression. Juergensmeyer notes that early Christians tended to pacifism, but St. Ambrose and St. Augustine developed the notion of just war, which justifies combat under certain conditions.

The myth of redemptive violence

Walter Wink (1998) believes that the myth of redemptive violence (a term introduced by Paul Ricoeur) has operated within the collective consciousness of the West for the last three thousand years. This myth splits the world into good and evil and makes a virtue out of violence, either to impose a divine fiat or as necessary for the restoration of social order. The myth suggests that when we are violated, we can strike back in self-righteous fury at our attacker because evil can be defeated by violence, which therefore can be redemptive, meaning that it has a transformative spiritual value. Wink sees one of the sources of this myth in a Babylonian text, the *Enuma Elish*, dated to about 1250 BCE, older than the Hebrew Bible. This myth describes the creation of the world and the human race in terms of violent conflict between rebel gods and the ruling gods. In the process, Tiamat, the great mother of that pantheon, is murdered and dismembered. From her corpse, the victorious rebel gods create the universe. In this mythologem, human beings originated from a violent act at the center of creation. This means that evil and aggression are primary, present from the beginning. Wink believes that this kind of creation myth is so prevalent that it is largely taken for granted and unquestioned. Needless to say, the idea that violence can be redemptive ignores the disastrous consequences of violence for victims of the resulting wars. One example of the application of the myth of redemptive violence was the attack on indigenous people in the Americas as the West was settled, while preserving the fantasy that this was for the best, part of the Manifest Destiny of the settlers. Another example is the analogous biblical story of the invasion of Canaan by the Israelites, who had to be destroyed because of their evil ways. The myth of redemptive violence permeates contemporary culture, not only in foreign policy but also in literature and movies. Wink believes that the way out of this myth is by acknowledging and transforming our own shadow rather than projecting it and by seeing divinity in the other as well as in ourselves.

The scapegoat complex

The Hebrew Bible (Lev. 16: 8, 21) describes how, in ancient Israel on the Day of Atonement, the sins of the community were ritually transferred to a goat that was then banished into the desert, as if sin and guilt were a physical burden that could be transferred. The goat substituted for and suffered on behalf of the community. Another goat was sacrificed to placate Azazel, a desert demon the people feared. In Isaiah 52–53, the Suffering Servant is a scapegoat who suffers for the sins of others. In the Jerusalem temple, scapegoat animals were slaughtered in elaborate rituals to atone for the people's sins and relieve their guilt. This archetypal theme is central to Christianity, where Jesus suffers for the sins of humanity; he is the ultimate innocent scapegoat.

The idea of the scapegoat suggests that we can project shadow aspects of oneself onto an animal, or onto another person or group, who then bears the burden of one's own shadow material or the shadow of one's group. Apparently, when disaster strikes, it is important to find someone to blame to avoid personal guilt and responsibility or to avoid the sense that there is no reason for what has happened. By projectively blaming an innocent victim, the community can maintain a sense of self-righteousness and moral superiority with no need for self-examination. Finding a scapegoat also distracts the community from the real source of its difficulties, which may be its own shadow. Scapegoating allows the projection of one's own toxic introjects and one's own violence, usually onto members of a hated group chosen by society to be attacked because its members seem threatening or too different. They then act as a target or container for the community's projected unwanted impulses. Scapegoating completely prevents any shadow integration while making the victim seem dangerous.

Scapegoating is an archetypal process that has continued throughout history, as when innocent victims, such as the Jews, witches, or other social outsiders in medieval Europe, were blamed for plagues and other problems. (The scapegoat motif is discussed in more detail in Perera, 1986 and Corbett, 2015.) Examples in modern times are legion, including Jews in Nazi Germany, Kulak peasants in the Soviet Union, Muslims in Serbia, Uyghurs in China, and immigrants in the USA. These groups become phobic objects that become culturally institutionalized targets for the projection of blame. They carry devalued aspects of the dominant group. At the same time, the oppression of an outgroup maintains in-group boundaries and stability, because scapegoating allows one's own internal bad objects and one's doubts to be attacked in projection. This mechanism is a narcissistic defense among people who cannot tolerate shame or guilt, which is dealt with by blaming the scapegoat. Scapegoating is also based on the fantasy of trying to maintain rigid boundaries between what is considered to be pure and impure, good and evil, or healthy and unhealthy, which is why sexual relations with the persecuted group are usually forbidden.

The psychological functions of religious beliefs

Religious beliefs are powerful influences within social groups and within the individual psyche. A wide range of theories try to explain the origin and function of these beliefs. Freud believed they are based on powerful wishes such as the need for a heavenly protector. For him, they are illusory, residues of infantile dependency, and an avoidance of painful reality. This attitude is now seen as a very limited way to understand religion. Later theorists such as Kohut see religious beliefs as ways to fulfill important selfobject needs. Such beliefs can be used to sustain the believer's sense of self. They bind anxiety, soothe the individual, and offer goals, values, meaning, and purpose in life. A belief system allows the believer to participate in a community of like-minded people, which also supports the cohesion of the individual members' sense of self. Attachment theorists believe that the fundamental dynamic underlying theistic religions is the need for the constant availability of reliable attachment figures such as Christ.

At the collective level, mythic religious beliefs answer fundamental questions about creation, salvation, and the afterlife. For skeptical observers, either religious beliefs are driven by the human need to answer these kinds of questions or such beliefs are defenses against existential anxiety. The skeptic might see a belief such as the resurrection of Jesus as a defensive (or more unkindly, a delusional) way to deal with death anxiety. However, such belief is shared by a large community of believers and is perfectly compatible with average mental health, because unlike a true delusion of the kind found in psychotic people, a religious belief is not arrived at by a pathological process such as schizophrenia. Yet there is some overlap; in people suffering from psychosis, delusions are often seen as having a defensive or adaptive benefit that explains unusual perceptual experiences, while religious beliefs may also be invoked for defensive and adaptive purpose.

The fact that many people share a religious belief only attests to its psychological usefulness and its importance within a religious subculture. The fact that a belief is shared means nothing in terms of its validity or truth. It is impossible to prove or disprove many religious beliefs; there is usually no definitive evidence on either side of the arguments for their validity. However, some religious fundamentalist and cultic subcultures share dangerous or bizarre beliefs that sound quasi-delusional or at least pathological from the point of view of the larger culture. The same phenomenon is seen among social conspiracy theories such as those promoted by QAnon, which sometimes have a delusional quality about them.[5] Some observers see such beliefs as examples of self-serving self-deception rather than true delusions, but extremes of self-deception shade into delusion.

Sometimes, religious beliefs can enhance mental health, such as when the conviction that one will eventually meet a deceased loved one in heaven softens the pain of grief. At other times, religious beliefs become incorporated into the individual's psychopathology or even produce psychopathology, such as when the depressed individual is tortured by his belief that he will spend eternity in hell. In such a case, the individual has blended a religious idea with a psychological difficulty, by using the idea of hell as a vehicle to express a delusional need for punishment due to unconscious or conscious guilt. A person who believes that there will be an apocalyptic final judgment in which unbelievers will be cast into burning lakes of fire may be using this religious mytheme to express his hatred and sadism or his need for revenge. It is not unusual for adherents to very rigid religious belief systems to be moralistic, self-righteous, prone to all-good and all-bad splitting and the projection of the shadow. These defenses protect the individual's vulnerability and supply structure that is not available internally. Such individuals are unable to question their beliefs; doubt is projected onto unbelievers. Emotionally fragile individuals need an unshakable system of beliefs of the kind found in religious systems in order to maintain their narcissistic equilibrium. A challenge to the validity of any one of these beliefs threatens the cohesion of the entire system. This dynamic is the source of much religious dogmatism.

Belief in the Devil

The Devil is a theological and mythic idea with important psychological consequences for religious believers. Many Christians believe that the Devil is responsible for much evil in the world and also for some of their own reprehensible behavior. Some Christians believe that the idea of the Devil is essential to Christian theology, pointing out that this figure has been part of the tradition since it began. The notion of the Devil makes evil something tangible and focused, especially for charismatic groups who stress the Devil's importance in the New Testament. Contemporary Church leaders such as Pope Francis refer to the Devil occasionally.

In the Hebrew Bible, the figure of Yhwh produces both good and evil (Isa. 45: 7). He orders destruction and sends plagues and defeats in war. Therefore, there was no need for the biblical authors to propose a separate figure causing evil. The figure of a Satan is found in three books of the Hebrew Bible, but this is not the Devil of later theology. This Satan is a member of the heavenly court, acting as an accuser or inciter of injurious behavior but not an adversary of God (Zechariah 3: 1–2; Job 1: 6–12; 1 Chronicles 21: 1).

During the First Temple period (circa 1000 BCE–586 BCE), the Israelites were polytheistic or henotheistic, believing that their God was the best of many. They became largely monotheistic during the Babylonian Exile and the subsequent Second Temple period (586 BCE-70 CE; Smith, 2004). At this time and during the Hellenistic (333 BCE–63 BCE) and Roman periods, the idea developed that there are rebellious, evil forces in the world that are opposed to God and his plans for the world. Otherwise, it was difficult to account for evil and for the disasters that had befallen the people.

Greg Riley (1999) suggests three important sources of the idea of the Devil and demons. In Genesis 6: 1–4, there is a story that the "sons of God" (Nephilim) took human wives. The Book of Enoch also tells the story that the sons of God bred with human women, giving birth to giants who died during Noah's flood. Their souls became demons. Another story is that when God commanded the angels to pay homage to Adam, because of pride one angel refused to do so because he had existed before Adam. This and other angels were cast out of heaven. A third source is inspired by stories in Isaiah, Ezekiel, and 2 Enoch about an angel expelled from heaven for wanting to be equal to God.

The Devil has played a significant role in Christian history, where it was seen as constantly disrupting human life and trying to move people toward evil. In the New Testament, reports of Jesus' exorcisms of devils (Luke 13: 16; Matt. 9: 32–33) suggest that he believed in the objective reality of evil forces. The Devil is said to have offered Jesus worldly power (Matt. 4: 8–9), and John 14: 30 speaks of the Devil as "the ruler of this world" because "the whole world is in the power of the evil one" (1 Jn. 5: 19). The Devil is even seen as the "god of this age" (2 Cor. 4: 4), and 1 Peter 5: 8 warns people to be vigilant because the devil is a "roaring lion" seeking to devour someone. The Devil is accused of entering into Judas to make him betray Jesus (Luke 22: 3). Saint Augustine said that "The human race is the Devil's fruit tree, his own property, from which he may pick his fruit." In the Gospel of John, the death of Jesus is said to result in the conquest of the Devil. However, the promise of the Devil's defeat obviously did not materialize, since evil continues to haunt the world for which Christ died. Accordingly, the promised final victory over evil has had to be postponed until the Second Coming of Christ.

For much of its history, especially in the medieval period, the Church typically accused heretics of being servants of the Devil and saw criticism of its authority as the result of the Devil's promptings. The Jews were regarded as servants of the Devil by notables such as Martin Luther and St. John Chrysostom. For many medieval Christians, bodily appetites were the link to the Devil. Many Christian ascetics have felt they are in a lifelong struggle against the Devil, which they often equate with sexual desire. They believed that the world has fallen and that, because sin is a deep aspect of human nature, we are vulnerable to the Devil's temptations. Asceticism, prayer, and denial of the body are their solutions. After the Enlightenment, literal belief in the Devil lessened but still persists. There seems to be a psychological need for a figure that we can make responsible for our own toxic complexes and shadow material, and blame for our negative behavior, instead of struggling with the shadow consciously. Pride, envy, and the need for power are particularly important in this context. In Christian iconography, the Devil was seen to be full of pride and envy. Pride is still seen as a potent cause of evil. Brennan (1997, p. 212) points out that in mythological stories of the Devil he always desires control, and "he feasts on power and the prospect of power." She also points out that the devil is especially envious of the creativity of others, which he would like to destroy.

The psychologist is tempted to reduce the idea of the Devil to the projection of intrapsychic shadow material onto a mythic figure, but people who claim to have experienced demonic figures describe an objective entity or presence (described in Corbett, 2018, pp. 142–143). In the absence of any overt mental illness or hysteria, these experiences cannot be summarily dismissed as hallucinatory or nothing but projective.

For Jung, the mythological Devil is the personification of archetypal evil. Jung believed that the dark side of divinity has been split off in the Christian tradition, in which Jesus is portrayed as perfectly good. Evil is therefore entirely attributed to the Devil, to the Antichrist, or to humanity. Jung therefore sees the Christian image of God as too one-sidedly benevolent. This split produced a metaphysical dualism in Christian doctrine, in which the Devil or the Antichrist became the adversary of God. In contrast, Jung's idea that the Self (the intrapsychic image of God) has a dark side maintains the unity of the Self. Here, it is important to reiterate Jung's caution that by describing the dark side of the Self we are discussing human experiences and images of the divine, not the divine itself.

Religion as a balm for suffering

One of the reasons that religion is popular is that it offers a way to find comfort and meaning when one is suffering. Christians may feel that their suffering brings them closer to Jesus or that it is a way to identify with him. The fact that God could suffer on behalf of humanity is comforting to many Christians.

For traditional theists, the problem produced by widespread evil and suffering is that if God is omnipotent, and so could prevent unnecessary suffering and evil but does not do so, he cannot be all good. He is therefore either not entirely good or not omnipotent. In response to this problem a variety of theodicies, attempts to justify God, have evolved. Typical are the books of C.S. Lewis (2015a, 2015b). Lewis deploys the traditional free will defense, which suggests that God gives people the ability to make choices that result in either good or evil, and God does not interfere with this choice. Lewis believes that pain is transformed when it is seen as a radical form of God's love and God's discipline, to make human beings humble by realizing their dependency on God, making them less rebellious and more loveable by God. He refers to pain as God's "megaphone to rouse a deaf world" (2015a, p. 91). This is a kind of soul-making theodicy that suggests that suffering somehow improves us spiritually. Lewis adopts the traditional Christian view of human fallenness, that we suffer because we sin. Suffering corrects this tendency and awakens us to our wickedness and abuse of free will. For Lewis, pain is remedial and essential, and we never know its ultimate effect on the personality. Somehow, God's presence makes the difference when we suffer. This type of theodicy was also developed by John Hick's *Evil and the God of Love*, which suggests that without suffering we would not develop virtues such as courage and compassion, because spiritual maturation requires suffering. Simone Weil (1951) makes the case that if it is accepted, affliction can be a way to give total assent to God and so reach the height of the love of God. She believes that if the situation is accepted one can hear the word of God from the depths of the affliction, which in her words is "a marvel of divine technique." This attitude would be of help only to people already committed to the spiritual life.

This kind of theological explanation does not deal adequately with the effects of chronic pain on the personality. Nor does it explain the need for so much suffering, the intensity of human suffering, or the suffering of animals and children, which often makes no sense. Suffering is sometimes soul-destroying, resulting in nothing but bitterness. Neither does this theodicy address the old question of why the wicked prosper and good people suffer, except by saying that we cannot accurately judge others' characters and behavior, and the books will be balanced in the afterlife. Pain may make us feel we are surrendering to a loving God, but the skeptic will wonder whether we are surrendering to the superego, the sense that we deserve punishment. The very notion that a loving God has to inflict severe pain to mold his creation suggests a sadistic God-image and defensively idealizes suffering. The idea that God allows or inflicts pain to test people or to demonstrate his love of humanity is intellectually tortuous and verges on sadomasochism. It is akin to the "for your own good" rationalization of parents who abuse their children.

Writers such as Jung and Victor Frankl believe that the discovery of meaning in suffering allows us to bear situations that otherwise would be unbearable. Jung therefore refers to religions as "therapeutic myths" (CW 18, para. 1231) that try to deal with suffering. He believes that a philosophical or religious view of the world is a psychological method of healing (CW 18, para. 1578). Religions may indeed offer such meaning, but sometimes intense suffering causes people to lose rather than strengthen their faith. Similarly, all religions offer comfort for death anxiety, whether through belief in an afterlife or in karma, but the other side of that coin is that the prospect of what happens after death may produce considerable anxiety.

Notes

1 In the same paragraph, Jung criticizes Freud's idea of religion as illusory, since this idea destroys the bond between humanity and their gods, severing people from the very basis of the psyche.
2 Several previous saviors had been born of a virgin. Dionysius was born of Zeus and the human Persephone, Horus was born to the virgin Isis, and so on. The Church Fathers discredited these earlier accounts as devices of the Devil.
3 In this context, it is worth remembering that the biblical Yhwh may have originally been a volcano god. For example: "Smoke went up from his nostrils/and devouring fire from his mouth: glowing coals flamed forth from him" (Psa. 18: 8). At the giving of the law at Mt. Sinai, the text emphasizes how the mountain was wrapped in fire and smoke, which rose "like the smoke of a kiln" (Exod. 19: 18).
4 Christian Identity is a white supremacist, religious ideology that believes that white people can be traced back to the lost tribes of Israel. Non-white or "mud" people were created before Adam and Eve. Many adherents are virulently racist and anti-Semitic. Many believe that the world is in its last days and Jesus will return after a period of tribulation. Adherents often believe that there is a Jewish conspiracy to rule the world.
5 Some QAnon followers believe that the world is controlled by a cabal of Satan-worshipping, blood-eating, pedophiles. This movement still has large numbers of followers.

Chapter 3

The psyche expresses itself in the Bible

The Bible through a psychological lens

The Bible's historical importance is incalculable; it has been a major influence on the Western psyche and the Western intellectual tradition. That is why Jung declares that: "We must read our Bible, or we shall not understand psychology. Our psychology, whole lives, and language and imagery are built upon the Bible" (1976, p. 156).

The interpretation of the Bible has always been controversial. Biblical scholars and theologians of different religious traditions understand the text very differently. The Bible was written over a long period of time by many authors in cultures very different from our own, so that even for adherents to one of the biblical traditions, much of it needs explanation and interpretation. Such interpretation can be carried out from the point of view of preexisting doctrine and dogma; from a literary, linguistic, sociological, or historical-critical viewpoint; or from a psychological point of view. Some biblical scholars deplore the attempt to talk about religion psychologically, as if doing so ignores its transcendent source, but Jung's approach allows us to locate the source of the experience of transcendence within transpersonal levels of the psyche rather than in a heavenly realm beyond the psyche.

Biblical stories seen from a psychological perspective are manifestations of different levels and different processes of the psyche, both human and archetypal. Biblical stories describe the interaction of the authors' consciousness with archetypal level of the unconscious or with the Self. Jung believes that these experiences are indistinguishable from traditional accounts of the experience of the divine (CW 12, para. 9). It is crucial to Jung's approach that when the unconscious produces religious experience, it expresses something real, because the psyche is real.

The archetypal dimension of the psyche reveals itself by producing mythic themes such as the trinity, a dying and resurrecting god, a virgin birth, and the apocalypse. Much of this kind of archetypal material found in the Bible was appropriated from earlier mythological systems, re-written to support the emerging worship of Yhwh. For the depth psychologist, biblical stories can be approached in the same symbolic way that we discuss myths and folklore, which have been repeated over and over again from generation to generation until finally they crystallize in canonical forms, at which point they are said to represent an underlying truth. Edinger writes that "the events of the Bible, although presented as history, psychologically understood are archetypal images" that erupted into space and time and require a human ego to live them out (1986, p. 13). These images can be amplified by locating them within world mythology at large rather than restricting their meaning to one theological system. Edinger points out that stories of numinous experiences such as Moses at the burning bush depict encounters of an ego with the Self. These encounters are then interpreted, and their meanings embellished and elaborated, over a long period. The interpretation of the numinous experiences described in the Bible often becomes incorporated into theological doctrine and dogma, but such interpretation is also colored by human psychodynamics. The Bible therefore reveals not only archetypal material but also a range of personality dynamics. The human level of the psyche and human mental mechanisms are important because features of human psychology are frequently projected onto divinity by the biblical authors, in an attempt to explain otherwise inexplicable historical events.

J. Harold Ellens (1997) points out that the psychological lens reveals features of the Bible that are not seen using other paradigms. From a depth psychological point of view, the psychological approach to the Bible is fundamental, since all religious imagery, including the Bible's description of numinous encounters and the subsequent doctrine and dogma to which they gave rise, originates in the psyche before it is elaborated by theologians. Edinger (1986, p. 11) points out that the Bible is "a self-revelation of the objective psyche." For him, this is the sense in which it is "inspired." He sees the Old Testament as "an exceedingly rich compendium of images representing encounters with the numinosum" (1986, p. 12). Edinger notes that the archetypes hitherto appeared as metaphysical aspects of religious dogma, but, in Jung's terms, now they can be seen to be psychological processes projected into "metaphysical space and hypostatized" (CW 9i, para. 120). That is, metaphysical entities such as gods and goddesses can now be seen as psychological phenomena rather than as divinities existing in an extra-psychological realm and occasionally intervening in human lives. The divinities of world religions are the personified projections of archetypal processes. Theologians assume that these divinities emanate from a metaphysical reality such as a God in heaven. However, the existence of such a metaphysical divinity is entirely unprovable, largely based on socially transmitted beliefs and the authority of sacred texts. In contrast, the experience of the archetypal level of the psyche produces numinous experiences that have been documented time and again and are empirically demonstrable (Corbett, 2020). For Jung, all direct experiences of the sacred either originate within the transpersonal levels of the psyche or, if they emanate from a divinity beyond the psyche, are at the very least mediated or transmitted by means of the psyche. We do not know if there is a divinity beyond the psyche, and we cannot know, since the psyche would be the inevitable medium of its expression to humanity.

Von Franz (1980) sketches the historical development of the projection of the archetypal psyche, initially onto demons and spirits, then onto a principle such as water, air, or fire conceived of as deities, and then onto mythical gods and goddesses. In antiquity, states of mind such as rage were attributed to the influence of external deities. She points out a general psychological law:

> The statement of the new truth reveals the previous conceptions as 'projections' and tries to draw them into the psychic inner world, at the same time as it announces a new myth, which now passes for the finally discovered 'absolute' truth.
>
> (pp. 38–39, italics in original)

She believes that this reinterpretation is an act of *"assimilation through reflection"* (italics in original) in which, when the projected content is taken back, the human level of consciousness is raised. When Christianity insisted on a historically real incarnate Christ-figure, it was as if "the whole mythical heaven full of gods had come down into one human being" (p. 41). Von Franz (1980) believes that with the advent of Christ, the mythic world "took on real form and definition."

The biblical image of God often reflects human psychology

There are many passages in the Bible that are objectionable or horrifying to modern ears, in spite of assertions that the text is divinely inspired. They represent the projection of problematic human personality traits and psychopathology onto divinity. There are innumerable such examples, including the killing of a rebellious child,[1] corporal punishment of children,[2] the killing of "witches,"[3] and slavery.[4] The book of Leviticus commands the death sentence for homosexuality (20: 13) and for adultery (20: 10), attitudes that presumably reflect the local mores of the time. One wonders why Moses is regarded in an idealized light, given that, under the impression that Yhwh orders him to do so, he says: "Now therefore, kill every male among the little ones, and kill every woman who has known man by lying with him/ But all the young girls who have not known man by lying with him, keep alive for yourselves" (Num. 31: 17–18). The text goes on to say that thirty-two thousand women were essentially made into sex slaves. Apologists insist that such laws and commandments must be seen in the overall context of the Bible as a whole. They cannot be understood in isolation, and they were in keeping with the standards of the times. However, biblical stories that display brutal behavior or overt psychopathology characteristic of human beings are often sanctioned and rationalized by attributing these actions to a divine commandment. Sometimes, these passages are ignored, explained away as part of the local culture, necessary to defeat evil, or glossed over by pious believers.

Corbett (2021) suggested that if a human being were to behave like the Yhwh of the Hebrew Bible, we would consider him to be a borderline personality. This is because Yhwh seems to be emotionally unstable, prone to rage attacks and unpredictable, fluctuating, unstable moods. He is narcissistically fragile, constantly afraid that his people will prefer other gods to him. He suffers from envy of other gods and insists he is greater than they are, and their followers must be eradicated, violently if necessary. It is noteworthy that the liturgy of the Abrahamic traditions often refers to praise and the "glory" of God, as if his devotees sense that he constantly needs reassurance about how important he is—a distinctly human need. As Corbett (2021, pp. 191–192) put it,

> He [Yhwh] seems to need his people, as if he is lonely or suffers from abandonment anxiety. His insecurity is visible on many occasions, for example when he allows terrible suffering to be inflicted on Job just to see if Job is truly faithful to him, in the process betraying his own lack of faithfulness. He tries to force his people to love him, partly through threats and promises and partly by regulating all aspects of their lives. He can be impulsive, paranoid, and defensively inflated. He is prone to all-good and all-bad splitting, leading to large scale, ruthless massacres.

The harshness of Yhwh's either-or judgment, a splitting defense typical of borderline personalities, is seen in the long list of offenses that he believes deserve the death penalty, such as sacrificing to another god (Exod. 20: 20), a child who curses his parents (Exod. 21: 15, 17), and working on the sabbath (Exod. 35: 2). If the daughter of a temple priest should become a harlot, she is condemned to be burned to death (Lev. 21: 9). Yhwh offers his people the choice of only fidelity to him or death. In Deuteronomy 27–28, he tells the people that they will be blessed if they are obedient but will be cursed if they disobey. When they rebel, frightful threats are made: "Their infants will be dashed in pieces/ before their eyes/their houses will be plundered/ and their wives ravished" (Isaiah 13: 16). It is very typical of narcissistic rage to maintain the need for revenge for a long period of time. Yhwh's narcissistic vulnerability is also seen in his unforgiving, long-standing, vengeful grudge against the Amalekites, people who attacked the Israelites on their way to Canaan from Egypt. Several generations later, Yhwh tells King Saul to "smite Amalek, and utterly destroy all that they have… kill both and woman, infant and suckling" (1 Sam. 15: 3). When Ahab, the king of Israel, shows mercy to a conquered foe that Yhwh had ordered to be destroyed, Yhwh is enraged, and says to Ahab "therefore your life shall go for his life, and your people for his people" (1 Kings, 20: 42). In other words, Yhwh wants his people to mirror his own vindictiveness. His narcissistic rage makes him threaten to punish the descendants of people who worship other gods "to the third and the fourth generation" (Exod. 20: 4–6). The prophets Ezekiel (18: 20) and Jeremiah (31: 30) protested this injustice but to little avail. As well as the radically unfair transmission of generational guilt, there are also biblical examples of mass extinction and collective guilt, such as in the story of Noah's flood, as if Noah was the only good person on earth. Yhwh is said to "love justice" (Isa. 61: 8) and "all his ways are justice" (Deut. 32: 4), but he often seems not only unjust but also irrational. He sometimes gets angry for unknown reasons, even looking for an excuse to be punitive, such as when he tells David to carry out a census and then punishes him for doing so (2 Sam. 24). Yhwh is said in many places to be merciful and "slow to anger" (e.g., Ps. 103: 8; Exod. 34: 6), but the evidence does not support this assertion. He becomes angry readily, massacring thousands of his people when he gets enraged, such as when the Israelites worship a golden calf (Exod. 32). He buries alive the rebellious Korah, his supporters and their households (Num. 16). He slaughters the Israelites who consort with the priestesses of a Canaanite god (Num. 25).

Yhwh glorifies war, never expressing regret that it is necessary, clearly reflecting a cultural value. Exodus 15: 3 says that "The Lord is a man of war." The image of the divine warrior is often reflected in the prophetic tradition. Isaiah 42: 13 says, "like a man of war he stirs up his fury...he shows himself mighty against his foes." In the Psalms, Yhwh "shatters the heads of his enemies...that you may bathe your feet in blood" (Psa. 68: 21–23). These attitudes reflect the human propensity to violence expressed in projection as an attribute of divinity.

David Penchansky (1999, p. 54) notes that the biblical writers "frequently depicted Yhwh as a dangerous, unpredictable force liable to break out in violence with no warning or provocation." Because the rabbinical tradition believed that God is always good and just, the rabbis, when faced with the manifest injustices and suffering Yhwh causes, tried to soften his image in various ways, such as by explaining the toxic material in terms of the social practices of the time. Instead of acknowledging Yhwh's capricious, often incomprehensible behavior, the rabbinical tradition absolves Yhwh from any wrongdoing by rationalizing his violence as necessary for some greater good or for reasons that we cannot perceive. It is too easy to interpret Yhwh's command to Abraham to sacrifice his son or Job's unwarranted suffering as tests of faith. Like much biblical interpretation, these rationalizations try to maintain a benevolent image of God. They are defenses against unconscious anger at the punitive father God or ways to deny his abusive behavior. This is so prominent and causes so much suffering that Jung insisted that our image of God must acknowledge his dark side.

The dark side of the biblical God-image

The dark side of the biblical God-image is seen in many stories of his violence, jealousy, and vengeance, threatened by prophets such as Jeremiah (45: 4–5): "I am bringing evil upon all flesh." Yhwh's dark side is often seen in the psalms, such as "for thy sake we are slain all the day long…and accounted as sheep for the slaughter" (Psa. 44: 22). God both destroys and saves humanity; he both punishes and is a refuge for the oppressed in times of trouble (Psa. 9, 107) because of his loving kindness. That is, the mercy and anger of God are intermingled, producing a piety that is a mixture of fear and gratitude.

In the biblical story of Job, at the behest of a Satan,[5] a member of the heavenly court, God is persuaded to allow Job to suffer terrible losses of his family, his property, and his health, as a test of his faithfulness and sincerity. The wager between the Satan and God was whether Job's piety was due only to how much God had given him. In his *Answer to Job*, Jung suggests that Yhwh's doubt about Job's faithfulness is really the projection onto Job of Yhwh's doubt about his own faithfulness. Jung describes Job's experience of Yhwh's savagery as a paradigm for the human experience of the dark side of God. Jung points out that, in his treatment of Job, "Yahweh displays no compunction, remorse, or compassion, but only ruthlessness and brutality" (CW 11, para. 581). Given what Job went through for no obvious reason, Jung believes it is a mistake to assume that God is only loving and benevolent; God is a totality that contains all the opposites, including justice and injustice, good and evil, ruthless cruelty as well as mercy and love. Jung attributes God's ill treatment of Job to God's unconsciousness, his lack of awareness of his own dark side because of a lack of self-reflection. For Jung, therefore, Job acted as a reflecting consciousness for God. By maintaining his innocence, Job forced Yhwh to become conscious of his shadow. Jung believes that Yhwh's need to catch up with the level that human morality had achieved forced God to incarnate in Christ. In this way, God experienced the kind of suffering he inflicts on human beings. The incarnation is therefore an "expiatory self-sacrifice" (CW 11, para. 740).

One clearly sees the dark side of God in the Hebrew Bible when reading all the atrocities he is said to have commanded. Isaiah 45: 7 says that God creates evil, and it is clear from Amos 4: 7–12 that God uses famine, plagues, and droughts as punishments. Amos (3: 6) says that evil does not befall a city "unless the Lord has done it." As Lamentations 3: 38 puts it, "is it not from the mouth of the Most High that good and evil come?" Furthermore, at least in our eyes, the level of punishment imposed on human disobedience in biblical stories often exceeds the gravity of the offense. Apologetic writers see all this as the use of evil for creative purposes or to further God's plan for humanity.

If one acknowledges that some suffering and evil result from the dark side of God, humanity is not responsible for all the world's evil; some evil has archetypal roots and is more than human. Nevertheless, the transpersonal level of moral evil sometimes has to be mediated by human hands, and one gets the distinct impression of willing human collaboration in some of the genocidal behavior described in the Hebrew Bible.

One of Jung's critiques of the Christian image of God is that because it assumes that God is only loving, responsibility for evil and suffering either is projected onto the Devil or the Antichrist or is thought to be entirely the result of the misuse of human free will. Christianity has insisted on the notion of God as the *Summum Bonum*, the supreme good, and also on the doctrine of evil as *privatio boni*, the absence of good, as if evil has no substance of its own (Hick, 2010). Our experience of history contradicts both these ideas. To account for the presence of horrendous evil while insisting that God is only good, the tradition requires a splitting defense. To avoid the cognitive dissonance that acknowledging the dark side of God would produce, theists find explanations for evil in the form of theodicies that try to justify God, such as by saying that he has his own reasons for allowing evil, reasons that human beings cannot understand, or by insisting that free will requires the presence of evil. These kinds of rationalizations try to avoid the uncomfortable evidence that the divine has a dark side. Jung believes that, rather than see God as being only benevolent, we should radically change our image of God to incorporate our experience of divine darkness. However, this perspective has not been widely adopted by biblical scholars, who usually see Job's story as a test of his piety.

When human parenting dynamics and human psychology are projected onto a God-image, suffering and evil are typically imagined to be the result of divine anger because of human disobedience. Like the behavior of a human parent, God's anger is seen as part of the way he relates to humanity, but according to the tradition, it always has a salvific end. Traditional theists often insist that if God carried out destructive actions, they must be morally correct. I wonder if the long history of violence carried out by theists may be unconsciously modeled on Yhwh's behavior or if his actions seem to justify the theist's own violence. There is a good deal of worthy moral teaching in the Bible, but its permissive attitude to slavery, cruelty, genocide, and intolerance also makes it useful as a Rorschach test in which we value the biblical material that corresponds to our own psychology.

In the New Testament, the dark side of God is clearly expressed in the book of Revelation, which describes the punishment of non-believers in harsh detail. However, according to Jung, the dark side of the divine has largely been repressed within Christianity, leading to a metaphysical dualism, as if God and the Devil are two spiritual powers (CW 9, ii, paras. 74–76). Christian doctrine therefore does not correspond to the human experience of divinity, which could see the work of God in events such as Hiroshima and the Holocaust. Nevertheless, many Christians resist the idea of the dark side of God. Certainly, Jesus' depiction of God indicates that his personal image of God was radically different from the way Yhwh is depicted in the Hebrew Bible. Jesus tells people to love their enemies, turn the other cheek, and be merciful "even as your Father is merciful" (Luke 6: 36). However, at the same time, the Christian tradition insists that Christ is the same God as Yhwh, suggesting some kind of personality change, since the God of the Hebrew Bible, to whom Jesus was referring, is sometimes not at all merciful. Jesus wanted to transmit this changed God-image to his followers. His focus on kindness is a good example of how one's personal psychological preferences color one's image of God.

Presumably, Jesus was a loving and compassionate individual, so those qualities are projected onto his God-image, but many of his followers in the subsequent history of Christianity were much more blood-thirsty and violent than he was. They transformed Jesus into a vengeful holy warrior (Revelation 19: 11–16) while also proclaiming him as Isaiah's (9: 6) Prince of Peace. These radically conflicting images of divinity are completely irreconcilable except through rationalizations such as "For as the heavens are higher than the earth, /so are my ways higher than your ways/and my thoughts than your thoughts" (Is. 55: 8–9). The reality is that one's image of God reflects a combination of one's character structure, childhood indoctrination, one's cultural and family background, and one's favorite sacred text. This image is often nothing more than a human construction. Because human images of God reflect human psychology, we often see biblical images of God that are typical of human autocrats who are territorial, paranoid, narcissistic bullies, demanding conformity in the service of preserving power.

Bertrand Russell (1967) pointed out that the most extreme cruelty and immoral behavior have been carried out during historical periods of dogmatic religious beliefs. Examples are the Inquisition, the persecution of witches and heretics, and other forms of sadistic behavior practiced in the name of religion. Much moral progress has been opposed by organized churches, so much so that Russell saw Christianity as "the principal enemy of moral progress in the world" (p. 15). An example is the resistance of southern white Christian ministers to President John F. Kennedy's attempt at racial integration and civil rights legislation. Although it is sometimes claimed that the basis of Western morality is derived from the Bible, in fact many of our current moral, legal, and ethical standards are actually not biblical. They have evolved with the development of social consciousness, and they are sometimes antithetical to biblical teachings.

Deceit and self-deception in the interpretation of the Bible

Traditional Christians adhere to the idea that in several places the Hebrew Bible prophesized the coming of Christ (e.g., Isaiah 10: 13; 9: 6; Micah 5: 2). However, historical criticism of the Bible has shown that this appropriation is mistaken. A typical "fulfillment prophecy" is Isaiah 7: 14, which was and still is sometimes translated as "a virgin shall conceive and bear a son" (Matt. 1: 22). The original text refers to a young woman and not a virgin, which are quite distinct words in Hebrew, so this is a deliberate mistranslation in the service of a theological belief. Contemporary scholarship believes that the actual text refers to an event that occurred during the lifetime of King Ahaz of Judah, when the prophet Isaiah reassures the King that a son will be born to him as a sign that he need not fear the enemy kings who had advanced against him (Lüdeman, 1996). Similarly, the Suffering Servant theme of Isaiah 53: 3 refers to a man who is despised and rejected, who bears the people's grief and is "wounded for our transgressions, he was bruised for our iniquities...and with his stripes we are healed...the Lord has laid on him the iniquity of us all." The Jewish tradition sees this verse in its original context as a reference to the suffering of the people of Israel during the Babylonian Exile. The writers did not have in mind a figure such as Jesus in their distant future, and Jesus did not see his task as liberating exiled Israelites and bringing them back to Israel. Yet the meaning of the Servant Song has been applied to Jesus by saying it was a prophecy that fulfilled itself in a different way than was expected. Lillian Freudman (1994) shows how similar deliberate misquotes and misinterpretation of the Hebrew Bible have been used to justify anti-Jewish hatred.

In order to use the Hebrew Bible as if it forecasted the advent of Jesus, it had to be misread or mistranslated. It is difficult to know to what extent the translators and theologians who misused such material were doing so deliberately and consciously. If it was conscious, it was a power play in bad faith, in the service of promoting and validating their theological beliefs about Jesus, which, ironically, he would not have shared. If these misappropriations were not conscious but involve a form of self-deception, the process required that the part of the interpreter's mind in which he knew he was being false was compartmentalized, denied, or split off from the rest of his mind, to avoid disturbing his conscience. Perhaps it was a form of motivated ignorance. Alternatively, the deception may have been conscious and deliberate but piously rationalized as serving a good cause. It was important to the early Christians that their tradition represented the continuation and fulfillment of the tradition of the Hebrew Bible, partly for political reasons since at the time Christianity was emerging, ancient traditions were given particular cultural value. Christians wanted to demonstrate that they were the new chosen people and that the original covenant between God and the Jews had been replaced or superseded by a new covenant with the Christian Church. Christian theologians believed that, by rejecting Jesus, the Jews had forfeited their original privilege of being chosen. This meant that the Christians no longer had to be envious of the Jews because the Christians had replaced the divine father's original favored child. In the process, the Jewish tradition had to be devalued and persecuted. In this way, Christians' resentment, and sibling envy at being initially not chosen, could be denied by projecting any sense of being devalued onto the Jews. Christianity also dealt with the Jewish claim to be chosen by claims of being saved rather than chosen, by insisting that there is no salvation except in Christ (Acts 4: 12), and by adding theologically derived sayings by Jesus such as "no one comes to the father but through me" (Jn 14: 6).

Not only have Hebrew Bible's prophecies been re-interpreted as if they refer to Jesus, but as an additional way to maintain his continuity with the earlier text, his reported miracles are usually adaptations of analogous miracle stories in the Hebrew Bible. For example, Elisha multiplied bread to feed a hundred people (2 Kings 4: 42–44), just as Jesus fed many people with a small amount of bread and fish. Elijah and Elisha both revived dead people (1 Kings 17: 17–24, 2 Kings 4: 31–37), so Jesus raised three people from the dead.

The idea that the story of Jesus is continuous with the story of Yhwh in the Hebrew Bible is made very unlikely by the fact that the mythological motifs of a dying and resurrecting divinity or a virgin birth are entirely incompatible with Yhwh's attributes. He has no known provenance, he does not die, and he has no gender. The idea of a crucified God would have been unimaginable to the authors of the Hebrew Bible, who saw Yhwh as omnipotent and not a physical entity. That is, the image of divinity in Christian theology is radically different from the God-image of the Hebrew Bible, so from the point of view of that text, claims that the traditions are continuous are dubious.

Is the New Testament the continuation of the Hebrew Bible?

Murray Stein (2018) has suggested looking at the Bible as if it were a long dream arising from the collective unconscious. This material has been filtered through the experience of the biblical authors and the egos of scribes and copyists, guided by the Self. Stein (p. 32) believes that the "Old and New Testaments" can be seen as "one whole and undivided developmental narrative" of the personality of a dreamer, such that the historical Jesus is the endpoint of the development of the Yhwh figure of the Hebrew Bible. Stein sees the story as a movement from "preconscious potential to conscious actualization," confirmed by Jesus' affirmation that he and the Father are one, so that that Jesus represents the individuated ego of the mythic figure that began as Yhwh. However, Stein thereby adopts a perspective that is valid only from a Christian point of view that sees the Old Testament as part of the Christian canon. In fact, the relationship of the Hebrew Bible and the New Testament, a contentious issue since the traditions diverged, cannot be taken for granted.

In the early years of the Christian tradition, it was important for Christians to insist on the continuity of the two texts as a way to maintain the antiquity of the emerging religion. Theologians therefore asserted that the New Testament fulfills the promises of the Hebrew Bible, especially with regard to the coming of a messiah, as if the two books are one story of the history of salvation. This view sees the two traditions as continuous and sees Jesus as the goal or fulfillment of the Hebrew Bible. However, within the Christian tradition itself, there have been several attempts to see the two Testaments as discontinuous, beginning with the rift between the early church and the synagogue, clearly seen in the early patristic literature (Hagner, 2016). Gnostics such as Marcion also saw the God-images of the Old and New Testaments as completely antithetical to each other. The later Christian Church tried to unite them by carrying forward Old Testament themes and models and applying them to the life of Jesus, albeit in a manner that is often based on dubious interpretations of the original text. In the history of New Testament scholarship, opinions about the question of the continuity of the Old and New Testaments have swung back and forth. Some Christian theologians have distanced themselves from the Hebrew Bible.

The Jewish tradition has always resisted any continuity between the Hebrew Bible and the New Testament, seeing Jesus as a false messiah because he did not fulfill the Hebrew prophets' messianic promises such as a peaceful world order and the restoration of a triumphant Davidic kingdom. Micah 5: 4 says that the messianic ruler's dominion will reach "to the ends of the earth," and a glorious temple will arise in Zion to which many nations will flock to worship Israel's God (4: 1–2). Christianity's eschatological promises have also not been fulfilled, although the hope that they will be remains alive. From the Jewish perspective, the New Testament is not a new covenant, and the notion that the traditions are fully continuous cannot be substantiated. The Yhwh of the Hebrew Bible is invisible; in that tradition, no image of God is permissible, so the Jewish tradition could not possibly see Jesus as the "image of the invisible God" (Col. 1: 15). Jewish theology would deny any such continuity between Yhwh and Jesus.

As an alternative to the notion that the two testaments are a continuous dream or that they are analogous to the individuation process of a personality, we could see the two traditions as manifestations of sibling rivalry for the divine Father, deploying competing but incompatible mythic representations of the image of God. This development of the human religious impulse continues with Jung's approach to religion, which is an emerging myth of God in its own right, quite distinct from Judaism and Christianity. Jung's work on the Self as an intrapsychic image of God is also important because the biblical traditions' images of divinity may not continue to develop. Jerry Wright (2018, pp. 118–119) has suggested that it may be too late for Christianity to change. As he puts it, "the religious corporation it has spawned may be too big to fail or to admit its failure." Wright suggests that "centuries of repetition have worn theological and Christological ruts too deep" for Christians to be able to extricate themselves. He points out that if the monotheisms persist in their inflated claims of absolute truth, and do not face the fact of their idealized projections onto their religious leaders and their projections of the archetypal psyche onto a metaphysical divinity, they are acting as "the greatest down-drag on the evolution of religious consciousness" (2018, p. 120).

A more inclusive religious myth is gradually emerging, to which Jung has made a significant contribution. In his approach, rather than depicting revealed truth from a metaphysical monotheistic deity, the gods (archetypal processes) are returned to their source within the archetypal psyche, which gradually unfolds itself (incarnates) into the consciousness of each individual. This process is no longer projected onto a savior figure or contained within a received text.

Notes

1 "If a man has a stubborn and rebellious son...Then all the men of the city shall stone him to death" (Deut. 21: 18–21). There are many other biblical instances in which the killing of children is condoned or ordered. Hosea 13: 16 says that as punishment for rebellion against God, "their little ones shall be dashed in pieces, and their pregnant women ripped open." This sounds like pure narcissistic rage and human hatred. Filicide may have been culturally sanctioned at the time, but today

it is regarded as pathological and criminal. The sources of child killing are typically revenge against a spouse, parental hatred of a child, the fact that the child is unwanted, or parental depression or psychosis. Filicide in the Bible is described in a simplistic manner as the result of stubbornness and rebellion, which ignores the psychological underpinnings of this behavior.
2 Proverbs 23:14 says that if the child is beaten, he is saved from hell.
3 Exod. 22: 18.
4 Slavery is condoned in several places. Lev. 25: 44–46 says: "As for your male and female slaves whom you may have: you may buy male and female slaves from among the nations that are round about you." It is noteworthy that Leviticus forbids having an Israelite slave but allows slavery among non-Israelite people (Lev. 25: 44–46). Ephesians 6: 5 says: "Slaves, be obedient to those who are your earthly masters, with fear and trembling, in singleness of heart, as to Christ." Colossians 3: 22 says: "Slaves, obey in everything those who are your earthly masters." These texts have been used to justify slavery by many Christians. Such passages are rationalized by saying that the word "slave" did not have the same connotations as it does today, often referring to people who were in service to pay off debts. However, the Greek words for slave and servant are different. Authors such as Augustine and Aquinas believed that slavery was God's punishment for sin.
5 This figure is not the Satan of later theology.

Chapter 4

The Bible as a mythic text

The Bible as myth, not history

Much of the Bible's supposedly historical material is seen by skeptics as mythic or legendary. Writers such as Thomas Thompson (2000) point out that there is little or no historical or archeological evidence for the existence of the early biblical patriarchs or for the existence of the united monarchy of David and Soloman in the middle Bronze Age (about 2000–1500 BCE). Neither is there evidence for the military exploits of Joshua. Thompson (p. xv) therefore believes that the Bible's story of Israel is a "literary fiction." He shows that there is no independent history with which to compare the biblical stories until about the ninth and eighth centuries BCE, when there is some confirmation in Assyrian records of the existence of the separate kingdoms of Israel and Judah. Within this school of thought, much of the biblical text, including its legal codes, the psalms, and the prophetic books, is considered to be a literary creation not older than the sixth-century BCE Babylonian Exile. This is a very controversial opinion that has increasingly gathered adherents since it was first proposed. In part this view is based on the fact that there is little or no archeological evidence for the Israelites' slavery and exodus from Egypt, for their 40 years wondering in the desert, for the military conquest of Canaan, or even for the existence of Moses (Finkelstein & Silberman, 2002). The question of the historical accuracy of these biblical stories is still debated, but today few archeologists believe that the history described in the Hebrew Bible is reliable (Dever, 2006, 2017). Many scholars now believe that the history told in the Bible is ideologically colored by theological, partisan interests. The problem is made more difficult because these debates are colored by the theological claim that God gave the Israelites the land of Canaan and by the contemporary political importance of this story.

A typically skeptical view of the historicity of the Bible is the controversial text by Giovanni Garbini (1988), who points out that not only is there little evidence for the historical truth of what the Old Testament reports, there are indications that these accounts have been fabricated to support theological positions. In fact, the available archeological evidence, such as of the invasion of Canaan, often contradicts the biblical stories. This invasion probably did not happen as the Bible describes. The evidence is that ancient Israelites were nomads who actually arrived in Canaan peacefully over several generations, which means there was no need for an Exodus as a historical event. They settled in areas that were sparsely populated, beginning about 1200 BCE. The archeological evidence suggests that the area was thinly populated by people living in small, unfortified villages, and accounts of major victories such as the destruction of Jericho are mostly propaganda (Finkelstein & Silberman, 2002). There was no violent conquest of Canaan as described in the book of Joshua. Any conflict that did occur was with small military garrisons. The biblical dates of the destruction of cities do not correspond to the archeological evidence; the destruction of the city of Hazor described in the Book of Joshua has been dated archeologically to a period 200 years later than the biblical account. Finkelstein believes that the people who formed early Israel were mostly local Canaanites. Archeology has not confirmed much of the patriarchal tradition, and there is little or no evidence for the existence of figures such as Abraham. King David is not mentioned in ancient inscriptions,[1] and there is very little convincing archeological evidence about him. On the basis of what can be known, Bob Becking (2009) has suggested that David was probably a local warlord who controlled a small area and was not the founder of a nation. In this view, which is, of course, controversial, the idealized attributes of Kings David and Solomon are ideological projections onto them. Furthermore, according to Garbini, worship of Yhwh was not confined to Israelites.

Contemporary scholarship suggests that most of the Hebrew Bible was written much later than the traditional history of the people of Israel claims. Much of this history was actually written in the post-exilic period (later than 538 BCE), purportedly describing events that had happened hundreds of years before then, so distortion of the historical account is inevitable. Theological ideas that were developed much later than the events described were retrospectively inserted into earlier historical accounts to explain what had happened in terms of the tradition's developing theology. The priestly writers in Jerusalem who were devotees of Yhwh tried to expunge mention of the earlier gods and goddesses that continued to be worshipped in the old tribal sanctuaries by local cults. Priestly authors rearranged, edited, and rewrote the earlier stories in order to justify their own theology, insisting that worship of Yhwh at the temple of Jerusalem was the only divinely ordained form of worship. All this was an attempt at unifying the nation by means of a common religion while maintaining the priests' own importance, since only they had custody of the word of God and were able to teach and interpret it. In spite of these findings of modern scholarship, the mythic account of the handing down of the law at Mt. Sinai, as described in the received text, is very important to traditional believers who treat it as historical fact.

Traditional religious believers sometimes argue that the historical accuracy of the biblical accounts and even the question of whether they refer to actual events are not important because of the stories' moral and spiritual importance and their expressions of timeless truths that were emitted from a heavenly realm. In contrast, authors such as Joseph Campbell (2001) believed that the mythic power and the symbolic meaning of the Bible's stories are actually more important than their historical truth. Campbell reads biblical stories as products "not of God's literary talent but of man's" (1964, p. 95). However, crucial stories within traditional religions, such as the Exodus, the giving of the law at Mt. Sinai, or the crucifixion and resurrection, are so foundational that the traditions are based on their historical truth. If these stories are mythic and not historically and factually true, the traditions are built on shaky foundations. Accordingly, for many traditional religionists, the literal truth of important events in biblical history is fundamentally important. For these believers, history is where God and humanity interact, so biblical stories are not simply symbolic teaching devices. However, the grounds for belief in the historical reality of biblical stories are largely a matter of faith since there is little or no evidence for most of them outside the Bible itself. For many critics, their credibility is very weak.

Traditional believers insist that their conviction that a biblical story is true might be obtained in ways other than by means of physical or historical evidence. The believer might feel his strong faith in the truth of the Bible arises as a religious intuition, or through a gift of the holy spirit, and this gives him good reason for his belief. Whether this type of knowing provides valid information is dubious, since any number of unverifiable ideas could be justified on this basis. Intuitions may be accurate, but they may also be a medium of self-deception, motivated by psychodynamic factors, needs, and fears. Presumably these factors affected the biblical authors as much as they affect their readers today.

Not just the historicity but also the unity of the Hebrew Bible has been rejected by hermeneutic approaches to it, such as historical criticism, which shows it to be not entirely trustworthy. For example, the idea that Yhwh had a female consort has been largely edited out of the Hebrew Bible (Patai, 1990) and so has early Israelite polytheism (Penchansky, 2005). A controversial episode is the story of a book that was reported to have been discovered about 624 BCE, during the restoration of the temple in Jerusalem. This "book of the law" was said to have been hidden since the time of Moses. It contained material that is now included in the book of Deuteronomy, and it became central to King Josiah's reforms described in 2 Kings 22–23. However, this material is alleged to have been written just before it was "discovered," and several scholars believe its attribution to a much earlier time was a rhetorical stratagem to enhance the credibility of its contents and promote Josiah's reforms. False attribution is a well-known feature of the Hebrew Bible. Examples include the attribution of the Psalms to King David or Proverbs to Solomon.

The New Testament has its own problems with credibility. Bart Ehrman (2012) has shown how much false attribution and outright forgery are to be found in early Christian writing, in an attempt to make the work look older and more authoritative than it is. The early Church created an image of the post-resurrection Jesus that corresponded to emerging Christian doctrine rather than to Jesus' actual teachings. This theology was then inserted back into the original versions of the Gospels. Jesus' image gradually became increasingly mythologized after his death, especially after reports of his resurrection. Over time, his status increased until he became divine, based purely on the opinions of church councils. Jung pointed out that archetypal projections, such as the expected Messiah, "the cosmic savior, the mediating God-man" (CW 11, para. 228), but especially projections of the Self onto Jesus, eclipsed the reality of the historical figure.

Myth as sacred story

Campbell and Jung see the Bible as a mythic text, but this description offends the sensibilities of traditional religionists who prefer to see their own tradition as authentic religion and other traditions as mythic. The problem is, as Campbell complained, that "myths tend to become history" (1964, p. 516), meaning that mythic imagery and metaphors are often misread as if they referred to historical facts. In this context, various authors have argued that the authors of the Bible were not necessarily trying to write literal history when they composed stories such as Adam and Eve. They were trying to transmit their philosophical beliefs, their experience of the sacred and spiritual truths, using story, metaphor, symbol, and allegory (Kuhn, 1940). This is the sense in which the depth psychologist reads the mythic imagery in the Bible. Jung's approach to scriptural imagery is to remythologize it, which means stripping away its traditional theological interpretations and understanding it symbolically. This approach could lead to a revivification of the traditions if they would allow it. However, among traditional religionists, there is considerable resistance to seeing religious imagery in mythological terms and developing it in a largely symbolic, psychologically oriented direction. This resistance is partly why many religious traditions are in decline, since many biblical stories and much doctrine and dogma are not credible if taken literally.

Mythology is integral to religion. Religious myths, stories of the gods and goddesses, describe and try to explain the human relationship to the spiritual dimension of reality. Myths orient us to the spiritual level and make it appear more knowable. The sacred dimension can be frightening and unpredictable, so myths reassure us about how to approach sacred reality and contain or channel its power. Myths also describe how the transpersonal dimension erupts into human space and time. Myths tell a story of order behind what otherwise would appear to be chaos. They symbolically depict themes that are important to the culture in which they arose, as if the culture was dreaming in the form of its myths.

A culture's dominant myths affect how the culture sees reality. Myths are culturally transmitted stories that depict events often believed to have occurred in historical time, usually as a way to explain a particular custom or religious belief or to explain why the world is the way it is. Myths answer questions about creation and how and why human beings exist. Myths are often genealogical, talking about the ancestors and how society began, usually in a manner that justifies contemporary cultural institutions. Myths can convey meaning and dimensions of experience that otherwise might be impossible to convey. Myths bypass conceptual thinking and appeal directly to our feelings and intuition, often at an unconscious level, in a way that cannot be accessed using conceptual thought. Myths also depict unconscious mechanisms, wishes, fears, and other important emotional needs in a symbolic or metaphorical form. Consequently, mythic imagery is very psychoactive, which is partly why the Bible has a powerful emotional appeal. To understand mythic imagery, we have to read it symbolically, as if it were a dream pointing to a deep reality, remembering Jung's view that symbols are expressions of "something that cannot be characterized in any other or better way" (CW 6, para. 816). The emotional appeal of biblical myths is part of the reason for their tenacity.

Myths can be usefully understood as metaphorical pointers to spiritual and psychological truths. Campbell (1991, p. 22) described myths as "metaphorical of spiritual potentiality in the human being." For Jung, all myths emerge from the archetypal or mythopoetic level of the psyche and reveal its dynamics. They convey ideas that may have no other way of becoming conscious. People appropriate mythic stories in a way that meets important psychological needs, such as in the mythic fantasy of being chosen by God, which gives the nation a privileged, idealized identity and a sense of moral authority. Important cultural rituals such as the Passover Seder or the Eucharist symbolically reenact a mythic story, keeping it alive for the participants. Some myths, such as the biblical notion of a forthcoming messianic era, promise a glorious future of perfect justice and harmony. This kind of mythic imagery connects people with their ancestry and helps people cope with loss and hopelessness.

Campbell believed that the purpose of myth is to open us to the transcendent dimension that informs these stories. He (2001) gives the example of the Virgin Birth, which within Christianity is taken to be a unique historical event but was in fact a favorite literary device among many pre-Christian traditions, deployed when they wanted to stress the importance of a historical figure. Campbell (1986) points out that many indigenous mythologies, including those of the Americas, have instances of virgin births. Within Christianity, the Virgin Birth has been seen as a unique and literal historical event or as symbolic of the sinlessness and perfection of Jesus. Campbell sees this story not as a reference to Jesus' biological birth but rather, in symbolic terms, as the birth of the spirit within the personality. Edinger (1987) understands psychological virginity as an attitude that is not contaminated by personal desires. Perhaps this mytheme symbolically refers to the birth of new spiritual insight born within a receptive area of the psyche.

The theme of divine impregnation by a god is also a recurrent archetypal motif that preceded Christianity, seen, for example, in the Greek story in which

Zeus impregnates the human Leda, producing the mortal Helen. Zeus also impregnated Danae in the form of a shower of golden rain, producing the hero Perseus. The divinization of a human being such as the Egyptian Pharoah or the deification of a human hero such as Hercules was also a well-known mythologem in pre-Christian religions.

The Hebrew Bible borrowed a range of mythic material from earlier Mesopotamian mythological traditions. Biblical authors used themes from this material to develop a historical account of their own tradition. For example, the Garden of Eden story originated in Sumerian myths; Eden was a district in Sumer. The creation story in Genesis contains themes from a Babylonian text, the *Enuma Elish*, where the same sequence of the stages of creation are found. The Babylonian myth appeared around a thousand years earlier than the biblical story. The biblical story of the flood is similar to stories in various Mesopotamian myths such as the Akkadian Epic of Gilgamesh, in which a heroic figure constructs an ark and is saved (Speiser, 1962). The themes of all flood myths tend to be similar; the gods find fault with the world they have created, so they try to destroy it with a flood, but one of the gods alerts his human favorite to build a boat. The story of Moses was borrowed from an Assyrian myth in which King Sargon 1 had been set adrift as a baby and rescued, a typical theme in hero myths. This kind of mythic imagery, borrowed from many earlier sources, was incorporated into the Bible, but each story was told as if it were a unique historical fact.

The New Testament contains a range of mythological motifs found in the mystery religions of earlier cultures. Many of the stories about Jesus reflect the appropriation of older Middle Eastern mythic images, such as the mythologem of the dying and resurrecting grain gods Attis, Adonis, and Tammuz and the Egyptian Osiris. Many Christian themes are found in earlier Egyptian stories (Mettinger, 2013; Harpur, 2004; Kuhn, 1940). The glorification of Mary is analogous to the worship of the goddess Isis in ancient Egypt, who mourned her husband and son, while Horus was the divine child of Egyptian mythology. There had been several miraculous saviors and healers before Jesus, such as Asclepius. Greek philosopher Apollonius of Tyana, a contemporary of Jesus, was reported to be a divine figure and miracle worker.

Harpur (2004) discusses the earlier work of Alvin Kuhn (1940), who shows multiple similarities between the mythology of Osiris/Horus and the Gospel stories of Jesus. Kuhn, Harpur, and David Tacey (2015) believe that the Egyptians saw these stories as allegories or myths that teach symbolic truths that could not be put into ordinary language. These authors believe that the ancient writers did not take their myths to be literal historical realities, but the compilers of the New Testament who applied mythic motifs to the life of Jesus mistakenly saw them as historical events, so that myth became biography. In this view, the Bible was written in the form of myth in order to stress the importance of significant stories, but the mainstream Christian tradition has misinterpreted this material as literally true, instead of understanding it symbolically and metaphorically. Tacey believes that the original authors of the biblical stories did not intend them to be read literally. They were written at a time when the mythic mode was the accepted way of describing important events, which is why scripture was deliberately written in a mythic mode. Scriptural stories contain mythic truth, or they describe spiritual rather than historical realities. In antiquity, the use of mythic imagery also served to protect the information in the story from falling into the wrong hands. From this point of view, seen in their first-century context, Jesus' miracles were not supernatural events, but literary devices deployed to convey the experience of divine presence. These stories, and mythic material such as Jesus' resurrection, require symbolic rather than literal interpretation.

Many Christian motifs are found in Mithraism. Mithra was a savior who was raised from the dead after three days. He could forgive sins and grant eternal life. Mithraism also included baptism, the story of an apocalyptic end of time, a virgin birth at the winter solstice, miracles, twelve disciples, and participation in a sacred meal consisting of the body and blood of the deity. Mithra was said to have been the son of Ahura Mazda, the Zoroastrian supreme god. It is therefore sometimes claimed that Christianity resulted from an amalgam of Mithraism and Judaism. Other contemporary scholars reject the idea that Christianity borrowed from Mithraism, in part because there are some features of Christianity that are unique, such as the claim that Jesus was the only source of salvation, which gave the emerging tradition an exclusive quality. Unlike early Christianity, the Mediterranean mystery religions were not exclusive; one could participate in more than one simultaneously, but this was not allowed by the early Christians, which is partly why Christianity succeeded in suppressing the other traditions.

Among traditional Christians today there is considerable resistance to the idea that these pre-Christian parallels influenced early Christianity, but there are certainly enough of them to provide thematic continuity between Egyptian and Graeco-Roman mythology and the emergence of Christianity, which may have made its acceptance somewhat easier. However, the pagan origin of Christian motifs was ruthlessly and violently suppressed by the early Church. The Church fathers assumed that in order to deceive Christians the Devil had created false religions with the same themes and rituals as those found in Christianity.

Traditional religionists often object to the description of biblical stories as mythic because of the cultural connotations of that word, implying that these stories are not true. However, it is possible to acknowledge the reality the myths are trying to point out without taking the myths themselves as literal truth. If we think of myths as sacred stories, the use of this term to describe biblical events is not disrespectful; it is a way of appreciating the text without treating it as literal history. Biblical myths have survived a long period of retelling and revision because they are psychologically and spiritually powerful. They are descriptions of the ways in which the biblical authors imagined that God interacted with them, or in Jungian terms how they encountered the Self, or how they projected the Self onto the biblical Yhwh or onto Jesus.

The Hebrew Bible's mythic imagery has traditionally been interpreted in historical terms. Both the Jewish and Christian traditions are very concerned with history; their ideas about divinity include its entrance into history on important occasions. For traditional religionists, therefore, myth has become historicized, and history is thought to express the tradition's sacred story. For the writers of the Hebrew Bible, every major event that happens was attributed to the will of God. That was their explanation for success and failure in wars and for famines and plagues. All this was done in the service of promoting a theological ideology that colors the Bible's accounts of historical events. This ideology developed much later than the biblical stories themselves and was retrospectively applied to the earlier events in order to explain them in terms of the tradition's emerging theology and soteriology. Since the nineteenth century, many scholars have suggested that stories in the Hebrew Bible are mythic attempts to provide historical justification for the religious practices of post-exilic Judaism, and these stories cannot be read as literal historical events. Historical and documentary biblical criticism (which tries to discern the original meaning of a text) has also established that many of the biblical stories either are inconsistent with each other or are clearly fictional or inaccurate. There are several examples of failed promises and prophecies in the Bible. For example, God promised King David that his kingdom and dynasty would last forever (2 Sam. 7: 4–13), but the Davidic house ended in 586 BCE with the destruction of Judah by Nebuchadnezzar. The compensatory concept of a future messiah of the house of David may have arisen as a result.

The Roman Catholic tradition has maintained a connection to its mythology, with a mythic attitude to transubstantiation in the Mass and to its shrines and relics. In contrast, the Protestant tradition has largely minimized the importance of myth, making this tradition lean toward rationality and a focus on ethics rather than metaphysical assertions. This attitude was based on the work of theologians such as Rudolf Bultmann (1960),[2] who believed that the myths and miracle stories described in the New Testament were superimposed on the life of the historical Jesus in order to enhance his messianic and cosmic importance. In the twentieth century, this attitude was developed by Christian existentialists and by people such as Bishop John Robinson in his 1963 *Honest to God* (reissued 40 years later), which wanted to rid the tradition of its mythic supernaturalism, which Robinson saw as unnecessary. He was offering what many observers saw as a revised form of Christianity. However, the Evangelical churches rejected this approach. They retain the authority of the Bible and reject any compromise about the literal reality of its stories. Since Robinson's book, a profusion of alternative theologies has appeared. Some of them include no metaphysics but instead see it as a moral duty to focus on theological approaches to social problems such as discrimination and the liberation of oppressed minorities.[3] Authors who want to diminish the importance of the Bible's supernatural imagery believed that a rational approach to biblical stories has become necessary to make Christianity acceptable in today's culture, in which theological assertions are increasingly challenged by science, which has replaced the authority of the church in most areas of life. Religions now have to fall back on claims about a spiritual dimension that science cannot observe, or they must insist that the laws of science and the values of important physical constants are divinely ordained.

Jung's approach does not abandon the mythic dimensions of Christianity. He believes that mythic imagery is often the only way to express material that emerges from the archetypal level of the psyche. Rather than demythologize religion, Jung reinterprets the tradition's mythic imagery to reveal its underlying symbolic meaning. Using this approach, we can see biblical myths as expressions of the archetypal psyche without the need for doctrinal or dogmatic interpretations of them.

The psychology underlying apocalyptic mythologies

Mythic imagery is relevant when it addresses existential anxieties around issues such as birth and death. However, mythic imagery may or may not resonate with the psychological structures of the reader. The myth of the End Times or Armageddon is accompanied by fantasies of a final battle between good and evil followed by the sadistic punishment of unbelievers, as we see in Revelation. This may appeal to people with violent, revenge-filled imagination, but this imagery is distasteful to people with less angry dispositions. Apocalyptic mythic imagery offers ultimate solace for believers who feel ignored by the larger culture and like to imagine retribution for perceived injustice. When the individual's current situation seems hopeless, when the world is indifferent to his plight and dismissive of his religion, the notion of a divinely ordained, ultimate confrontation with non-believers seems to be the only solution, even if it means widespread destruction and death. Apocalyptic mythology has been popularized by books about the Rapture, the mythic idea that at the time of the Second Coming of Jesus both living and dead believers will ascend to heaven. This story is accompanied by descriptions of the suffering of those left behind. The extreme violence meted out to unbelievers in the book of Revelation reflects the author's eruption of rage at them, which none of Jesus' teachings of love and mercy had been able to temper. The author's violence is projected as if it arose within God or Christ, who is depicted as seeking war against the unrepentant (Rev. 2: 16).

The Abrahamic traditions all nurse apocalyptic fantasies of the end of history as we know it, a day of judgment, and the arrival of a messiah who will begin a reign of peace, a new world order, "a new heaven and a new earth," and a "new Jerusalem" (Rev. 21: 1–2). The names and places are different in the different traditions, but the underlying mythic theme and its psychology are the same. Apocalyptic fantasies arise during historical times of despair, where there seems to be no possibility of deliverance within one's current reality, so one has to look to the future for justice. Apocalyptic thinking is often accompanied by projections about who will be the elect and who the saved. The apocalyptist is always one of the saved, revealing a narcissistic element. Apocalyptic fantasies tend to be seen among powerless, angry, oppressed people hoping for justice, revenge, and the defeat of evil. Notions of renewal or resurrection after a final destructive battle may also be related to the denial of death. Apocalyptic ideas are important to many fundamentalist Christians who see their tradition as under threat. They take the violent imagery of the book of Revelation not as myth but as a literal prediction of the end of the present era of history, followed by a paradisiacal future. Many sects have arisen that believed that "the time is near" (Rev. 1: 3).

The Hebrew Bible contains many references to a promised messiah who will deliver the people from their enemies and establish God's kingdom (e.g., Deut. 18: 15; Psa. 132; Jer. 23: 5–6). Apocalypticism became prominent among the Jews after the Babylonian Exile (586–538 BCE), following a series of defeats and disappointments. Perhaps they were worried that these disasters meant that God had deserted them. During their exile, the people had been told by their prophets that their sins had been forgiven and a glorious future awaited them. But when they returned to Jerusalem and rebuilt their temple, no such future materialized; they had lost their kingship and sense of nationhood because they had become part of the Persian Empire. They had to stop hoping for a better political future and instead concentrate on worship and obeying the law. After Alexander the Great conquered Palestine in 332 BCE, Hellenization became the prominent culture, although the Jews were allowed religious freedom, and in the early second century BCE, Hellenic Jews were in control of Jewish political and religious life. However, in 167 BCE, Greek King Antiochus IV tried to destroy Judaism by desecrating its temples and forbidding rituals such as circumcision. This triggered the Maccabean revolt of 162 BCE, which restored the Jerusalem temple, but occupation again followed. The Roman conquest of Jerusalem in 63 BCE and the subsequent Roman occupation of Israel ultimately led to the destruction of the second temple in 70 CE. Apocalypticism among the Israelites seems to have originated as a way to cope with these losses and with humiliating, constant foreign domination, accompanied by no prospect of improvement. It seemed that only total destruction by God and a new creation, under the leadership of a promised messiah, offered the Israelites justice, freedom from their conquerors, and hope for the future. The idea of an apocalypse was a fantasy of revenge nursed by the powerless. Perhaps this fantasy also represents a need for purity and a purging of all one's badness that will finally make one acceptable to the divine parent. From a symbolic point of view, apocalyptic fantasies also represent the wish for the emergence of a new sense of self, a renewal of the personality, or, as Edinger (1999) believed, the emergence of the Self into conscious realization. The apocalypse promises renewal and a new beginning or at least the hope for a better life. Apocalyptic fantasies also promise revenge and restitution for an unfair world, since only the faithful will be saved. In the process, rivals (such as other religions) have to be eliminated, if necessary, by violence. At the same time, apocalyptic fantasies can be used to threaten and manipulate people by insisting on the terrible events that will befall them if they are not believers. Some of the urgency and even threats within Paul's letters seem to have been due to his belief that the End Times were imminent, although some of his imprecations and his divisive rhetoric seem to have been based on the need to protect his authority.

Apocalyptic thinking imagines conflict between God and rebellious spiritual powers such as Satan or the Antichrist, who are seen as responsible for evil. Some human beings are thought to be particularly receptive to these forces. The book of Revelation symbolizes the Antichrist, the enemy of God, in the form of a dragon. The text says that although he is allowed victory for a period of time, characterized by famine and the persecution of the elect, eventually there will be a final eschatological battle in which the Antichrist is defeated, and the elect attain a new heaven and a new earth. The identity of the Antichrist has been projected onto a series of Roman emperors, popes, and evil dictators. One of the extraordinary aspects of the book of Revelation is that it ignores the fact that Christ's self-sacrifice was supposed to finally overcome evil. Furthermore, after the redemption of humanity because of Christ, one wonders why God would again unleash evil onto humanity and why the Lamb of God became so destructive in the book of Revelation. As Jung points out, the level of "hatred, wrath, vindictiveness, and blind destructive fury" in the book of Revelation "blatantly contradicts all ideas of Christian humility, tolerance, love of your neighbor and your enemies, and makes nonsense of a loving father in heaven" (CW 11, para. 708). This problem has to be rationalized by saying that evil is permitted by God for his own reasons.

Apocalyptic mythology is easily incorporated into political struggles between religious groups with conflicting ideas about who will emerge victorious at the End Times. This kind of mythic literalism encourages violence. The mythic image of a battle between good and evil resonates with intrapsychic conflict between different aspects of the personality. Mythic beliefs of this kind are particularly psychoactive when they correspond to such dynamics within the reader, which are stimulated by the story.

The problem of interpreting biblical myths

The Bible is a compilation of material that traditional believers assert was directly given by God. Traditional religionists therefore object to thinking about the Bible in terms of myth, or they are uneasy about subjecting biblical stories to the kind of symbolic, metaphorical interpretation that is applied to the mythology of other cultures. However, interpretation is inevitable. Over a long period of time, as texts were copied and recopied, editors, translators, and interpreters changed the original texts to accommodate the evolving theology of their tradition. James Kugel (1997, p. xiv) points out that interpreters sometimes felt obliged to explain why biblical characters behaved the way they did, and in the process, interpreters added to the text by "deducing" facts they believe to be implied within it. At the same time, they were trying to convey the Bible's message, but Kugel believes that the process of editing and interpolation tended to transform the original meaning of the text. He gives the example of how the story of Adam and Eve became transformed into the story of the Fall of Man, and the snake came to be identified with the Devil, both the result of later interpreters even though the story itself does not contain these themes. Over time, these kinds of interpretations became the official meaning of the text and were passed on to subsequent generations and canonized in the tradition, ignoring the original historical context of the story. Kugel therefore points out that it is the *interpreted* (emphasis in original) Bible that is central to Judaism and Christianity.

Translation of a text such as the Bible often involves interpretation and bias and usually conveys preexisting cultural and theological commitments, such as patriarchal prejudice against women. Thus, there are two accounts of the creation of Adam and Eve. In the first one (Gen. 1: 26), the emphasis is on the fact that the male and female are both created in the image of God. The second account has been used to claim that the male has priority because Eve was created out of Adam's rib (Gen. 2: 21–23), but the only reason to give the second account priority is the prejudice of the interpreter. Susan Schept (2021) shows that although the usual translation of the story of the creation of Eve from Adam's rib in Genesis 2: 18 makes it sound as if Eve was secondary to Adam, or only his helper, this translation does not get at the essence of the meaning of the text. Schept says that Genesis 2: 18 can also be translated as "I will make a power [or strength] corresponding to man," implying that God created woman equal to man. The damaging nature of the traditional translation contributed to the subsequent notion that women are subservient to men.

Schept believes that the rabbinic tradition projected their fear of women onto the mythic figure of Lilith,[4] a demonic figure who threatens women in childbirth and devours infants. Lilith is said to copulate with men in their dreams, and from their nocturnal emissions, she inseminates herself and produces hordes of demons who still plague humanity. Because of this fear, Jewish women used to protect their children using amulets and other apotropaic symbols in the child's bedroom. Schept views the origin of the need for such a demonic female figure in terms of various psychodynamic theories. One is based on early splitting mechanisms in infancy, when, according to Kleinian theory, the mother is experienced as either all good or all bad. Then, Eve represents the good mother and Lilith the demon-mother.

The Bible's mythic cosmology was taken literally by its authors and subsequent interpreters, such as when the text describes how Joshua asked God to make the sun stand still (Joshua 10: 12), implying that the sun revolved around an immobile earth. The biblical authors seem to have imagined the earth to be flat,[5] surrounded by a series of domes. The stars were seen to be objects that were contained within the vault of the sky and could fall to earth (Dan. 8: 10; Matt. 24: 29). In the Genesis creation story, on the second day a vault (some kind of support structure) was created that divided the waters, with some water above and some water under the land. Thus, Noah's flood was caused by an opening of the "fountains of the great deep" and the "windows of the heaven" (Gen. 7: 11).

There are many ways to interpret the Bible. The Roman Catholic Church believes it is the final arbiter of disputes over doctrine and the meaning of the text, but Protestants also have their own wide spectrum of interpretations. These range from fundamentalists who believe the Bible is infallible and inerrant to liberal theologians who dispute its factual and historical accuracy but believe it was divinely inspired. Fundamentalists are concerned that if any of the text is admitted to being mistaken, much of the rest of it, especially its supernatural and miracle stories, may be seen as not historical, thus undermining the truth of the tradition.

Biblical stories are traditionally viewed as descriptions of the acts of God intervening in history. These events are always interpreted in terms of preexisting theological ideas, heavily colored by the authors' projections onto their image of God and what they imagine God has in mind. However, like all myths, biblical texts can have a wide range of meanings. Feuerbach (2008) believed that faith in a historical text that is regarded as eternal, absolute, and universally authoritative is a product of superstition and sophistry, since such a text is "necessarily subject to all the conditions of a temporal, finite production" (p. 173). Feuerbach trenchantly remarked that if God can count the hairs on a human head and note the fall of every sparrow (Matt. 10: 26–31), he would not have left the biblical text to the "stupidity and caprice" of scribes to transmit his word. For skeptics, the fact that there are multiple interpretations of the Bible, not to mention its many internal inconsistencies and gratuitous violence, renders it even less likely to be a divine product with a single message. In summary, psychologically speaking, the Bible is a product of the mythic imagination and its archetypal processes, colored by human psychological dynamics, projected onto divinity.

Mythic elements in the story of Jesus

Various aspects of the Gospel stories about Jesus, such as the miracle stories, seem to be largely mythic, not historical, so they can be best understood symbolically and metaphorically. An example is the account in Luke 24: 50–53, in which Jesus blessed his disciples and then was "carried up into heaven." The ascension story is repeated in Acts 1: 9–11, with different details, borrowing from the myth of Elijah being taken up to heaven (2 Kgs 2: 1) in order to validate the story. The intention of the author may have been to make a theological point rather than describe a historical event. As Campbell (1991) points out, the literal denotation of the story is that Jesus went up into the sky, but there was no place in the sky for Jesus to go. The story therefore has to be read in terms of its metaphorical connotation, which is that "he has gone into inward space...into the consciousness that is the source of all things, the kingdom of heaven within" (p. 56). For Campbell, the literal reading of such stories is to make the mistake of taking the story as prose instead of poetry.

Stories about Jesus vary in the different Gospels because of their varying intentions directed toward different audiences, but they all report that Jesus told his followers that an apocalyptic event was to occur soon. He seems to have believed that he was its forerunner. He also spoke of the imminent arrival of the Kingdom of God on earth (Matt. 10: 7). This motif is central to the mythic image of Jesus, but his followers may not have understood the symbolic meaning of the Kingdom, which refers to a subjective connection to the presence of the Self, the inner divine, rather than the remoteness of the biblical Yhwh. This dimension of Jesus' teaching, which is available to everyone because it is the same Self in all people, has long been a feature of Eastern religious traditions that stress connection to the Ātman, the inner divine in the Upaniṣads. However, in Christianity, this idea was overshadowed by making Jesus the only exemplar of such closeness to divinity. This projection onto him may have been necessary at the time, but Jung's approach to the Self shows that it is no longer necessary. In some ways, Jung revives the Gnostic tradition that stresses direct intuitive knowledge of the divine. The harshness with which the Gnostics were suppressed speaks to the need of the early Church to discourage the idea that we have direct inner access to divinity and instead we require the ministrations of the Church.

Psychodynamics of the Garden of Eden myth

The story of the Garden of Eden is one of the foundational myths of the biblical tradition. Not surprisingly, it has given rise to a vast amount of interpretation, commentary, art, and literature. There has been much debate about how the story was put together by merging different traditions and sources. Many comparisons have been made with similar themes in earlier Near Eastern texts. I assume the story continues to interest people and evoke commentary because of its emotional resonance. In particular, I am concerned with its lingering harmful effects on the Western tradition. We can only speculate about the ideology and theology that the authors wanted to convey and the underlying attitudes and assumptions that affected their writing. However, the subsequent political uses of the story have been very important, especially the way it has been used to oppress women. Because of the misogyny of many interpreters of this text, Eve has been singled out for special condemnation. The subsequent theological elaboration of the story in terms of the Fall of Adam and the transmission of original sin reflects the psychology of early Christian writers such as St. Augustine and St. Paul; these themes are not found in the story itself.

D. Andrew Kille (2001) has provided an overview of multiple approaches to this story. Here, I have selected a few themes that contrast the use of the story in the Christian tradition with the Jungian understanding that the story is about the development of consciousness. Some of the early Church fathers (such as Origen) saw the story of Adam and Eve as an allegory, but others (such as Tertullian) insisted on a literal interpretation. The predominant Christian view of the story became that of St. Augustine, who combined a symbolic and a literal interpretation of the story. He believed that Paradise represented the Church and that the four rivers in the garden represented the Evangelists. He also believed that as a result of Adam's disobedience, a fundamental change in human nature had occurred that was transmitted to subsequent generations. In his view, because of Adam, human beings are conceived and born in sin. Consequently, sin is inevitable and requires redemption.[6] Augustine's approach led to the devaluing or sometimes demonizing of sexuality, a theme that is not present in the original story, which does not say that sexuality is sinful. At most, we could read the story as saying that when Adam and Eve became aware of their sexuality, they felt shame about it so that they hid behind fig leaves, which tells us only that the writers' culture saw sexuality as shameful. However, theologians such as Augustine saw sexuality as a powerful source of sin that taints all human beings. This attitude became one of the major damaging effects of the biblical tradition.

The idea of intrinsic human sinfulness produced by Adam's disobedience has dominated subsequent Christian thinking. Augustine built on his understanding of St. Paul, who also had a sense of the inevitable nature of sin because of the behavior of the original couple. Thus, he writes that "In Adam all die" (1 Cor. 15: 22) and "Sin came into the world through one man" (Romans 5: 12). Paul could not have derived the idea of inherited original sin because of the Fall of Adam from the teachings of Jesus, nor could he have discovered in these teachings the idea that faith in the atoning death of Jesus was necessary to avoid the resulting eternal damnation of humanity; these were his own ideas. In 1546, the Council of Trent ratified Augustine's idea that there is a direct connection between Adam's sin and humanity's inherent sinfulness. This is still the official opinion of the Roman Catholic Church. However, although Paul and the subsequent Church interpreted the story of the Garden of Eden to mean that human beings are born into unredeemed sinfulness, the story itself does not say that; it says that the disobedience of Adam and Eve brings death and certain forms of suffering to the world. Disobedience has several other sources besides willful badness, including curiosity, the desire to explore, and a need to differentiate oneself from oppressive authority. These aspects of the story have not been adequately discussed.

By agreeing to eat the forbidden fruit, Adam and Eve learn that that they are able to disobey God. From the traditional point of view, this disobedience means that sin is the result of human behavior, but this view avoids the fact that God deliberately placed the serpent in the Garden from the beginning. The serpent plays an essential role in the unfolding story and links it to the ancient snake cults of the Middle East, which were still active at the time the story of Eden was written. The serpent was widely revered as a symbol of the goddess in that area. Merlin Stone (1976) writes: "In several Sumerian tablets the Goddess was simply called the Great Mother Serpent of Heaven" (p. 199). Stone therefore believes that the negative view of the serpent in the Garden of Eden myth was designed as part of the suppression of the worship of the goddess. The ancient Hebrews were struggling to make Yhwh the only God, so the snake had to be depicted as inducing evil and hence the enmity between Yhwh and the serpent described in the story. Priests of the emerging religion of Yhwh made the serpent a scapegoat and represented it as an enemy of humanity for propaganda purposes. The story implies that listening to the goddess in the form of the serpent caused the expulsion of humanity from Paradise, which served the function of adding to the need to suppress goddess worship. Stone believes that the tree symbolism in the myth is also a link to the goddess. She believes the tree of the knowledge of good and evil was in fact a fig tree, which was sacred to the goddess in various traditions. Eating its fruit was a form of communion with the goddess.

Stone notes that the story in Genesis is a modification of Sumerian traditions in which men and women were simultaneously created from clay by the goddess. A thousand years later, the worshippers of Yhwh modified the creation story so that a male God created Adam before Eve, who became only a helpmate, thus asserting divine sanction of the primacy of men. This was necessary for political reasons such as male kinship rights, which are certain only if paternity is known. At the same time, women were cast in the role of temptress. Eve was largely blamed for the couple's disobedience, and this attribution, combined with her secondary status having been created after Adam, evolved into the silencing of women that persists in the tradition (1 Tim. 2: 11–14; Eph. 5: 22–24; 1 Cor. 11: 3, 7 9; 1 Pet. 3: 1). There have been attempts to support a more woman-friendly account of Genesis 2–3, such as by saying that the initial Adam was androgynous or sexually undifferentiated (Trible, 1979) and that male domination was a corruption of this ideal. However, these accounts have not been convincing for traditional readers of the text. The androcentric reading of the story, in which Adam is dominant, is quite vivid, such as when God tells Eve that "he [Adam] shall rule over you." This patriarchal interpretation of the Eden story persists and is used to justify the reduced status of women in some traditions. The placing of blame onto Eve has also been used to explain why women are sentenced to suffer in childbirth.

Another dimension of the story is its narcissistic element. Yhwh becomes worried that since the couple now know the difference between good and evil, they have "become like one of us" (Gen. 3: 22), meaning in possession of divine knowledge. If they were also to eat from the Tree of Life, they would live forever, as Yhwh does, apparently becoming a narcissistic threat to one of the attributes that made him special. Therefore, Adam and Eve had to be banished from the Garden and punished to prevent further hubris or competition with Yhwh. Erich Fromm (1996) believed that the reason God did not want them to become like him was to safeguard his own omnipotence and superior status.

Fromm is here noticing the narcissistic element in the personality of the Hebrew Bible's God-image. Fromm points out that the act of disobedience in the Garden of Eden was not simply a sin but a rebellion against an authoritarian God and the beginning of human freedom. Fromm points out that Adam and Eve develop individuality, maturation, and consciousness as a result.

According to Mircea Eliade (1975), the nostalgic myth of a long-ago paradise or an effortless, bountiful Golden Age is universal. Depth psychologists tend to see the archetypal fantasy of paradise as a connection to the memory of the pre-egoic, conflict-free reality characteristic of early infancy. The Garden of Eden then represents a stage of life without effort or labor. Neumann (1954, p. 114) points out that as the ego emerges in childhood, "the paradisal situation is abolished; the infantile condition, in which life was regulated by something ampler and more embracing, is at an end." That is, the myth of Paradise is a symbolic representation of the early infantile experience in which everything is provided for. With the "knowledge of good and evil," meaning awareness of the tension of the opposites and the beginning of conflict, paradise is lost.

Jung (CW 5, para. 396) believes that the Garden of Eden motif is about the birth of consciousness. Before Adam and Eve ate the apple, they were at one with nature. They were in a paradisical state of completion, but they were unconscious. By eating the apple, they acquired the knowledge of good and evil, which refers to the capacity to discriminate between opposites and be self-reflexive, albeit at the cost of guilt and suffering. By becoming conscious in this way, they disturbed the original unity of creation, but for Jung the dawn of new consciousness always requires the evolution of an original unity into pairs of conflicting opposites. He writes that "the emancipation of ego consciousness was a Luciferian deed" (CW 9i, para. 420), meaning a rebellion against the established order, but it was necessary for humanity's ongoing development. Edinger (1972) points out that the Eden myth can be read to depict the birth of consciousness as a crime that alienated humanity from God. However, it seems strange to many readers that wanting knowledge and consciousness should be regarded as negative by God. The couple's punishment seems overly harsh. Sanford (1981) points out that the behavior of Adam and Eve is clearly the result of a deceptive practice by God. God created beings who were curious, gave them free will, goaded their curiosity by placing a serpent in the garden for the express purpose of tempting them, and then expressed surprise at how they behaved. The serpent seems to possess a kind of knowledge or intelligence. It could represent the unconscious, which often wants to rebel against authority or question received truths, which is essential for development to occur. Rivka Kluger (1967) sees the serpent as an aspect of the dark side of God, of which he was apparently unaware. The serpent is also a kind of trickster figure that instills doubt and upsets the established order. The serpent is often associated with Satan in subsequent literature, but its actions in the Garden were essential for the progression of consciousness, so it cannot be seen as entirely malign.[7]

From a psychological point of view, the snake can be seen as symbolic of the urge to new consciousness. Jung therefore sees the serpent motif as part of a "therapeutic myth" because life needs opposition, without which there is no energy. He finds it particularly important that God placed the serpent in the Garden; it implies that the potential for evil is present at the beginning of creation, so that evil cannot be entirely attributed to humanity. It is indeed strange that God creates the serpent and then punishes it for acting according to its nature. God told Adam about the tree of knowledge and forbad him to eat from it but also provided the serpent, producing a set-up obviously designed to stimulate curiosity. However, subsequent Christian theologians saw Adam's and Eve's action as nothing but prideful rebellion against the will of God, ignoring God's obvious role in the story. The snake was seen as a personification of the Devil, urging disobedience to God.

It is interesting that Jewish commentators on this story did not develop the idea of inherited sinfulness; in fact, they saw procreation as a fulfillment of the commandment to be "fruitful and multiply" (Gen. 1: 28). It is worth noting that during the Babylonian Exile the Hebrew Prophets promised a future paradisical state, heralded by the advent of the messiah and brought about by God, who would ensure the people's ultimate victory (Isa. 41: 18–20; Ezekiel 36: 35). This was a compensatory fantasy, given the parlous state of the Israelites at the time. The analogous idea is found in the Christian notion of a coming Kingdom of Heaven or the Heavenly Jerusalem of the book of Revelation. These promises have not materialized.

The failure of the Bible's mythic promises

Jack Miles (1995, 2001) retold the biblical story as if it were the story of God's development, including Yhwh's failure to fulfill his triumphalist, grandiose promises to the Israelites of the Hebrew Bible, which ends with God's total silence. God did not rescue them as he had promised. He did not give them a peaceful kingdom, and he overreacted to human weaknesses and failures. Miles therefore sees the New Testament story as God's attempt to rectify the situation. He does so by acknowledging his own guilt and responsibility for evil and suffering, consequently dying in a self-inflicted manner. At the same time, he introduces the idea that only grace and love are effective. The story reaches a climax in the crucifixion, which is seen as a triumph for this God. However, for many people today, these biblical promises and attempts at reparation have entirely lost their appeal. Christianity has been unable to overcome the essential dissonance at its heart: an act of horrifying violence allowed by a loving God. To critics, the crucifixion does not seem like an act of grace, even though it is portrayed as an act of loving sacrifice; it seems rather like an act of gratuitous cruelty and, at bottom, child sacrifice.

The failure of the biblical promises was inevitable. There was no metaphysical heavenly father who was choreographing the drama behind the scenes.

That idea was a human construction. The traditions used the historical events described in the biblical story for theological purposes. The biblical authors developed post hoc explanations for these events, as if they had been divinely ordained. However, even catastrophic events like the Holocaust, the failure of a messianic era to be established, the failure of Christ's Second Coming, the failure of apocalyptic fantasies, the failure of evil to be conquered, and the failure of promises such as "he will wipe away every tear from their eyes" (Rev. 21: 4), all seem to be unable to dislodge traditional believers' faith that the biblical promises will one day be fulfilled. To maintain the illusion provided by theological interpretations of the biblical myths, the stories have been constantly reconceptualized, re-visioned, reinterpreted, and seen from a series of new perspectives, all to help believers understand why God's promises have not materialized and help them keep the faith. New explanations are required to deal with cognitive dissonance, which accompanies the painful sense that the historical evidence belies the believer's cherished beliefs. A psychologically oriented, mythopoetic, symbolic view of biblical stories that does not take them literally would avoid such distress and would open the traditions to new levels of meaning.

Notes

1 There is one exception: In 1993, in Tel Dan in northern Israel, an archeologist found an inscription that refers to the "House of David." The significance of this finding is debatable. What the inscription refers to is uncertain.
2 The theologian Rudolf Bultmann famously advocated a progressive approach to religion that saw most biblical stories, especially miracle stories, as mythic rather than literal history, which he believed made them unintelligible to modern people. He wanted to get rid of the mythic elements in religion and replace them with philosophical thought. However, myths have important spiritual and psychological meaning when they are read with a symbolic and metaphorical sensibility. Conceptual, rational thinking is the wrong approach to religion. The biblical writers used mythic imagery because it was the best way to express their experience of the sacred.
3 Conservative religionists dismiss this kind of theology as socialism in disguise, and they lean toward right-wing politics.
4 Lilith may have originally been a Babylonian female demon known as Lilitu.
5 The Devil took Jesus to a high mountain and showed him all the kingdoms of the world (Matt. 4: 8), which would be possible only if the earth was flat. In Daniel 4, 10–11, the king sees a huge tree at the center of the earth. The top of the tree reached to the sky and was visible to the ends of the earth, implying it is flat. When the Bible talks about the four corners of the earth (e.g., Rev. 7: 1), this may have been meant literally rather than metaphorically.
6 The alternative view, proposed by the Greek theologian Irenaeus, was that rather than having been created perfectly, human beings are initially imperfect and grow into the likeness of God. Therefore, the Fall is due to immaturity and is not due to malice.
7 Freudian readings of the story see it as disguising its latent content, which is that Eve represents the primal mother. Adam and Eve have offsprings, so the story is about incest with mother and Adam's aggression against God the Father.

Chapter 5

Psychopathology in religious traditions and texts

Masochism in religious traditions

The term "masochism"[1] in this chapter is used to describe a pattern of recurrent self-harming behavior and the constant renunciation of pleasure, carried out for the sake of some greater good such as a religious cause. This pattern is often the result of unconscious guilt, such that the individual feels he has to suffer in order to assuage a harsh superego. He unconsciously seeks suffering because he believes he deserves it. The masochist suffers consciously but is gratified unconsciously when he subordinates his behavior to the interests of others or to his larger cause. This behavior becomes a way of life. Masochists may be self-sacrificing to the point of being martyrs. Moral masochists (Freud's term) of this type have a sense of self-righteousness and moral superiority because of their ability to tolerate their suffering. They often portray themselves as victims and complain about their misfortunes, but their complaints are actually a form of boasting. They enjoy the attention and respect they receive for their suffering, which sometimes makes them seem saintly. The unconscious agenda of a masochist includes the control of those around him, who are often made to feel guilty about his suffering. Masochistic surrender may feel like the only way to maintain a relationship that requires tolerating abuse, self-depreciation, or ingratiating oneself to an important other, including the individual's image of God. Sometimes, masochists attempt mastery by deliberately repeating painful experiences. St. Paul is a case in point.

Was St. Paul masochistic?

The following discussion of Paul is based on the portrait provided by his letters, bearing in mind disagreements about the authorship of some of them by experts, and the question of whether these texts were edited by subsequent followers. Our approach must also be tentative because we assume that current psychological theory can be applied to someone who lived in a very different culture. Paul's personality in general has been discussed by several authors (Callan, 1990, Corbett 2021).

Paul suffered a great deal during his ministry. He was repeatedly attacked and derided by groups who saw him as a traitor to their tradition and a supporter of false doctrines. In the face of considerable hardships, including flogging, stoning, near drowning, fasting, and imprisonment, he managed to maintain his hope and faith. However, characteristic of moral masochists who are willing to suffer for some greater good, at times he seems to take pride in suffering, and he expresses a kind of moral superiority: "For the sake of Christ, then, I am content with weakness, hardships, persecutions, and calamities; for when I am weak, then I am strong" (2 Cor. 12: 9–10). To the psychoanalyst, this sounds like a compensatory attitude, as if Paul was making a virtue out of a difficulty by turning weakness into strength. Masochistic people who expect punishment from authority figures will sometimes provoke the kind of behavior that will elicit punishment, because this relieves the anxiety of waiting and allows the individual to choose the time and place of his punishment. Paul repeatedly placed himself in dangerous situations (2 Cor. 11: 25–27), as if he had an unconscious need for punishment. This element in his personality helps to explain why he repeatedly preached to congregations he knew would attack him. Paul believed that hardship is necessary to enter the Kingdom of God and encouraged his followers to "share in suffering for the gospel" (2 Tim. 1: 8). Paul appealed to his followers to "present your bodies as a living sacrifice," as a form of worship (Romans, 12: 1).

Consciously, Paul believed he was suffering to advance belief in Christ among his followers. Moral masochists are willing to suffer for this kind of worthy cause, and they may demonstrate saintly behavior while suffering in the service of an ideal that is more important than their own safety. There is often an element of moral triumph in being able to tolerate the necessary suffering, which is a way of supporting the individual's self-esteem.

Paul welcomed his suffering because it made him feel closer to Christ. He also sounds as if he felt that being persecuted conferred prestige. Paul sometimes inflicted discomfort on himself: "I pommel my body and subdue it" (1 Cor. 9: 27). This suggests either that he suffered from self-hatred or that he was enraged at his body,[2] and he seems to have generalized this into distaste for bodies in general. We see this in his negative attitude to sexuality, shown in his preference for chastity, celibacy, and the unmarried state, which he wishes others would adopt (1 Cor. 7: 8). This attitude contravenes the attitude of the Judaism in which he grew up, which greatly favors the married state. One has to wonder if he had some kind of sexual difficulty which he rationalized by spiritualizing his distaste for sexuality and the body, but that is a speculation. There is, by the way, no indication that Jesus' taught Paul's attitude to the body, but Paul's mistrust of the body and sexuality became incorporated into subsequent Christian attitudes.

My view of Paul's masochism in the service of his religious beliefs disagrees with Jacob van Bruggen (2007), who denies that Paul was masochistic. Van Bruggen believes that Paul disliked hardship and suffering and tolerated these experiences only to promote the Gospel. But this is a misunderstanding of the masochistic character dynamics; the moral masochist dislikes suffering as much as anyone, but he feels it is necessary for a greater good, so he unconsciously and repeatedly puts himself into situations that will incur it.

Paul's preoccupation with sin

Paul constantly emphasized his personal sinfulness, suggesting unconscious guilt and a harsh superego. He felt he was a "wretched man" who serves "the law of sin which dwells in my members" (Rom. 7: 23–25), which helps to explain his need for divine grace and the importance of Jesus, who atones for human sin. Because of Paul's literal reading of the story of the Garden of Eden, he believed that humanity had been condemned by the Fall of Adam, so that God decreed death for mankind because sin rules the entire world. Paul saw human beings as passive victims of sin that controls their behavior (Rom. 5: 12–12; 13–25). His sense of being powerless in the face of his sinfulness suggests he was in the grip of a powerful complex. Paul's teachings on sin reflect his own psychology, but they became woven into Christian theology's emphasis on human sinfulness.

Paul's self-criticism is typical of people with (introjective) depression, who have internalized harsh, critical parents. They feel that at their core they are bad, and they bewail their negative personality traits as evidence of their badness. They try hard to be good but fear that their underlying badness or sinfulness will be exposed. Paul saw God as a strict father who demands sacrifice and atonement, perhaps based on the harsh behavior of the biblical Yhwh. Speculatively, this image of God may also have been the result of the projection onto God of characteristics of Paul's personal father.

Paul's kind of depressive masochism is often associated with resentment, anger, and aggression, especially when the individual feels unfairly treated. We see Paul's rage and intolerance when he says that a day of God's wrath and judgment will occur (Rom. 2: 5), when angels in "flaming fire" (2 Thes. 1: 7) will pursue vengeance on non-believers. He blinds a man he considers to be a false prophet (Acts 13: 11) and he wishes that "those who unsettle you would mutilate [sometimes translated as castrate] themselves" (Gal. 5: 12). Anyone who preached a contrary message to that of Paul: "let him be accursed" (Gal. 1: 9), and "If anyone does not love the Lord, let that person be cursed!" (1 Cor. 16: 22). The projection of Paul's own feelings onto God is seen in Paul's threats of divine retribution onto those who afflict his followers and those who disobey Jesus. Paul's vituperation may have occurred because unbelievers threatened his intense need for Christ, or they stimulated his own doubt. Paul insisted on ideological compliance among his followers, saying, for example, "what I write to you is a command of the Lord" (1 Cor. 14: 37). Paul's aggression may have been deployed to counteract feelings of helplessness, but his polemics and rage at unbelievers contradict Jesus' teaching of love and forgiveness.

Paul's behavior after he became a follower of Jesus was similar to the way he behaved prior to his conversion, when he harshly persecuted Jesus' followers. Before Paul's Damascus road experience, he attacked Jesus' followers in a "raging fury" (Acts 26: 11), encouraging their deaths (Gal. 1: 13; Acts, 7: 60). Paul says that he believed himself to be "the foremost of sinners" (1 Tim. 15) for this earlier behavior, but he believed he received mercy because he acted ignorantly. However, one wonders if residual guilt remained because he abandoned the faith of his ancestors. He may have dealt with this problem in part by insisting that God chose him before he was born to preach to the Gentiles (Gal. 1: 15–16), thus absolving him of guilt.

Paul writes that before he followed Jesus, he was a strict, even obsessive observer of Jewish law, but apparently this diligence did not alleviate his anxiety and sense of sinfulness. Religious rituals carried out with extreme scrupulousness are often driven by guilt or anxiety; they can be used as an effort to atone for a sense of badness. Paul believed that the Jewish law he used to follow actually increases sin (Rom. 5: 20), probably because it could not be followed exactly. That is why Jesus' atoning death was so important to Paul; it ended the need for the strictures of Mosaic law, which can be burdensome for obsessional people who try to follow it very meticulously.

Paul was able to deal with his anxiety by making Jesus a highly idealized selfobject, such as by speaking of Jesus as "the man of heaven" (1 Cor. 15: 48), divine before birth, in whom "the whole fullness of deity dwells bodily" (Col. 2: 9). Idealization deals with anxiety because it seems that the idealized figure, who is seen as strong and wise, soothes the individual, gives answers, and provides a sense of direction. Primitive idealization often leads to intense merger or identification with the idealized figure, so that Paul says, "it is no longer I who live but Christ who lives in me" (Gal. 2: 20). By identifying with Christ so intensely, he may have made it difficult for his followers to disagree with him, since this identification gave him enormous charismatic authority, as if he was a proxy for Christ. This radical identification with and internalization of Christ may also be a defense against a fear of abandonment by the needed selfobject.

Paul inflated the image of Jesus into a figure of cosmic proportions that Jesus himself would not have recognized. Idealization is a process by which a human figure is seen as perfect, more than human, and in this case as divine. From a Jungian point of view, this means that Paul projected the Self onto Jesus. People who are hungry for such an idealizable figure lack a meaningful internal sense of direction, goals, and values. These are provided by the idealized figure, who represents the individual's perfect self. Idealization hungry people are often anxious and unable to soothe themselves. Idealization is normal and necessary in childhood when parental figures are seen as strong and powerful, but if the childhood need for such a figure is not adequately met, the individual has a lifelong need for an idealizable selfobject, with whose perfection and omnipotence he can merge. The idealized selfobject is not seen realistically. Paul's inflated image of Jesus persisted and was adopted by the Christian Church. The Church developed a sense of its own importance by insisting that its teachings are in the true tradition of the Apostles, and the Pope was declared to represent God's will on earth. His authority was declared to be based on the supposed episcopal succession through Peter as the first Pope.[3]

Psychodynamic aspects of moral masochism displayed in religion

There is a range of psychoanalytic theories about the origin of masochism. Relational masochists unconsciously believe that the only way to obtain love is to allow themselves to be abused, or they believe that attachment requires being abused, so that masochism in relationships defends against separation anxiety. From the point of view of psychoanalytic self-psychology, masochism is an attempt to "restore and maintain the structural cohesion, temporal stability, and positive affective coloring of a precarious or crumbling self-representation" (Stolorow et al., 1980, p. 30). Masochism can also be the unconscious protest of a helpless individual against an aggressor, and at the same time it can be a plea for help. A charitable view of religiously based asceticism, which is often regarded as masochistic, sees an ascetic lifestyle as a way to reduce the hegemony of the ego and allow the emergence of the transcendent dimension into consciousness. (This question is discussed in Corbett, 2015.) Karen Horney believed that such masochism is ultimately directed toward the goal of oblivion, "getting rid of self with all its conflicts and all its limitations" (2000, p. 248). Among professional religious, the hope seems to be that by suppressing the needs of the personal self, asceticism will allow a vision of divinity.

Because masochists believe that punishment is certain to come, instead of prolonged waiting for it, which increases their anxiety, they may provoke others to hurt them, thus conjuring up what they fear while allowing some control. This kind of masochism is a strategy of powerless people. Christians who were traumatically abused in childhood may identify with Paul's attitude of accepting abusive treatment for the sake of his cause. Some may serve others in a way that is religiously and culturally sanctioned but is actually excessive because it is driven by masochism.

Theodore Reich (1941) makes the point that groups that have endured suffering in the course of their history often connect the idea of being loved by God with punishment, as if God distinguishes them in this way. This is analogous to the abused child's fantasy that "father beats me because he loves me." Similarly, Richard Rubenstein (1972) sees the idea that the Jews are a chosen people as a masochistic rationalization of their long-standing national suffering. The notion of the nation as a Suffering Servant (Isaiah 53) seems to accept suffering as proof of their special status in the eyes of God. Rubenstein points out that masochistic people may see abuse as a sign of love, and he sees this as a common dynamic in Western religions. A certain amount of denial operates to maintain this illusion. For example, the book of Lamentations, chapter 3, has a long list of the ways the speaker has been afflicted by God:

> He has made my flesh and my skin waste away, and broken my bones; he has besieged and enveloped me with bitterness and tribulation; he has made me dwell in darkness...put heavy chains on me...he has made me desolate...I have forgotten what happiness is

and so on. In spite of this grievous suffering, the speaker then consoles himself by saying: "The steadfast love of the Lord never ceases, his mercies never come to an end" (3: 22). The obvious cognitive dissonance between this statement and the writer's previous complaints is not addressed. The same dynamic is seen in Isaiah 63: 3–7, where God says: "I trod them in my anger...their lifeblood is sprinkled upon my garments...I poured out their lifeblood on the earth," but the writer immediately goes on to say: "I will recount the steadfast love of the Lord...according to the abundance of his steadfast love." Here, too, the cognitive dissonance in the last phrases is ignored. Paul offers the same theme in Romans 5: 3–5: "we rejoice in our sufferings...because God's love has been poured into our hearts." The Epistle to the Hebrews (12: 5–6) approvingly quotes Proverbs 3: 12: "the Lord disciplines the one he loves/and chastises every son whom he receives."

Masochists believe that too much pleasure now will bring future punishment, and the more they suffer now, the greater will be their future happiness. Suffering is therefore a promise of happiness to come. The Hebrew Prophets typically assure the people that although they are suffering now, there will be a future period of greatness and restoration (e.g., Jer. 33; Ezek. 36; Job 5: 17–18). Reich (1941, p. 427) sees this as a strategy of victory through defeat, and he sees the glorification of suffering in Judaism and Christianity as a form of masochism. This attitude is particularly noticeable in the idea that Jesus' suffering was actually an ultimate victory. It is also seen in comments such as "Blessed are you when others revile you and persecute you...Rejoice and be glad, for your reward is great in heaven" (Matt. 5: 11–12). Jay Haley (1969) pointed out that, as a strategy, masochistic surrender ("turn the other cheek") can be seen as a way for the powerless to assert defiance and moral superiority. Haley believed that Jesus deployed this strategy as a power tactic against authority. However, there are more sophisticated reasons for Jesus' teaching not to return evil with evil.

Paul and Christian martyrdom

Religious martyrs are willing to give up their lives for their beliefs. Paul's martyrdom is described in the apocryphal book *The Acts of Paul*, written toward the end of the second century by Paul's admirers. According to this story, the emperor Nero, who was afraid that the Roman Empire might be overthrown by the Christians, ordered that Paul be beheaded, part of a series of attacks on

Christians following a fire in Rome in 64 CE. Early Christian writers such as Clement of Rome also attested to Paul's martyrdom. It seems that Paul had been willing to die for his faith, exemplified by Philippians 1: 21–24:

> For to me to live is Christ, and to die is gain/ If it is to be life in the flesh, that means fruitful labor for me. Yet which I shall choose I cannot tell/ I am hard pressed between the two. My desire is to depart and be with Christ, for that is far better/ But to remain in the flesh is more necessary on your account.

In this passage, Paul seems to struggle with the tension between his desire for martyrdom and his need to serve his community.

In the Christian tradition, martyrdom has been greatly valued and honored when it is seen as sincere, especially if it is involuntary, less so if it is deliberately and unnecessarily sought. From the second to the fourth century CE, Christians experienced persecution because of their religious beliefs. Many of them chose death rather than abandon or betray their beliefs. Within their community, they were seen as powerful, not as passive victims of the Romans. Their religiousness was not considered to be abnormally intense; they were seen as heroic by their contemporaries. They often had visionary or rapturous experiences, dissociative states, or dreams that presaged their deaths and arrival in paradise.

The Christian tradition associates martyrdom with its etymological root, the Greek *martus*, meaning to witness, since the martyr bears witness to the truth of the faith. Early Christians used this term to describe people who submitted to death as a witness to their faith in Christ. These Christians believed that the sacrificial pattern of their death followed that of Christ. As well, the manner of their deaths challenged the Roman state gods and the political authority of Rome. Christian authorities such as Aquinas have seen martyrdom as an example of virtue, charity, moral perfection, and courage. Skeptics have seen martyrdom as a political strategy used by people in a position of weakness or as a way to gain prestige within their community. Christian martyrs have also been seen as exhibitionistic, psychologically disturbed, depressed, or even suicidal (Tam, 1997). It is, however, an oversimplification to see all religious martyrdom as nothing more than a form of moral masochism. It is important to remember the martyrs' cultural context at a time when eschatological fantasies of immanent divine judgment were prevalent, but Christians had no political power. They had a vision of a paradisiacal afterlife for those who died faithfully, and they assumed that the divine father would love them and punish their pagan persecutors. Martyrs saw themselves as helping to establish the Kingdom of God.

Masochistic elements in religious ascetical practices

Paul's ascetical attitude was carried over into the later Christian tradition, on the assumption that denying or mortifying the body brings one closer to God. However, it is sometimes difficult to distinguish religiously based asceticism from characterological masochism. Gordon (1987) discusses the possibility that there may be a connection between characterological masochism and surrender to a deity taking a pathological form. She postulates an archetypal need to venerate and worship an object that transcends our personal being. Masochism is then the shadow side of this need. Gordon quotes Masud Kahn's idea that human beings need to have their psychic pain witnessed silently by an "other," and this need leads to the creation of an omnipresent God. Gordon points out that many religious rites, rituals, and ascetical practices frustrate or deny physical and emotional needs. In this context, one thinks of self-flagellation, fasting, self-mutilation, abstinence from sexuality, and other forms of self-sacrifice. Postures adopted during religious practices, such as kneeling, prostration, and bowing, also express surrender and humility, but these are not necessarily masochistic. Gordon contrasts pathological masochism with healthy surrender to the holy. She notes that by scrutinizing the projected nature of the object worshipped, we can discern material in the individual's unconscious. The object of veneration—the individual's God-image—carries the projection of the individual's personality traits, be they benevolent or punitive, loving, or violent.

Gordon tends to see masochism as an end in itself, in which case pain is its primary objective. However, this is mistaken; moral masochism usually occurs for some larger purpose. It may be seen as an essential means of connection to the sacred because a masochistic stance was the only way to stay connected to an abusive parent. In childhood, the future masochist had to submit to an abusive parent to maintain any sense of love and connection, and this dynamic may obtain in the transference of parental attributes to divinity. For some theorists, Christ's self-sacrifice is itself an example of religiously based moral masochism, characterized by suffering in the service of a transcendent idea.

Emmanuel Ghent (1990) sees masochism as a perversion of a natural wish to surrender, which should not be confused with the kind of submission in which one is powerless in the hands of another. He points out that submission to a religious authority or to a set of religious doctrines and dogmas may be a form of masochism in the service of feeling protected and safe. Masochism is then the shadow side of authentic spiritual surrender.

Religious systems may take advantage of masochistic character traits to impose ordeals on their adherents. The physical austerities described in world religions, such as fasting, are said to enhance spiritual development, purify the soul, and lead to self-transcendence. These traditions imply that the body is a barrier to spirituality and must be suppressed. Sometimes, the tradition insists on the necessity for suffering: "through many tribulations we must enter the kingdom of God" (Acts, 14: 22). Christian mystics have therefore tortured themselves in order to identify with the suffering of Jesus.

Infanticide in the Bible

A biblical examples of child sacrifice is found in 2 Kings 3: 27, which describes how, when the King of Moab was besieged, he offered his son for a burnt offering. This theme is found in the mythology of many cultures in which a son was sacrificed when the society was in danger (Frazer, 1919).[4] Trying to convince his contemporaries to stop the practice of child sacrifice, the sixth-century BCE Jeremiah (19: 5) says: "They have built the high places of Topheth in the Valley of Ben Hinnom to burn their sons and daughters in the fire—something I did not command, nor did it enter my mind." Jeremiah (32: 35) complains that children were being sacrificed to Baal.

In ancient Israel, the first-born male, animal or human, was consecrated to Yhwh (Exod. 13: 2). The first-born male child had to serve Yhwh in the Tabernacle. Martin Bergmann (1992) believes that the demand to sacrifice the first-born was due to the projection of murderous parental wishes onto Yhwh, and this sacrifice was transformed or sublimated into the rite of circumcision. In contemporary Judaism, to symbolically redeem the child from the biblical obligation to serve in the temple, a descendent of the priestly caste is ritually given five shekels to absolve the child of this service. David Bakan (1971, p. 104) also believes that the ritual of the redemption of the first born may be interpreted as an effort to counteract an infanticidal impulse in the culture of early Israel. He points out that this impulse is seen in various places in the Hebrew Bible, such as the story of the binding of Isaac.[5] Bakan points out that the biblical Job would continually sacrifice to propitiate God in case his children had sinned. Bakan sees Job's continuous ritual sacrificing as an obsessional defense against an unconscious fantasy, or wish, that his children might be killed. Bakan sees the subsequent attribution of Job's children's deaths to God or Satan as "a thin disguise" (p. 106) of this fantasy. Bakan sees such latent infanticidal imagery in various other parts of the Book of Job. For example, Job 39: 13–18 describes how the ostrich neglects her eggs and is "hardened against her young ones," suggesting that God creates infanticidal creatures. When, following the death of his children, Job (1: 21) says, "the Lord gave and the Lord hath taken away," Bakan sees this cry as a veiled reproach that tries to justify the divine father's infanticidal act. Bakan sees the sacrifice of animals in the Jerusalem temple as an appeasement or displacement of the infanticidal impulse. He notes that this practice had lost its social importance by the time of the book of Job even though the impulse had not disappeared. Bakan points out that while Freud stressed the Oedipal desire to kill the father, the Bible much more commonly stresses the infanticidal impulse. Bakan believes that the notion that child sacrifice was demanded by God, such as in the Abraham–Isaac story, is an example of the human impulse to infanticide. Bakan believes that in the rite of circumcision the use of a proxy to carry out the procedure rather than the baby's father is a precaution against a dormant infanticidal impulse.

Bakan believes that Christianity also tries to counteract the cultural tendency to infanticide, exemplified by the slaughter of infants ordered by King Herod, described in Matthew 2: 16–18. Bakan thinks that the sacrifice of the Mass is such a preventive device. He sees Jesus as the victim of an infanticidal impulse, because according to Christian theology the sacrificial death of the Son of God cancels the debt men owe to God. In his discussion of the ritual of baptism, Richard Rubenstein (1972) suggests that baptism "promises escape from the hostility of the Divine Infanticide; baptismal rebirth thus involves the hope for a noninfanticidal Parent."

Bergmann (1992) suggests that the custom of child sacrifice has been a driving force in the development of Western religions. He believes that the development of a loving God-image was an attempt (only partially successful) to ameliorate this practice, which he also believes was once part of the worship of Yhwh as it was for many early traditions such as the worship of the god Moloch. Hence, the Levitical prohibition against sacrificing children (Lev. 18: 21). The biblical commandment that "every firstborn male" should be consecrated to God (Ex. 13: 2) may have referred to the practice of infanticide in early Judea. It was transformed into the practice of the redemption of the first born described above. Bergmann argues that the biblical tradition was only partially successful in abolishing child sacrifice by developing an image of a loving God. The murderous wishes (entirely human) projected onto Yhwh led to the belief that Yhwh demands the sacrifice of the firstborn and the consequent need for the redemption of the firstborn male child in the Jewish tradition. Bergmann shows how child sacrifice evolved into the idea of the scapegoat and the crucifixion of Jesus. Bergmann thinks that child sacrifice, or cruelty toward children, is still alive in the unconscious; it is therefore part of human nature, so that the biblical tradition is a victim of the human archaic past. It is true that evolutionary psychologists believe that during early human evolution, infanticide was adaptive during periods of food scarcity. Such cognitive programs developed in the human phylogenetic past may have persisted and appear in disguised forms in religious traditions.

In this context, we are reminded of the tragic story of Jephthah in the book of Judges (11–12), who sacrificed his daughter to Yhwh in return for victory in battle. This murder is defensively rationalized in various ways by subsequent interpreters,[6] but it clearly indicates the existence of child sacrifice at the time. It is possible that the story of Abraham and Isaac was written to stop such sacrifices. The book of Hebrews (11: 32; 11: 17) values the actions of Abraham and Jephthah.

The tradition of child sacrifice comes to the fore in the story of Jesus. It is difficult for non-Christians to understand the notion that God requires the sacrificial death of a son except as a monstrous feature of human psychology projected onto divinity. This ideology is part of the larger notion that sacrifice in the form of suffering and pain is somehow pleasing to God. Given this ideology, it is not surprising that Christianity has been viewed as an enemy of life. It seems that the warnings of the biblical prophets such as Hosea (6: 6), Isaiah (1: 11), and Micah (7: 21–23) that God does not require sacrifices but prefers justice, humility, and kindness have been forgotten, eclipsed by the human need for blood. (The psychology of sacrifice is discussed in Corbett, 2015.)

Before leaving this topic, I should also point out the story of parents in the Hebrew Bible who, it is predicted, will cook and eat their children or their placentas during a famine. (Deut. 28: 53–57). Yhwh threatens this punishment because "you did not serve the Lord thy God with joyfulness and gladness of heart." The book of Lamentations (2: 20) asks "Should women eat their offspring," and "The hands of compassionate women/have boiled their own children;/they became their food" (ibid. 4: 10). During an extreme famine described in 2 Kings 6: 24–30, maternal cannibalism is described again during a siege. Why these texts specifically threaten cannibalism to stress the severity of divine punishment is unclear, but perhaps this behavior reflects child hatred and Bakan's infanticidal impulse, here rationalized by attributing it to God. Maternal infanticide still occurs but usually in the setting of a delusional depression or a postpartum psychosis. This is evidence that the impulse persists in the depths of the unconscious.

Child abuse in the Bible

The physical abuse of children is part of the violent legacy of the biblical tradition. There are many exhortations to child abuse in the Bible (Greven, 1992). To name a few: "He who spares the rod hates his child, but he who loves the child is careful to discipline him" (Proverbs 13: 24). "Folly is bound up in the heart of a child, but the rod of discipline will drive it far from the child" (Proverbs 22: 15). "Do not withhold discipline from a child; if you punish the child with the rod, the child will not die. Punish the child with the rod and save the child's soul from death" (Proverbs 23: 13–14). "The rod of correction imparts wisdom" (Proverbs 29: 15). Harsh discipline is recommended in Hebrews 12: 5–11: "the Lord disciplines those he loves, and he punishes everyone he accepts as a child." In these passages, abusive treatment of children is rationalized and justified as good for the child's soul. This religious rationalization has allowed if not encouraged sadistic punishment of children, especially among fundamentalists. Donald Capps (1995) points out that James Dobson, the evangelical Christian and founder of Focus on the Family, recommended beating children (Dobson, 1996). Dobson had been beaten as a child and was compulsively repeating what was done to him, so his advice was not purely based on scripture. This is a good example of the way in which religious teaching can be coopted to serve a pathological process, in this case the need to repeat cruelty inflicted on the individual as a child.

Abraham and Isaac

The biblical story of Abraham's willingness to sacrifice his beloved son Isaac (Gen. 22: 1–19) is an example of child abuse that has given rise to many interpretations. The fact that at the last moment Isaac was saved is often understood as a way that the biblical authors discouraged the child sacrifice practiced at the time. The incident may also have been an attempt to soften the murderous image of God in the Hebrew Bible. This episode is often seen as a test of Abraham's faith, because the text says that "God tested Abraham" (Gen. 22: 1), and he is typically lauded for passing the test. The episode is also rationalized as a model of obedience to God. Dreifuss and Riemer (1995) unconvincingly argue that because Abraham was deeply identified with Isaac, Abraham's willingness to sacrifice his son was the same as his willingness to sacrifice himself to God, so this was part of his individuation process. More likely is the possibility that some primitive impulse toward child sacrifice remained in Abraham, and he projectively attributed this impulse to God. Suspicion of Abraham's fathering is raised by the fact that he sends his other son, Ishmael, and Ishmael's mother, into the desert to fend for themselves (Gen. 10: 21). In fact, the command to sacrifice Isaac has been seen as a divine punishment for Abraham's treatment of Ishmael, although God ordered Abraham to listen to Sarah's demand to expel Ishmael. Abraham is typically idealized rather than condemned for initially acceding to God's command to sacrifice Isaac. Kierkegaard's opinion in his *Fear and Trembling* that Abraham was a "knight of faith" is justifiably regarded as abhorrent by many commentators. These kinds of pious rationalizations of a potentially heinous act are unconscious defenses against its horror. They also defend against feeling conscious rage at the brutal father God who commands it. Secular critics of the story have suggested that Abraham did in fact sacrifice Isaac, but the episode was edited by later redactors in a way that met the moral code of their times, which substituted animal for human sacrifice.

On their three-day journey to the place of sacrifice, Abraham may have begun to doubt the rectitude of his intention, and when he saw the ram caught in the bush, he imagined this as an angelic intervention. We cannot help imagining what kind of image of God would make such a demand on Abraham, and why he did not protest, as he had done when he argued with God about the destruction of Sodom and Gomorrah (Gen. 18). If the scene is literally one of divine command, one could see this as an example of the dark side of the biblical image of divinity, analogous to the suffering inflicted by God's testing of Job's piety.[7] These are both stories that give the lie to the biblical image of God as "merciful and gracious...abounding in steadfast love and faithfulness" (Exod. 34: 6).

According to the rabbinical tradition, Isaac was an adult when Abraham tied him to the altar. We cannot tell why Isaac did not protest or try to run away. However, one can imagine that he was intimidated by his father. It is difficult for sons to rebel against authoritarian fathers who demand submission; the son's compliance is a way of maintaining the relationship, but one can barely imagine how Isaac felt about his father's willingness to sacrifice him. Psychoanalysts have seen Abraham's behavior as the result of an Oedipus complex in which Abraham saw his son as a threat (Sugar, 2002). He treated Isaac as if he was Abraham's property, which may have been a cultural norm.

It may not be an accident that Abraham rebelled against his own father, Terah, who then took his son to Nimrod, a local ruler, who, according to tradition, cast Abraham into a fire from which God saved him. Although the sacrifice of Isaac is said to have been ordered by God, like many biblical commandments its source sounds like a component of human psychology projected onto God.

Bergmann (1992) shows that the origin of archaic religion included the need to placate the anger of the gods by sacrificing children. He believes that this dynamic has been repressed and sublimated, but child sacrifice still has an unconscious influence in Western culture. He agrees that the substitution of an animal for Isaac represents a shift away from child sacrifice, but Bergmann believes that such practices are still alive in the unconscious of modern people; it is an aspect of human nature that Jung would call archetypal. Although the biblical prophets tried to stop the practice of child sacrifice, some Israelites continued to practice it at least until the fall of Jerusalem in 586 BCE (e.g., Jeremiah, 32: 35; 7: 31; Ezekiel 15: 21). As the tradition matured, it finally ended the practice, which is forbidden in various places in the Hebrew Bible (e.g., Deut. 18: 10). This motif appeared in Christianity as the sacrifice of the Son of God, which is rationalized as necessary because of original sin, which makes humanity guilty because they inherited Adam's sin (Romans 5: 12–21). This interpretation of an entirely mythic story rationalizes Jesus' sacrifice and appears to give it some moral legitimacy.[8]

Sexism and misogyny in religion and sacred texts

Misogyny in religious traditions is easily disguised and often sanctioned by religious teaching, as if it was ordered by God, illustrating the general point that people are attracted to religious material that corresponds to their own psychological structures and preferences. The question is why men have seen women as so dangerous that they must be contained, restricted, and given no authority.

The authors of sacred texts develop their image of God in the form of their own unconscious needs, desires, and fantasies, so given the cultural preference for men at the time the Bible was written, the biblical image of God is depicted as male. In ancient Israel, discrimination against women was part of the culture. In the biblical tradition, in matters such as rape, divorce, laws of purification, childbirth, menstruation, and laws of inheritance, it is easy to see the enactment of this discrimination. Prejudice against women is still present, even inherent, in some branches of the Jewish and Christian traditions. This bias is usually rationalized within the traditions by saying that men and women have complementary but distinct roles.

The place of women in Christianity

The New Testament's devaluation of women is a good example of the way in which human psychology and psychopathology may become incorporated into theological systems and a tradition's image of God. Paul wrote that "I want you to realize that the head of every man is Christ, and the head of the woman is man, and the head of Christ is God" (1 Cor. 11: 3). Apparently, he believed in some kind of hierarchical order of creation, based on the story of the Garden of Eden, which says that woman was created for the sake of man and woman was made from man. Paul took literally the story of Eve being deceived by the serpent (1 Cor. 11: 8–9; 2 Cor. 11: 2–3; 1 Tim. 2: 13–14), which may be both a symptom and also one of the sources of the misogyny he demonstrates. He preferred women to be submissive, insists that women should cover their heads in church, and says "it is disgraceful for a woman to speak in the church" (1 Cor. 14: 35). He writes: "As in all the churches of the saints, women should be silent in the churches. For they are not permitted to speak, but should be subordinate, as the law says" (1 Cor. 14: 33–34). Contemporary Bible scholars approach this material in different ways. Some believe that because Paul is reflecting the cultural misogyny of his time, these passages are irrelevant today. It is also possible that Paul never wrote some of this material, in which case it's an interpolation by a scribe who copied his letters. Nevertheless, Paul's theology clearly includes a hierarchy of male dominance, which he sees as God given. At the head of the ranking is God, followed by Christ at the head of men and men at the head of women. Paul believes that while men reflect the glory of God, women reflect the glory of men (1 Corinthians 11: 2–16). Paul therefore does not see women as equal to men, even though in Galatians 3: 28 he says there is no longer male and female "for you are all one in Christ Jesus." Paul's preference for silent, obedient, covered women, may reflect a difficulty with sexuality that was stimulated by his seeing women's hair. Paul's antipathy to homosexuality (Rom. 1: 27) and his aversion to the body and sexuality permeated the subsequent development of the Christian tradition. Most authorities believe that Paul did not write the later Pastoral letters, 1 and 2 Timothy, which reflect the conventional patriarchal attitudes of their time, requiring women to be modest, quiet and obedient, subject to their husbands, and not allowed to tell men what to do.

The relevant New Testament justification for men's domination of women is found in multiple phrases such as

> I permit no woman to teach or to have authority over men; she is to keep silent/For Adam was formed first, then Eve/ and Adam was not deceived, but the woman was deceived and became a transgressor (1 Timothy 2: 1–14).

Or, in 1 Cor. 11: 3: "the head of the woman is man, and 1 Cor. 11: 9 says that woman was created for man. Women are instructed to keep silent in churches and are commanded to "be under obedience" (1 Cor. 14: 34–35). Women are also denied authority in the family: "Wives, be subject to your husbands as you are to the Lord. For the husband is the head of the wife just as Christ is the head of the church, the body of which he is the Savior" (Ephesians 5: 22–23).

(Contemporary Christians who believe that the Bible is inerrant ignore the following verse, which justifies slavery: "Slaves, obey your earthly masters with fear and trembling.")[9] The biblical rationale for the superiority of men looks like a defense against the fear of women, which apparently is as prominent now in some quarters as it was among the biblical authors, who imagined that their personal fears and prejudices were divine commandments or natural laws. This attitude continued in authors such as Martin Luther, who spoke of women as that "stupid vessel" in his *Vindication of Married Life*, where he sees men as "higher and better than she."

Feminists have pointed out that New Testament attitudes to women, in comments such as "wives, be submissive to your husbands" (1 Peter, 3: 1), contribute to domestic violence and the physical abuse of women. This attitude is not only the result of the Church teaching the inequality of women. It is also due to Christianity's focus on the redemptive value of suffering. Because of this combination, women in the Christian tradition were long acculturated to accept abuse. Child abuse was also considered necessary (Carlson-Brown et al., 1989). Christians are admonished to share joyfully in Christ's suffering and follow his example (1 Peter 4: 13; 2: 21–22). The usual defense of these passages is to point out that they were written in a very specific cultural context. However, their baleful influence has persisted in some branches of the tradition.

Paul's personal ideal is the asexual life and unmarried state (1 Cor. 7: 8, 27, 38, 40). He says that unmarried people can serve God single-mindedly without being encumbered with family problems (1 Cor. 7: 1; 26, 32–35). Paul rather grudgingly allows marriage as a concession, if celibacy is impossible, because he believes it is better to marry than to be "aflame with passion," but he wishes everyone was like himself in in being celibate (1 Cor. 7: 7–8). He recognizes that this is his own preference and not Jesus' teaching, but he believes that his opinion is trustworthy "by the Lord's mercy" (1 Cor. 7: 25). The reasons for Paul's attitude to sexuality and the body are not clear. He may have dissuaded people from marriage because he believed in the approaching eschaton: "the time is short…For this world in its present form is passing away" (1 Cor. 7: 29, 31).

A charitable view of the Christian anxiety about sexuality is that it is a distraction from the spiritual life. The Gospel of Matthew suggests that it is preferable to be one of the "eunuchs for the Kingdom of Heaven" (Matt. 19: 12), one of those who remain celibate or even castrate themselves. (It is by the way incredible to believe that Jesus would have recommended this practice, given the high value placed on marriage and family within Judaism.) Belief in the perpetual virginity of Mary is another example of the phobic aversion to sexuality found in the tradition, in which virginity is associated with purity. Because of this bias, the early Church tried to present James, the brother of Jesus, as his cousin, to justify the dogma of Mary's perpetual virginity. Ranke-Heinemann (1994) points out the deduction of Augustine and Aquinas that Mary must have given birth without labor pains, and the immaculate conception meant that she had not experienced the "shame" of sexual pleasure. The damage that this neurotic attitude to sexuality has caused to people in the Western tradition has been enormous. Psychotherapists still see the reverberations of this attitude to sexuality among people recovering from fundamentalism.

The patriarchal bias within Christianity became dominant. Augustine suggested that although women's soul has a spiritual nature, and it is made in the image of God with the capacity for redemption, the woman's body is not in the image of God but is carnal and prone to sin, so she is created to be subject to males. During the Reformation, Luther and Calvin continued the tradition of the subordination of women as if it were a divinely ordained social order. In this view, women deserve punishment for Eve's sin, and women are viewed as intrinsically sinful. As a result of these attitudes, women have been marginalized in the Christian tradition and were not allowed leadership positions until relatively recently. The suffering this attitude has caused is incalculable. The prejudice against women appears whenever they violate patriarchal norms, such as by claiming the right to become priests. Fundamentalist clergy still try to limit the role of women in the church using the rhetoric of biblical inerrancy.

The ideal biblical image of women is a passive, acquiescent, silent creature, devoted to service. In their more conservative branches, none of the major monotheistic traditions treat women and men equally. In orthodox Jewish circles, women do not participate in some major rituals, and they are not encouraged to study sacred texts such as the Talmud. Men hold the positions of authority. Women raised in traditions that see the status of women as less than that of men, or who believe that women must submit to the authority of men, are conditioned from birth to accept this situation as biblically justified. Needless to say, feminist scholars have strongly and cogently criticized this situation (Gross, 1996), so that within these traditions feminism in any form is seen as dangerous to the faithful and subversive to the tradition. Men are seen as spiritually superior. Women are often blamed for the difficult aspects of human life because of the behavior of the mythic Eve in the Garden of Eden, who was blamed for the Fall of man and for bringing sin and death into the world. Thus began the never-ending myth of female evil, perpetuated by Christian theologians such as the second-century Tertullian, who referred to women as "the devil's gateway" in his *On the Apparel of Women*. This idea was developed by subsequent Church Fathers such as John Chrysostom, Clement of Alexandria, Ambrose, Thomas Aquinas, and writers such as Augustine, who warned about Eve the temptress. Augustine identified women with concupiscence and lust. St. Jerome saw women as a tool of Satan and a pathway to hell. Tertullian referred to women as a temple built over a sewer.[10] The Church Fathers were so averse to anything to do with sexuality that they imagined that somehow Mary delivered Jesus while remaining a virgin.[11] In other words, these men's personal sexual anxieties and fears were projected onto the danger of women rather than being acknowledged as personal vulnerabilities.

The same male insecurity contributed to the biblical preference for chastity, as expressed by Paul in 1 Cor. 7: 2–3 and continued within the tradition, which tended to see something shameful about sexuality. Women were construed to be temptresses. The tradition's idea that sexuality is sinful was clearly seen when unbridled sexuality, including intercourse with the Devil, was projected onto "witches" in the Inquisition's *Malleus Maleficarum* of 1487. This book saw witchcraft as the result of "carnal lust," which was said to be insatiable in women. Medieval Christian monks and nuns practiced all manner of asceticism to try to repress their sexual feelings, which they regarded as impure or demonic. Clement of Alexandria believed that demons enter men's bodies because demons do not have sexual organs of their own, so this is the only way they can obtain sexual pleasure. Therefore, abstinence and suffering are necessary to get rid of them (*Clementine Homilies*, 9: 10). The Council of Mâcon in 585 CE debated whether women had a soul.

Rosemary Ruether (1981, 2014) pointed out that Christology has been frequently used against women. She discusses Thomas Aquinas' argument that men are the normative type of human being, and only men represent the fullness of human potential. For Aquinas, women are by nature physically, morally, and mentally defective. Thus, the incarnation of the divine Logos had to occur into a man, and all priests must therefore be men. She points out that this means that God is male, and words like "Father" and "Son" are typically understood literally. Ruether (1993) points out that patriarchy is a form of idolatry since it idolizes the male as a representative of divinity. She also believes that the prophetic tradition implies a rejection of the elevation of one social group against others and the use of God to justify social domination.

Feminists have tried to develop female images of Jesus to compensate for the tradition's emphasis on his maleness, but the tradition's savior is clearly male, and its concept of divinity still tends to have a masculine quality. Divinity is usually referred to using masculine pronouns, although it is possible to see the term "Son of God" as a metaphor rather than a biological statement. The fact that Jesus is typically depicted as white contributes to the racism that has been noticeable among some Christians.

Psychological and historical origins of the religious suppression of women

The suppression of Goddess worship

There are controversial theories about the ways in which worship of the goddess was supplanted by the worship of a male sky-God. One theory is that during the Bronze Age there were waves of invasion by northern, patriarchal warrior groups into the Near and Middle East over a period of about 2500 years, beginning about 3000 BCE (Stone, 1976; Gimbutas, 2005; Lerner, 1986). These invaders are variously known as Indo-Europeans or Aryans; they may have been Kurgan nomads from southern Russia. They saw their sky-father-storm-gods as superior to the goddess. They brought with them an androcentric culture with masculine images of God such as Yhwh, who was originally a storm god. An alternative idea was proposed by Leonard Shlain (1998) who suggested that the invention of writing and literacy, which reinforced the more masculine left hemisphere, led to the dominance of masculine modes of thought. This led to the devaluing of the right hemisphere's more imaginative approach, which shifted the balance of power toward men, a devaluing of the status of women, and suppression of the worship of the Goddess. Political and psychological factors also made male supremacy very important to the worshippers of the male sky-God.

Political reasons for the suppression of women

Merlin Stone (1976) believes that the misogynistic and anti-sexual attitude of the patriarchal traditions originated for political reasons. A patriarchal system requires absolute knowledge of paternity for purposes of inheritance and kinship, but the goddess worshiping cultures were matrilineal. These cultures practiced forms of sacred sexuality, in which women living in the temple of the goddess would have sexual intercourse with men in honor of the goddess or as her representative. For them, sex was sacred. These societies had little or no concern for the paternity of children. Accordingly, these ancient sexual customs were condemned by the emerging priesthood of the male sky-God. These priests wanted a male kinship system. To be sure of the paternity of a child they insisted on premarital virginity and marital fidelity for women, and they insisted that extra-marital sex is sinful and shameful. Women could not be allowed to retain control of their own property and had to be firmly under the control of men. Uncertainty about paternity led to such insecurity among the biblical authors that if "the tokens of virginity were not found in the young woman, then they shall bring out the young woman to the door of her father's house, and the men of her city shall stone her to death" (Deut. 22: 20).

Uncertainty about paternity may be in part related to uncertainty about partner fidelity. Male jealousy may have evolutionary roots in a fear of the extinction of the man's genes if he could not be sure if he is protecting his own children or those fathered by another man. These kinds of anxiety are given ideological form by insisting on virginity at marriage and on monogamy, both of which try to ensure paternity.

Such is the narcissistic rage and need for revenge that adultery produced among biblical writers, it was punishable by death (Lev. 20: 10: Deut. 22: 24), a practice that was of course attributed to a divine commandment. Men's emotional vulnerability and the political necessity that led to this grotesque overreaction were never acknowledged. Instead, a mythology developed that insisted that Yhwh had demanded the suppression of women and worship of the goddess, usually referred to in the Bible as "other gods" whose altars had to be destroyed (Deut. 12: 2). Nevertheless, this suppression was only partially successful, as we see throughout the Hebrew Bible, whose authors constantly complain about the practice of goddess worship and insist that Yhwh condemns it. So intense was the pressure to suppress the goddess that the Israelites were commanded to kill even their own family if they worshipped "other gods" instead of Yhwh (Deut. 13: 6–8). The priests of Yhwh destroyed as many of the shrines of the goddess as they could reach, and they developed a creation myth which tells the story in terms of a male deity. The myth of the Garden of Eden was used to further justify the claim of male dominance. In the process, the priests had to convince the followers of Yhwh that sex was immoral unless strictly regulated, and everything to do with procreation was potentially suspect.

The biblical writers went to great lengths to try to eliminate worship of the goddess and replace her with a male sky God. This replacement helped to solve the biblical writers' fear of women by eliminating the power of the goddess and removing the need for the creativity of a divine Mother, since the male God creates through his word. As the divine became male, the societal power of women was concomitantly reduced. The incarnation of God into a male furthered this process. Some of the need for the repression of the goddess might have to do with psychological factors such as an archaic fear of the power of the devouring mother.

Psychological factors underpinning men's fear and envy of women

Men's fear of women is an important psychological reason for patriarchal religions' misogyny and attempted suppression of women. This dynamic is rarely admitted among men because it seems to admit an attitude or weakness regarded as unmanly. Nevertheless, among some men there is an unconscious fear of being weakened by women, or a fear of men's need for women, which feels like a narcissistic wound to men's masculinity. One of the ways that men are devalued in Western cultures is to call them effeminate. The need for power over and domination of women is used as a defense against the narcissistic vulnerability that women induce in men. Male dominance in society reinforces and demonstrates cultural stereotypes of masculinity.

There is a range of psychoanalytic ideas about the historical origin of the male attempts to dominate women, and why women typically do not need to dominate men. Most theorists suggest that the suppression and marginalizing of women in patriarchal traditions is due to the fear of women, which led to a compensatory need for male domination in order for men to feel safe from women's power. Control of women is actually a way of controlling men's dependency on women. Melford Spiro (1997, p. 149) suggests that when men's sense of superiority is threatened, they create the narrative of the dangerous woman, a narrative that suggests that women may try to control men not because of "superior talent or ability but because of deceit and treachery (ranging from sexual wiles to magic and sorcery)." Wolfgang Lederer (1968) collected large numbers of ancient images and myths that seem to glorify women on the surface but actually depict them as full of deadly elements. One medieval statue depicts a peaceful woman in front, but the back of the statue is covered in sores, worms, and "all manner of pestilence" (p. 37). Lederer believes that the largeness of the maternal vagina compared to the boy's small penis engenders the fantasy that to enter it would be disastrous; "the boy himself would sink in, would be submerged, would be devoured" (p. 6). The fear of women may also be at the root of patriarchal attempts to control female sexuality, possibly including the contemporary attempts to restrict access to reproductive rights.

Freud described the fear of women in several places (e.g., *Standard Edition* xiii, p. 396) and noted that women's genitals are often uncanny or somehow horrifying for men (*Standard Edition* xiii, p. 259). He believed that this fear was due to a childhood belief that the female had been castrated, so this might happen to the male child. In a 1922 essay titled "Medusa's Head," in a rather forced comparison, Freud connects the sight of adult female genitalia to the terrifying sight of the decapitated head of the Medusa. He equates decapitation with castration. Freud mistakenly assumed that his era's culturally determined, patriarchal attitudes toward women were innate biological and psychological necessities. Freud's theory that the penis is somehow superior to the clitoris, and the importance of girls' discovery that they lack a penis combined with boys' castration anxiety, became his central explanations for the differential development of men and women. Few contemporary analysts take this phallocentric idea seriously, and feminists point out that it is oppressive. The opposing, gynocentric theory focuses on the early pre-Oedipal period of the very intense mother–child relationship, with its concomitant fear of material abandonment or rejection, which is a terrifying prospect since the child is totally dependent on mother. Men may experience difficulty establishing a secure sense of masculine identity because they have difficulty separating from mother.

Melanie Klein locates the fear of women in the infant's early experience of mother, when the baby projects its own aggression onto mother and thus experiences her as hostile, especially when the mother does not meet the baby's needs, making her seem potentially malevolent or unreliable. Karen Horney suggested that men see women as especially sinister and mysterious when they are menstruating. For Horney, the fear of women relates to the mystery of motherhood and men's envy of this ability, combined with the fact that a little boy "judges that his penis is much too small for his mother's genital and reacts with the dread of his own inadequacy, of being rejected and derided" (1973, p. 142). Horney believed that Freud's phallocentric theory was a defense against womb envy, and that men's creativity and cultural achievements were the result of their envy of women's ability to create children. Winnicott (1986) also believed that the fear of women stems from the infant's early experience with mother, who had absolute power to provide what the baby needed: "the woman figure of primitive unconscious fantasy has no limits to her existence or power" (p. 253). Perhaps men's devalued attitude toward women is then an unconscious form of revenge.

Bruno Bettelheim (1962) believed that men may be envious of women's ability to bear children, so called "parturition envy." One line of evidence for this hypothesis is the Couvade syndrome, in which men display symptoms of pregnancy such as nausea, vomiting, abdominal swelling, and backache, especially in the first and last trimesters of their wives' pregnancy. The situation usually improves after the birth. This syndrome is often ignored, undiagnosed, or ridiculed. Psychoanalytic theorists believe this syndrome is due to envy of women's procreative ability or even rivalry with the fetus, which produces a narcissistic injury. There are other etiological possibilities for the Couvade syndrome, such as a hysterical conversion syndrome or men's identification with their wives' anxiety about the impending birth. A more mundane possibility is simply that men may become marginalized during their wives' pregnancy and birth, which gives women a sense of achievement and social recognition not available to men. (Feminists have pointed out that the rise of men's gender roles during pregnancy and childcare have somewhat changed this dynamic.) Bettelheim also points out that in tribal cultures male initiation rituals sometimes make the initiates mimic women in childbirth, apparently in envy of women. Bakan's (1966) *The Duality of Human Existence* noted that one of the pervasive themes that runs through the Bible is its stress on the importance of the male role in the conception of children, as if women's role had to be downplayed because of men's envy of women's ability to bear children.

A range of psychoanalytic papers reviewed by Daniel Jaffe (1968) offer clinical evidence for men's envy of women's procreative ability. Donald Capps and Nathan Carlin (2009) suggested that the exaggerated ages of men in the Bible are the result of men's envy of women because in fact women have a longer life expectancy than men. These authors provide evidence that bearing and caring for children produces biological hardiness in women. Harold Tarpley (1993) suggested that men may envy women not only because of breast and womb envy but also because of unconscious vagina envy. He points out that male genitalia are exposed to physical injury, and men are vulnerable to criticism of penile size, but female genitalia are hidden and safe from comparison.

The vagina dentata as a mythic source of the male fear of women

The mythology of the vagina dentata, the vagina with teeth that could bite off the penis during intercourse, is a culturally widespread manifestation of the fear of women and male sexual anxiety. The idea implies a dangerously predatory form of female sexuality. This archetypal motif[12] is reported in the folk literature of many cultures (Thompson, 1997) and has been described by several anthropologists (Chamberlain, 2010). The myth is found in the folklore of south and north America, including several First Nation groups. Among the

Tsimshian and Kwakiutl Native Americans of the northwest Pacific, the vagina is compared to the mouth of a rattlesnake (Minton et al., 1969). The myth is also described in Japan, Siberia, Polynesia, Africa, and Australia. Verrier Elwin (1943) collected stories about the vagina dentata in the Madhya Pradesh area of central India. The goddess Kali is sometimes seen as a terrible mother with a vagina that devours the penis of the god Shiva. Some creation myths about the origin of the first humans depict the original women with sharp teeth in their vaginas. In one such myth, a culture hero has to break off the teeth of the vagina of the Terrible Mother, turning her into a human woman (Neumann, 1983). Neumann believes that the destructive, devouring side of the feminine appears "most frequently in the archetypal form of a mouth bristling with teeth" (Neumann, 1983, p. 168). In some myths, the vagina is thought to contain a meat-eating fish, an eel, a demon, or a snake. In some of these myths it seems as though the vagina is autonomous, not under the control of the woman herself. The idea that the female genitals are an entrance to the underworld, or to hell, is found in Christian imagery and also in other mythologies in which death is imagined to be a return to the womb of the goddess (Gimbutas, 2005). The mythological motif of vagina as mouth is explored by Barbara Walker (1983), who believes that castration fears are derived from mouth symbolism that is transferred to the vagina because of their similarity. This fantasy may contribute to the idea of the devouring mother. Walker (pp. 1035–1036) also notes that "Christian authorities of the Middle Ages taught that certain witches, with the help of the moon and magic spells, could grow fangs in their vaginas." Psychoanalysts typically see this motif as a representation of the fear of castration inside the vagina, which sometimes manifests itself as a fear of female sexuality. (A wide range of psychoanalytic approaches is reviewed by Otero, 1996). Barbara Creed (1993) sees the vagina dentata motif as a version of the monstrous feminine, men's fear of the deadly castrating woman. The folklorist Alan Dundes (1993) has suggested that one possible origin of the vagina dentata myth might occur in early infancy when the baby bites the breast, which is a phallic object, and later in life the man fears that a woman might bite back on his own phallus.

The vagina dentata theme was prominent among Surrealist artists in the 1920s (Markus, 2000). It became an urban legend among American soldiers in Vietnam, in stories that Vietnamese prostitutes placed broken glass or blades in their vaginas in order to shred their customer's penis (Caputi, 1988). The fact that this story was believed is evidence of the persistence of the underlying fear. Michelle Gohr (2013) believes that the idea "not only pervades American culture but has also become rampant in its level of subliminal occurrences" (p. 33). Indeed, the mythologem persists in contemporary culture in the genre of horror movies such as *Teeth*, in which a rape victim discovers that she has a vagina dentata. The practice of female genital mutilation may have developed as a reaction to the mythology of the dangerous vagina (Gohr, 2013, p. 40). Jill Raitt (1980) suggests that the image of the vagina dentata is one of the foundations for the caricature of dangerous women that is dominant in Christian theology, in which the ideal woman is passive.

The fear of women is one source of the medieval fear of witches. Raitt (1980) notes that, according to the *Malleus Maleficarum*, one source of witchcraft is carnal lust, which makes witches consort with devils. Apparently, it was believed that witches could enchant men into believing that they had lost their penis, and witches collected penises. In other words, male sexual fragility was projected onto the power of women. Raitt believes that this fear could make men feel unnecessary and could psychologically castrate them, which she sees as the problem behind the male inability to deal with the "mysterious 'otherness' of women" (p. 423). As a result of this fear, women were locked into mythic stereotypes and not seen as human beings. Raitt believes that for men the vagina dentata symbolizes the fear of entry into unknown dangers that must be controlled. Raitt suggests the male-dominated Church neutralized the female threat in various ways in order to make women only a procreative partner, illustrated by the Church's preference for virginity and asexuality, insisting on tying women down to motherhood, or by insisting she is a whore and a temptress. Women are therefore either denigrated or "set on pillars marked 'virgin/mother,' where they are safely out of the way" (p. 424). In Jungian terms, the Church defensively split its image of women into a Madonna-whore fantasy.

Psychological factors underlying the fantasy of ritual purity

Religious systems typically have rituals of purification that are deployed whenever a sacred order or a moral code has been violated, or as part of a ritual process. These rituals typically use water, as in baptism, or blood, as in the Jerusalem temple's animal sacrifices. Leviticus 16: 2 says that once a year the temple had to be ritually purified with the bloody sacrifice of a bull. In some traditions fire and smoke are used as agents of purification and cleansing. The Hebrew Bible's authors were very concerned to avoid anything that might be a source of defilement, anything that could desecrate something sacred or pure. When there was a risk of defilement, people used rituals to protect themselves from it or to purify themselves if they had become impure.[13]

The meaning of purity and defilement in the spiritual sense is entirely metaphysical. Ritual purity has an invisible quality that is not directly perceptible, so that it is not synonymous with ordinary physical cleanliness, since an object or person might be physically clean but ritually impure.[14] The notion that certain objects cannot be touched because of their spiritual power is found in the biblical story of Uzzah, in which his inappropriately touching the Ark of the Covenant caused his death (2 Sam. 6: 3–8), as if holiness has an unseen, deadly power, and Uzzah crossed a forbidden metaphysical or magical boundary.

In the Hebrew Bible, a ritually impure person is not eligible to participate in religious rituals or enter the temple and would be cut off from the presence of God (Lev. 7: 19–21: 22: 3–7). An unclean person would contaminate everything with which he or she came in contact, and so could not offer sacrifices. Descriptions of Yhwh's obsession about ritual purity among his subjects seems to reflect the biblical authors' need to separate themselves from other groups, projected so that this need seems to be a divine commandment. Perhaps the focus on ritual purity is also a way to deal with personal shadow material by "cleansing" it as if it were external. Laws about ritual purity served the function of allowing the people to feel special and unique, as well as ritually warding off evil. The social system of ancient Israel was partly structured around the maintenance of ritual purity. The laws of purity and their associated rituals helped to consolidate the community around a common set of values, and they acted as social regulators.

The biblical ideas about ritual purity gave rise to complex ritual structures. These have been explained as an instrument of social control by an elite class of priests who were regarded as socially superior. They claimed they were able to mediate between the people and Yhwh because he gave the priests the authority to describe his preferences and wishes in his relationship to his people. The priests could decide what was clean or unclean and they had the power to decide who could participate in temple rituals. To indicate their special status, the priests had an even stricter purity code for themselves than the code for the general public.

The book of Leviticus describes a set of laws intended to achieve holiness in the eyes of Yhwh. Because Yhwh is holy, his people have to be holy, and being holy means being pure, which requires ritual laws of purity (Lev. 11–15). Yhwh would not allow anyone in a state of impurity to approach him, as if he or his sanctuary could somehow be defiled. This is an interesting projection of the human fear of pollution onto the divine. Pollution was sometimes used as an explanation for misfortune; Hosea 5: 3–7 announced that because the people had become defiled, God had withdrawn from them. To illustrate how seriously the purity laws were taken, more than a hundred years later, Ezekiel (5: 8–12) described the defilement of the temple by idolatrous practices, leading to horrible punishments such as parents eating their children, children eating their parents, plague, and famine.

There were two categories of purity in ancient Israel. Moral purity was about avoiding certain types of behavior such as idolatry or sexual transgressions, while ritual purity was about avoiding defilement due to childbirth, infectious diseases such as leprosy, contact with dead bodies, and discharges from the body such as menstrual blood. The main concerns seem to have been about boundaries, involving material that escapes the body or that may invade the body in the form of impure food. It is noteworthy that the categories that produced ritual impurity often had to do with the body, disease, sexuality, and death, which Yhwh did not experience himself, so by purifying himself the worshipper becomes closer to Yhwh.

It seemed that certain types of material could have a kind of spiritually contagious effect on whatever it touched, passing on a negative spiritual power.

The contagious effect is seen in the fact that if a wrong doer is not punished, the entire community is implicated in his guilt. Impurity was equated with being sinful. The effects of being impure might result in being cut off from the community or even in death, such as if a priest were to approach anything holy in a state of impurity (Lev. 22: 9). Moral defilement was so serious that it led to expulsion from the land and separation from Yhwh (Numb. 35: 33–34). Because the land of Israel was declared to be holy, everything beyond it was somehow impure.

An important source of pollution according to the biblical text was eating the wrong foods (Lev. 11). There are many attempted explanations for the resulting dietary laws. One view is that they promote hygiene and public health, but that does not account for all the laws. The anthropologist Mary Douglas (1966) suggested that the idea of holiness is connected to physical wholeness or completion; to be holy is to be whole. Holiness is given physical expression in the wholeness of the body, which is why all sacrificial animals had to be without any physical defect (Lev. 22: 17–24), and the priesthood is forbidden to men who are deformed, crippled, blind, lame, hunchback, or disfigured in some way (Lev. 21: 17–21). Certain occupations, such as being a tax collector, made the individual impure. Tithing, or taxes on agricultural products, was also part of this system since produce on which tithes had not been paid was impure.

Biblical purity was partly about not mixing species or categories, such as wearing clothes made of both wool and linen, the mating of different types of animals, or sowing a field with two kinds of seeds (Deut. 22: 11; Lev. 19: 19). According to Douglas, human beings have an innate tendency to classify experience into discrete phenomena, so the biblical authors try to impose boundaries and clear symbolic patterns onto messy experiences. Ambiguity is experienced as dangerous. Everything had to be in its correct place. Cultures create order and unity by organizing their worldview into binary categories or classifications such as clean or unclean. An unclean animal is one that does not conform fully to its class. If it does not clearly belong to either air, water, or land, it does not demonstrate wholeness and cannot be ritually pure. This classification excludes animals whose nature is ambiguous such as amphibians or those whose boundaries are unclear. Such a hybrid or transitional animal feels dangerous because it threatens the order that holds the society together. "Holiness requires that individuals shall conform to the class to which they belong...different classes of things should not be confused" (Douglas, 1966, p. 54). Thus, "rituals of purity and impurity create unity in experience" (p. 2). Douglas claimed that the cultural association of a substance as polluting, or ritually impure, is linked to its perception as anomalous within a symbolic classification. Danger is found at the margins or when crossing the boundaries of categories. Because the human body mediates between the person and the external environment, everything that either enters or leaves the body such as food or excreta can be experienced as dangerous or polluting. Certain types of behavior were seen to be defiling because they seem unnatural, or not the way things are supposed to be according to divine precepts.

Douglas believed that the biblical dietary laws were about the maintenance of symbolic boundaries between types of animals. She rejects the idea that the biblical prohibition about eating pigs had to do with hygiene. She suggests that although the pig has a cloven hoof, like the other members of the Israelite flocks of sheep or goats, unlike them the pig does not produce milk, and unlike the pig these animals also chew the cud. Therefore, the pig is anomalous, and anomaly produces anxiety because it resists classification and so is forbidden in a culture that values classification. In her later work, Douglas decided that this was not a strong enough argument for the Levitical dietary laws. Her later view was that taboos reinforce oppositions that seem to structure the universe and make it rationally comprehensible, in order to avoid chaos. The animals that can be eaten are those that can be sacrificed in the temple; the pig cannot be sacrificed. There is a parallel between the altar and the human body or between table and altar.

There is a range of alternative explanations for the Hebrew Bible's prohibition against eating pigs. This taboo may have arisen because of pigs' association with pagan cults in which pigs were sacred to Baal and Ishtar. Alternatively, the laws are designed to teach discipline and restraint, and to distinguish Israelites from other people such as the Philistines, who consumed large amounts of pork, so this became an ethnic marker and a boundary. Or some animals are unclean simply because Yhwh said so. The underlying principle of the dietary laws seems to have to do with Yhwh's need to separate Israel from other nations "that you should be mine" (Lev. 20: 26). This emphasis on separation seems to be a form of maintaining national self-esteem by feeling unique, just as (in the people's projection onto him) Yhwh is unique, so the people must mirror his specialness, which is partly reflected in his commandments.

The New Testament stresses moral defilement (2 Cor. 7: 1). When Jesus annuls the dietary laws (Matt. 15: 10–20) he points out the need for people to be pure on the inside, to cleanse the heart, and to be concerned with what comes out of the individual instead of worrying about what is taken into the person (Mark 7: 15). In 1 Cor. 7: 12–13, Paul rules that when a Christian is married to an unbeliever, they should not divorce because "the unbelieving husband is consecrated through his wife, and the unbelieving wife is consecrated through her husband," and their children are holy. This indicates a sense that holiness is contagious; the non-believing spouse is sanctified by the believing spouse, as if holiness can be transferred. A related idea is found in the practices of baptism and the sprinkling of holy water, as if water transmits blessing, purity, and holiness or divine agency. This is a kind of magical practice that may be understood symbolically because water is associated with life, but several traditions treat it literally, as if holy water has special properties.[15] There is a tradition that Jesus was baptized not to be purified by the water but to make the water holy, to purify the water.[16] In the Christian tradition, salvation given through Jesus' death is a form of purification from sin (Heb. 9: 14, 22). In both the Jewish and Christian traditions, therefore, there is a belief that spiritual perfection or sanctity is attained by avoiding or controlling defilement by the body and its passions, or by using the body incorrectly, which is a source of pollution. This control is thought to allow contact with the spiritual dimension.

By applying laws of purity only to one's own group, it is distinguished from polluted others, thus establishing ethnic boundaries, as if ethnicity and genealogical purity are an essence rather than simply a type of social group. Therefore, various forms of contact with other groups, such as intermarriage, are forbidden in the Hebrew Bible and the subsequent tradition, since they are seen as essentially polluting. So serious is intermarriage that Numbers 25 describes a serious plague that resulted from relationships between Israelite men and Midianite women, followed by the divine commandment to wage war against the Midianites (Num. 25: 17; 31). Sometimes the danger of intermarriage with foreign women was seen as dangerous because it might tempt men to worship gods other than Yhwh (Deut. 7), but sometimes intermarriage seems to be intrinsically defiling (Gen. 34, Ezra 9–10). Such marriage is seen as an act of disloyalty to Yhwh (Ezra. 10: 10), as if he were a potentate who requires his subjects' loyalty. The wives and children of such marriages were rejected. Deuteronomy 23: 3 forbids the descendants of mixed marriages from entering "the assembly of the Lord" for ten generations. This latter type of "defilement" seems to be the conscious expression of unconscious tribalism, stranger anxiety, and xenophobia, which are said to have evolved to keep people within their own group because of the competition for resources among groups of early hominins. The inevitable result of such ethnic division is conflict. Religions almost inevitably foster an in-group/out-group psychology, thus promoting divisiveness and conflict between people. The biblical story attributes the Israelites' xenophobia to a divine commandment; it was more likely to have been a projection onto Yhwh of their need to be his unique nation.

Tribalism continued in the early Christian tradition when, at the Council of Elvira (circa 306 CE), the Catholic Church forbade marriage between Christian and Jews. The Nazis used the same prohibition in their Nuremberg Laws. The underlying psychology is the same; a sense of superiority and specialness, with a concomitant need to devalue other groups in order to maintain an ingroup sense of superiority. Societies typically project their undesirable qualities onto other groups, and by treating them as less than human, assume that they may be justifiably persecuted and abused. The dynamic has not changed, especially when ethnic and racial differences are involved, because of the inbuilt human intolerance of otherness. Stranger anxiety and the resulting xenophobia seem to be unfortunate parts of our evolutionary endowment.

The biblical fear of menstrual blood

The Hebrew Bible prescribes strict laws for the isolation of women during menstruation, because menstrual blood is ritually unclean: "When a woman has a discharge of blood which is her regular discharge from her body, she shall be in her impurity for seven days, and whoever touches her shall be unclean until the evening" (Leviticus 15: 19). Leviticus states that while menstruating anything a woman touches becomes unclean or polluted, and anyone who touches any of those things becomes unclean themselves. Sexual relations are forbidden during menstruation (Lev. 18: 19). (Presumably, this is also because there is little chance of a woman becoming pregnant at this time and enjoying sex for its own sake was disapproved of.) The priests claimed that women were dangerous or defiled during menstruation, and this pollution is contagious. After childbirth the woman was required to offer either two turtles or pigeons to the priest, who "shall make atonement for her, and she shall be clean" (Lev. 12: 8). (Ejaculation of semen was also a form of impurity, but the man was unclean only until that evening [Lev. 15: 16].) Furthermore, according to Leviticus 12: 1–5, a woman who had given birth to a male child is impure for 33 days but remains impure for twice that period having delivered a female child. Having a baby rendered her ritually impure and having a female baby even more so. No reason is given to explain why childbirth renders a woman so impure that the situation can be rectified only by the blood sacrifice of an animal.

Menstruating women were excluded from the Jerusalem temple. In the tradition of menstruation contaminating holy places, based on the strictures of Leviticus 12, from the late Middle Ages until the late nineteenth century in the Roman Catholic tradition, the custom of "churching" forbad women entrance to a church for 40 days postpartum, apparently because they were spiritually impure. The unconscious fear of contamination by menstrual blood may contribute to the reluctance of the Roman Catholic church to ordain women, although this is also a way to maintain men's control of the Church's central ritual. Menstruation and the anxiety it triggers in men seem to be among the main reasons that women in Judaism and Christianity are excluded from positions of authority (Phipps, 1980). The Roman Catholic Church and the Eastern Orthodox Church still list the "moral impurity" of menstruation as a reason for resisting the ordination of women priests (Anthony, 2020).

St. Jerome saw menstruation as "God's curse" on women (Phipps, 1980, p. 300). Menstruation was considered to be one of the curses inflicted on Eve for her rebellious behavior. This fear has been widespread. There is a horror of menstrual blood in many traditions, in part because of the mystery involved; human beings tend to respond to mystery with anxiety. In the folk tales of the Yuki Indians of California, the dangerous venom of the rattlesnake is said to be menstrual blood, and in Zuni and Hopi folklore menstrual blood attracts serpents, while the Makuxi of Guyana believe that a menstruating woman can be seduced by serpents (Minton et al., 1969). The anthropologist Rita Montgomery (1974) studied menstrual taboos among 44 different tribal cultures, across the Americas, Africa, Asia, and the Pacific Ocean. In many of them, this blood is either a source of unease or a frank taboo. Lederer also (1968) lists many cultures where the fear of menstruation persists. He gathered some of this information from James Frazer's 1890 *The Golden Bough* (vol. 2, p. 238 *passim*), which describes many tribal cultures who show this fear and insist on secluding and avoiding menstruating women, who are not allowed to touch weapons. Just one example; an Australian group tells boys that if they see menstrual blood, they will become prematurely grey, and their strength will fail prematurely. Frazer writes that in Pliny's *Natural History* (77 CE), the touch of a menstrual woman is said to have many baleful effects; it turns wine to vinegar, blights crops, dims mirrors, blunts razors, and so on. Frazer reports that in various parts of Europe the touch of a menstruating woman turns beer, wine, or milk sour, and causes buds to wither. Menstrual taboos that violate human rights by contemporary standards are still common in many societies and religions (Anthony, 2020; Kamat and Tharakan, 2021), leading to restrictions and psychological and emotional stigmatization. The continuation of this fear suggests that the anxieties that afflicted the biblical authors still persist.

The origin of the laws about the "impure" nature of menstrual blood are complex and uncertain. Early people believed that babies were made of their mother's blood, which stops flowing during pregnancy and was thought to "coagulate" into a baby (Neumann, p. 31), thus giving women mysterious transformative power. Perhaps it is not a coincidence that the word "Adam" can mean "made of blood." It seems that the biblical authors viewed blood with a mixture of numinous awe and fear. They felt they had to control its mysterious power, perhaps because it was too redolent of the power of the goddess they were trying to suppress. The sight of menstrual bleeding has also been said to induce castration anxiety in men.[17] It looks as if depicting menstruating women as "unclean" is a defensive way of saying men are afraid of them. A more skeptical view is that asserting the negative effects of menstruation may have simply been an excuse for their domination of women. Such is the taboo against menstrual blood that the orthodox Jewish tradition still forbids direct physical contact with a menstruating woman, which would cause ritual impurity. Apologists argue that the ritual separation of women during menstruation described in Leviticus is not misogynistic but is intended to be protective of them and offer them privacy.

The Garden of Eden story of Eve born of Adam's rib, as if she is delivered from his body, suggests the biblical authors' need to compete with women's ability to bear children. The fact that Eve was a product of Adam, combined with the primitive fears of women described above, contributed to the devaluation of women in the biblical tradition. Stories such as Adam and Eve are still regarded as relevant among fundamentalists, but the male-centric cultural sources of these stories are often ignored, and these kinds of biblical sources are still used to insist on the male domination of women. A good example is the decision in 2023 by the Southern Baptists, America's largest Protestant denomination, to remove women from church leadership. Conservatives in that tradition were angry that churches had ordained women pastors. This argument began in other denominations several decades ago, and the move to prevent women from having positions of power persists among evangelical Christians. The ostensible basis for this position is partly that God created Adam first, and then Eve (Gen. 2: 18–25). However, several feminist scholars have deconstructed the androcentric reading of that text by suggesting that it can be read to mean that "the human" was originally created as a non-gendered being, which was only later divided into two genders. Using the logic of the biblical order of creation, since the animals and plants were created before humans, it could be argued that humans are inferior to animals (Young, 2009). Based on linguistic analysis, the text can also be read to say that the two humans are equal partners, and the woman is not merely created as a helper (Efthimiadis-Keith, 2010 discusses this literature). However, using traditional androcentric translations of the text, which ignore recent scholarship, this story is taken to mean that because Adam was created first, men must be more important than women. Furthermore, in Genesis 3: 16 God says to Eve that because of her disobedience "he [men] will rule over you." Overall, it seems that in patriarchal traditions men's fear of women, men's fear of maternal dependency, and a fear that men's sexual feelings will make them vulnerable, are projected onto women, who are then treated as if they were dangerous and must be contained.

The psychodynamics of blood sacrifice and ritual

Why did the religions of antiquity require so much killing in the name of their gods, as if killing could be made sacred? Why did the ancients believe they had to ritually kill in order to be in a right relationship with their gods? In the Hebrew Bible, there are accounts of untold numbers of animals being sacrificed to Yhwh, in part because he enjoyed the smell of burning flesh, which was a "sweet savor unto the Lord" or a "pleasing odor" (Lev. 2: 12; 3: 16), a phrase that occurs frequently. He was said to send his fire down to consume the offering on the altar (1 Kings 18: 38). The priests may have imagined that Yhwh would glory in gore, since blood was thrown around the altar to cleanse and purify it (Lev. 1: 1–7; 14: 19). Blood was used to purify the people and to make atonement for them (Lev. 4; 2 Chron. 29: 24). Since the blood of an animal refers to its life (Lev.17: 11), and Yhwh was said to give life, blood sacrifice may indicate some kind of visible bond between him and the people, or it was thought to ensure his presence in the temple. The people were threatened with his absence if the temple was defiled, so to maintain his presence it had to be purified with a bull and goat sacrifice during the annual celebration of Yom Kippur, a Day of Atonement (Lev. 16). The "sin offering" on this day was an expiatory sacrifice, an attempt to make amends for having sinned against Yhwh. The sacrifice probably had a powerful psychological effect on the sacrificer. The sacrificer put his hand on the animal as if transferring his sins to the animal, which was then killed before God as a substitute for the sacrificer, whereupon the priest spread the blood around, flayed the animal, and burned it so that it would ascend to God (Lev. 1: 6; 4, *passim*). The sacrificer had to have a sincere attitude for such offering to be effective, so that God would grant the necessary atonement or ritual purification (Noonan, 2021). The ritual process produced an intense emotional atmosphere in dramatic surroundings that enhanced its psychological effects.

There is a strong taboo in the Hebrew Bible about eating blood (Lev. 19: 26), and the blood of the temple sacrifices was dedicated to God alone. All this may have been a way to channel or sublimate the human lust for blood. One cannot help wondering about the attitude of the priests carrying out animal sacrifices, whether they reveled in the killing or whether they found it distasteful but necessary. Fascination with bloodletting and violence persists, in movies like *Apocalypto* and *The Passion of the Christ*, which contain distinctly sadomasochistic imagery.[18]

Contemporary anthropologists ask about not only the symbolic meaning of a ritual but also the functional question of what it does, what it achieves. Perhaps ritual killing channels, sublimates, domesticates, and contains human murderous impulses. Sacrificial rituals are also magical practices, in which the intention is to influence the higher powers. Skeptical psychologists see this as a regressive, unconscious attempt to obtain the good wishes or forgiveness of a parent figure, projected onto a deity. The hostility of the sacrificer is also projected and becomes a fear of being punished by the deity. Sacrifice can also be written off as merely superstitious behavior, which is understood psychologically in terms of magical thinking that presumes that thoughts can affect the physical world. A further motivation for superstitious rituals and magical practices is to provide the illusion of control over events, or to obtain supernatural help, especially in situations of danger and uncertainty, when a ritual practice seems better than inaction. Socially conditioned beliefs also play a part in the individual's participation in ritual behavior, due to pressure to conform combined with obedience to clerical authority. These systems of thought are difficult to discard when one has been conditioned from childhood to believe in them. Evidence that the ritual has no effect on whether the desired outcome occurs typically has no effect on the believer's faith in his system and can usually be explained in terms of the system itself.

Rituals such as the Jerusalem temple sacrifices suggest an underlying belief that if we shed blood, our own lives will be spared, as if something has to die to prevent more death. It is possible that people who sacrificed animals to Yhwh believed they were returning the life of the animal, which they identified with its blood, to its creator, so they would be allowed to eat its flesh. However, those dynamics alone might not explain the need for the shedding of so much blood, so the purpose of sacrifice and its possible psychological motivations remains to be explored.

The sacrifice of animals and occasionally of human beings was common to many religions in antiquity, in widely disparate geographical cultures and historical periods. Not all sacrifices involved ritual slaughter; at the other end of the spectrum, an object such as food or wine is offered on an altar as an oblation, a gift to the deity. There is a wide range of scholarly discussions of ritual sacrifice (Gane, 2022), but there is no single form of sacrifice, so it requires a range of explanations. There are anthropological, cultural, theological, and psychological ways to understand the phenomenon. Some social processes mirror deep psychological processes within individual members of the group, but some social and cultural processes are more a function of the group's history and societal structures than of individual psychology. Anthropologists sometimes complain that psychologists are too ethnocentric when they try to apply Western psychology to non-Western cultures, which may have very different psychological structures. However, if Jung is correct, the archetypal level of the psyche applies to all human beings, and sacrifice is so worldwide historically and geographically as to be clearly archetypal.

The practice of sacrifice is very old; it has been reported among reindeer hunters of ten thousand years ago who would throw their first kill into the sea as an offering (Feiner and Levenson, 1968). In part, this ritual slaughter is based on the sense that we can influence or even coerce the higher powers if we give up something of value to us. Sacrifice is then an exchange in which people hope to be given something by the deity in return for what they have offered. Sacrifice also acts as a form of purification, communication, and communion with a god, or it is an attempt at homage, thanksgiving, and praise to the god. Sacrifice also wards off the anger of the god, whose displeasure is appeased if an animal is sacrificed. Sacrifice thereby acts as an atonement or reparation, as if the animal dies for the sins of the individual. This is a principle of substitution, as if the gods require the life of an animal to preserve a human life, and the sacrificer vicariously experiences his own death in the death of the animal. The person sacrificing the animal symbolically dies, apparently in an identification with the animal, but is then transformed, purified, or reborn as the god receives the sacrifice. The sacrificer is then confirmed in his sense that the god is a reliable selfobject, one to which he can safely attach and idealize in a way that alleviates his anxiety. The eating of the sacrificial victim in a communal meal helps to establish social cohesion and bonding. In many archaic societies, public occasions and festivals required an act of ritual killing to ward off some deep-seated anxiety about whether the gods would approve of and bless the community. Ritual process in general seems to help people channel or contain intense emotions in a socially approved of manner. Ritual provides a sense of control or efficacy in an uncertain or dangerous situation.

It seemed to early cultures that sacrifice alleviates guilt and eliminates evil from the community. Alternatively, or additionally, ritual violent sacrifice may be a way of coping with the fear of death by appearing to control it. Jung (CW 5, para. 671) sees sacrifice both as a way that "man ransoms himself from the fear of death" and also as a symbolic renunciation of life in order to regain it. Sacrifice pacifies the deity to ward off impending disaster or to restore order and relationship with the god when things are going badly. Sacrifice thereby tries to maintain a sacred order, especially a moral order that is always in danger of being transgressed (Hubert and Mauss, 1964). A radically alternative view was suggested by the theorist Georges Bataille (1991), who believed that cultures always generate waste and excess and must expend this surplus energy. Historically this was achieved in war or spending on luxury, but also in sacrifice, whose function is unmitigated consumption or destruction for the sake of pure expenditure. In his view, sacrifice gives destruction its due; there is no expectation of reward or profit. Another societal perspective is that of Emile Durkheim who believes that gods exist because human beings sacrifice to them (Mizruchi, 1998). The worshipper survives by ensuring the survival of the god, who must not be allowed to die. At the same time, the ritual process reflects and legitimizes society's social order.

Animal sacrifice seems to be a primitive mental mechanism in which the animal's life is offered to the deity as if the life of the person making the sacrifice is preserved by taking the animal's life. It is striking that the sacrificial animal was often flayed and dismembered on the altar, unconsciously enacting the kind of rebirth motif often found in shamanic rituals in which symbolic dismemberment is followed by regeneration and being remade (CW 11, para. 346 note 9; para. 448). There is therefore an element of hoped-for re-creation in sacrifice, a kind of re-circulation of life energy between the human and divine realms, where life is given in the hope of it returning. Eliade (1961) believes that sacrifice is an act of creation that repeats and imitates an original sacrifice that created the world, and so is a form of rebirth. The burning of the animal is important because fire and smoke seem to be a connecting link between the human and the divine; fire made the animal sacred, and smoke transferred it to the realm of the gods (Edinger, 1990).

God and the people are symbolically united by participating in the flesh and blood of a sacred victim. Eating the animal creates a kind of blood covenant that is similar to human kinship bonds (Smith, 1972). By eating the sacrificial animal that has been consecrated to the god, the qualities of the god are incorporated, and the sacrificer can more fully identify with his idealized image of his god, and perhaps absorb some of the god's power. Hubert and Mauss (1964) believe that the purpose of sacrifice is to bring the profane level into relationship with the divine using the consecrated victim as a form of mediation or hinge between the sacred and profane worlds. They point out that sacrifice does not simply orient the sacrificer toward the god, it also alters the sacrificer. In Kohut's terms, sacrifice consolidates the self-selfobject tie, where the god is a necessary but also potentially threatening omnipotent selfobject. By affirming the relationship with his god, sacrifice helps to consolidate the cohesion of the individual's sense of self and wards off fragmentation anxiety. De Vos and Suarez-Orozco (1987, p. 327) see sacrifice to a god as a "primitive mode of coping with a need for security," as if the power of the god can thereby flow to mortals in a form of "divine reciprocity" (p. 322), especially when sacrifice is eaten, which symbolically ingests and incorporates the god's power.

They believe that feeding the god by offering a sacrifice tries to induce relaxation in a "potentially destructive being" (p. 321). This kind of sacrifice is relational. Edinger (1972, p. 96) describes a "sacrificial attitude," in which sacrifice indicates that the ego realizes its subordinate position to the Self, the image of the divine, and is prepared to serve it.

The origins of sacrifice can also involve a dynamic in which the individual offering a sacrifice has a kind of parental transference to the divine. Children are known to sacrifice themselves or their own needs to care for a parent, to prove their love or to gain parental love, to avoid separation from a parent, or as a form of masochistic surrender to reduce tension in the face of an angry parent (Feiner and Levenson, 1968). It is a short step to see this dynamic as the ground of the notion that divinity needs a sacrifice to maintain our connection to it. In a relationship with a fragile parent, a child may feel that the welfare of the parent is at stake, which requires that the child gives up something to stabilize the parent. Given the typical father projections onto the biblical Yhwh, the need to maintain secure attachment to him and avoid his anger seems to reflect some of these archetypal parent-child dynamics. Sacrifice is a way to obtain the divine father's goodwill and approval. Another possible factor is that from childhood we associate suffering with parental punishment, so that when we suffer, we try to mollify the higher powers or the divine parent by making an offering. It is as if human beings believe that a sacrifice will alleviate or avert their suffering, as if giving up something of value to them somehow affects the higher powers that are causing their difficulties. Perhaps this dynamic is part of our evolutionary inheritance, since early in human evolution, sacrifice for the sake of others or for one's children may have had value for the survival of the group.

The notion that sacrifice is essential to the relationship between God and humanity is expressed in Jesus' self-sacrifice, which is held to be a kind of universal sacrifice or a purification because "the blood of Jesus his Son cleanses us from all sin" (1 John, 1: 7, and Heb. 9: 13–14), although it is not clear how this historical act still applies to us. Hebrews 9: 23–28 teaches that there cannot be remission of sins without the shedding of blood, an idea that is surely the projection of the human need for revenge. The ritual of the Eucharist expresses themes of the incorporation of God, gratitude and allegiance to him, and identification with him. As Jung points out (CW 11), the Mass is a symbolic act of union and consecration through a ritual sacrifice; he sees this form of sacrifice as a deeply rooted archetypal phenomenon, as if the archetypal need to sacrifice has evolved to the point that it is now sublimated in the form of the Mass and in religiously motivated self-denial and asceticism.

Nancy Jay noted that, in many societies, only males may perform sacrificial rituals (1985, p. 283). The male Israelite priesthood had this exclusive privilege, and this priesthood was inherited from father to son, an ideology of genealogical continuity that keeps the lineage clear. Jay points out the affinity between religions that carry out blood sacrifice and social systems that stress patrilineal descent of authority and property. In these societies, women give birth but have no legal descendants. Paternity is never totally certain, so birth alone is not the sole criterion of patrilineal membership; an additional ritual is needed. In the biblical culture, a blood sacrifice (a lamb and a dove) was made after the birth of a child, and by participating in this ritual, the child is identified with the father in the moral and legal sense, creating certain evidence of paternity. The ritual serves as powerful evidence of patrilineal descent and maintains the continuity of social order. Jay suggests that by incorporating members into a patrilineal descent group by means of blood sacrifice, the group believes it can transcend mortality as well as transcending birth. "In this sense, sacrifice is doubly a remedy for having been born of woman" (p. 297). She notes that the traditional Eucharist is carried out only by a lineage of male members of a patrilineage, the apostolic succession of clergy from father to father, "in a line no longer directly dependent on women's reproductive powers for continuity" (p. 292), ensuring a male-dominated social order. A man can become a priestly "father" without needing a mother. Jay suggests that blood sacrifice is necessary to establish patrilineal descent because only killing is a serious enough counterbalance to giving birth. Unlike birth, sacrificial killing is under control, in contrast to the vulnerability and suffering of childbirth.

Magic and superstition in religious rituals

One usually sees some combination of magical thinking and superstition within ritual practices. Magical thinking is the illusory belief that thoughts can influence the material world. Magical thinking invents a needed reality to compensate for the actual reality that is too painful. This mental mechanism is in part a residue of infantile omnipotence and in part a regressive way to feel effective and ward off helplessness. Ritual practices are magical in the sense that physical actions are thought to influence spiritual reality. Ritual magic tries to induce a connection between a mental state and a desired physical effect. In religious settings, rituals are carried out in an emotionally charged atmosphere by a charismatic individual. The sacrifices conducted in the Jerusalem temple depended on this kind of magical thinking. Priestly trappings and the authority of the scripture imbued the priest with archetypal projections, so in the transference to him he was seen as a mana personality[19] who had superior spiritual power, which enhanced his effectiveness and social power.

The psychology of superstition has behavioral and psychodynamic explanations. Superstitions are based on a combination of magical thinking and belief in supernatural influences. Superstitions include beliefs that there is a causal connection between thoughts, actions, and unrelated physical events, although any connection between them is actually coincidental. The fact that the same practice, such as wearing a "lucky" charm during a sports event, sometimes seems to have an effect and sometimes does not, is unimportant as long as the result is occasionally randomly reinforced, which keeps alive belief in the practice. Superstition probably evolved among our early ancestors, who would invoke the presence of invisible supernatural factors to explain and try to control otherwise inexplicable natural phenomena. Human beings like to find patterns that give the world meaning, even if the patterns are actually psychological superimpositions onto phenomena that are random.

The boundary between faith and superstition is not sharp. Magical practices such as sprinkling with holy water evoke a dormant belief in and hope for the miraculous. These may be deeply unconscious beliefs, perhaps belonging to an archaic level of the psyche, a mythopoetic stratum that is more primary than the rational, conscious mind, but one that is able to have a powerful effect on the ego. Ritual objects give the believer a feeling that the object is spiritually special or powerful, even if its specialness is not perceptible by our ordinary senses. Examples are belief in the power of holy water, the aura around the reliquaries of saints, or the numinous quality of the eucharistic wafer or the Torah scroll. Once these beliefs are established, they are transmitted culturally. In many traditions, holy water is thought to transmit its holiness and transform impurity. For example, belief in the magical power of water is shown in Numbers 5: 16–31, where it is used ritually to determine the innocence or guilt of a woman suspected of adultery. She drinks holy water in which a scroll with a curse written on it has been dipped, and if she is guilty, she will feel pain and her body will swell. Rationalists assume this type of magical practice depends on effects that operate by means of the unconscious, including an idealizing transference to the priest, suggestion, expectation, or a placebo effect, which is known to be potent, able to activate brain mechanisms (Benedetti et al., 2005). Another biblical example of a psychological process that produces magical effects is the practice of looking at a bronze serpent to heal snakebites (Num 21: 4–9.) In the Roman Catholic tradition, the sacraments were said to work of their own accord, as if they have direct power regardless of the priest, strengthening the Church's claim to be able to invoke God's presence and power. Protestants denied this kind of magic on the grounds that it was blasphemous to claim such power. During the medieval era, outside the control of the priesthood, lay people used holy water for practical purposes, to cure illness, ward off the Devil, and for protection in general. This shows the fine line between magic and religion, and the aura of magic around water. There are many holy wells in Europe, some of which are thought to cure specific illnesses, either in humans or in animals (Bord and Bord, 1985). Belief in the healing power of sacred wells was prevalent at least until the second half of the twentieth century, according to the anthropologist Veronica Strang (2004). She found that in the county of Dorset in southwest England, belief in the mysterious power of water had persisted, and it was used in funerary rites and even exorcisms. Once belief in the importance of such a ritual has taken hold, it often becomes quite resilient and difficult to let go of, even when its efficacy fails. The illusion of control of an uncertain situation is powerful. Rituals seem to create order. Not only are they derived from sacred texts such as the Bible, they are also imbued with the authority of long tradition.

The destructive power of religion

Religions and their sacred texts can motivate people for good or ill. Religions foster acts of service to others, humanitarian relief, kindness, and charity, but religions may also lead to great violence, evil, authoritarian social control, and despotic behavior (Lüdeman, 1996). Charles Kimball (2002, p. 1) believes that religion has caused more violence than any other "institutional force in human history." The monotheistic traditions have been responsible for many abuses, including misogyny, the ill-treatment of minorities and indigenous people, and the killing of heretics. Colonialism, imperialism, racism, and slavery have all been justified in religious terms, and it is remarkable how many Christians have aligned themselves with authoritarian leaders such as Mussolini, Franco, Pinochet, Putin, and the like. Rwanda's Roman Catholic clergy were implicated in the 1994 genocide.

Religious violence

Regina Schwartz (1997) describes the historical and current violence and abuse sanctioned by Christianity and Judaism. She sees this violence as itself religious, not a perversion of religion. Religions lend supernatural authority to violent behavior, as if "God wills it," when in fact it is the product of a human proclivity. The level of violence that has been perpetrated against non-believers by religious establishments that claimed to do so in the name of God is striking, and suggestive of the projection of the believers' own doubt onto others so that it can be attacked externally. During the fourth century CE, as Christianity became the dominant religion of the Roman Empire, Christians became increasingly violent in their laws against non-Christians. Christians tried to eradicate earlier traditions by demolishing their temples or turning them into churches, burning their books, killing their priests, and other forms of physical persecution.

Warfare has long been associated with religion (Juergensmeyer, 2001), and so has terrorism. One might argue that religion itself is not to blame for the fact that its history is studded with conflict. Rather, it can be claimed, the all-too human behavior of its adherents is the problem. However, sometimes intolerance is built into religious systems when they insist that no other religion is valid, or theirs is the only path to salvation. These intolerant aspects of religion may provoke problematic aspects of the believer's personality, such as the justification found in sacred texts to express hostility toward non-believers or to adopt an attitude of superiority or contempt for them. Violently toned complexes can also find resonance within liturgy, homiletics, and hymnology that use battle imagery ("onward Christian soldiers") to describe conflict with Satan or with unbelievers. The biblical Yhwh is a God of war, and often settles disputes violently, setting an example for his followers.

It is easy to blend religious justification for violence with social and political goals. Murderous anti-abortion violence has been justified on religious grounds if it is carried out for a "higher" purpose. Juergensmeyer (2001, p. 2) has shown how the Christian anti-abortion movement is "permeated with ideas from Dominion Theology," an ideology that wants to turn the USA into a Christian nation, governed by biblical law. The extreme version of this ideology believes that Christians are the new chosen people and are destined to dominate the world. To achieve this end, some adherents to these views endorse violence, which they rationalize as a price that may need to be paid to achieve their goals. Christian Identity leaders often rest their violent beliefs on the authority of the Bible. Christian Identity theology is based on racism, anti-Semitism, and biblical law. This ideology is in the background of several white supremacist and militia groups that want to merge religion with the state. They often imagine that they are at war with the forces of evil, and some see themselves as at war with the larger secular society. They believe that violence is justified as a response to a repressive secular government. Many Christian nationalists feel they should be in control of their country because God established the USA as a Christian country. They believe they have a mandate to lead the country into godliness, which for them means alignment with biblical law. To achieve this end, some focus on apocalyptic fantasies of spiritual warfare against what they see as social decadence. Christian nationalism is sometimes accompanied by white supremacy, xenophobia, and a toxic form of masculinism. This ideology ignores Jesus' teachings about social justice and compassion.[20]

Religion and nationalism have often merged to support each other, thus politicizing religion. A typical example was the conflict between Catholics and Protestants in Ireland from 1968 to 1998. Extremist Israeli nationalists want to create a state entirely based on biblical law and re-establish the Jerusalem temple in preparation for the advent of the Messiah. Juergensmeyer (2001, p. 46) quotes a messianic Zionist who believes that it would be heretical to give up any land to the Palestinians, since according to the Bible the land was given to the Jews by God, and "the redemption of the whole world depends on the actions of Jews in creating the conditions necessary for messianic salvation."[21]

A characterological propensity to violence is easily spiritualized if it is believed to be sanctioned by God. The religious texts these messianic and nationalist groups use to justify their violence are open to interpretation, but violent people are attracted to violent interpretations of these texts. Violent interpretations give them a focus for their anger and allow them to feel part of a group with a high-minded purpose that transcends their individual lives. Once part of such a group, the power of group persuasion adds to their convictions. Such groups are often led by a charismatic, demagogic leader whom members can idealize. The leader promises to solve all their problems, usually by oversimplifying complex social issues using simplistic moral directives and primitive splitting defenses that seem to clearly demarcate good and evil. The individual's own conscience and critical thinking become subordinate to the ideals of the group and its leader. Some men identify with the strongman persona of narcissistic leaders, who often promote violence as a way to assert their strength.

These leaders often appeal to men who have unconscious doubts about their masculinity, or to those who need to submit to an authoritarian leader in a masochistic fashion. Authoritarian leaders are often misogynistic but may be nevertheless appealing to women who are attracted to what they perceive as strength. They prefer a patriarchal order in which women accept a secondary status as long as they are deemed superior to other races or religions.

Exclusivist forms of religion have sometimes led to missionary fever, which historically has been incorporated into political and cultural imperialism and conquest, as we saw in the cruelty of Spanish missionaries in eighteenth- and early nineteenth-century California. They thought the local people were savages who had to be civilized, and in the process of Christianizing them the missionaries severely abused the indigenous people.

The conquest of cities described in the Hebrew Bible as the Israelites occupied Canaan are typically seen by apologists as necessary justice or a means of purification of an area so that God would be present there (Copan, 2011). This purification required the destruction of the temples and altars of the gods of the local inhabitants (Deut. 12: 2–3). The invasion of Canaan is rationalized as an objective judgment on the local people because they were living immoral lives and worshipping pagan gods. They therefore had to be driven out (Exod. 33: 2), because of the danger that living among the Canaanites would tempt the Israelites to intermarriage and idolatry. Yhwh was seen as participating in these wars, intervening on behalf of his people miraculously, such as by stopping the sun's motion so a battle could be finished (Josh. 10: 14: 42). To rationalize their bloodthirsty behavior, these battles were carried out in the name of Yhwh, who claimed to be exclusive and was keen to eliminate his competitor gods. The archetype of the divine warrior was a cultural dominant in ancient Israel, so war became a sacred activity, and whoever did battle on Yhwh's behalf was declared to be holy. Wars with this kind of ostensibly religious motivation have often been used as a cover for colonial expansion.

"Holy" or "Just" War

The early Christians were largely pacifists who resisted military service because they believe that human life was sacred and God prohibits killing, even in a just cause (Ferguson, 1978). However, as Christianity became more involved in the politics of the Roman Empire, military service was increasingly seen as a duty to the state, and it was seen as naïve to fail to resist aggression. After the fall of the Roman Empire, European Christians were constantly at war with each other, and the Church became increasingly militarized. In the fourth and fifth centuries CE, war was rationalized by Saints Ambrose and Augustine, leading to the idea of a just war, meaning war whose intention was to restore peace and avenge injury. According to this doctrine, war must avoid unnecessary violence, damage to temples, looting, and massacres. The idea of just war was clarified and finalized in the sixteenth century, insisting that it must be ordered by a lawful authority, its cause must be just, the belligerents should intend to advance good and avoid evil, innocents should not suffer, and it must be undertaken as a last resort with a reasonable chance of success. Needless to say, the only definition of whether a war was justified was the decision of the ones who declared it. The theory sounds reasonable in theory but ignores the catastrophic losses and suffering incurred in war.

With the blessing of the Pope, in the eighth century CE, various pagan groups were forcibly converted to Christianity by Charlemagne. Enemies of the church, pagans, and heretics were seen as opposing the law of God and thus were not protected by just war theory, as we saw during the Crusades, which tried to liberate Jerusalem from Muslim control beginning in the late eleventh century. They were convinced that "God wills it." Large numbers of Jews and even Eastern Orthodox Christians were massacred by crusaders on the way to Jerusalem. They perpetrated a series of savage acts of torture, murder, and even cannibalism. Once in Jerusalem the crusaders burned people alive and massacred the inhabitants, all in the service of their God. Apparently, they had forgotten Jesus' admonition that "all who take the sword will perish by the sword" (Matt. 26: 52). This episode reveals how powerless is spiritual teaching in the face of the human shadow. All that was needed was a rationale to express it. The religious excuse for the Crusades was actually a convenient cover for the church's political and economic motives. A few Christians, such as the Franciscans, remained pacifist, and this stance was adopted by later groups such as the Quakers. During the religious wars that followed the sixteenth-century Reformation, Roman Catholics and Protestants each believed that theirs was a holy war against God's enemies. During the English Civil War of 1642, the Puritans under Oliver Cromwell massacred thousands of people in the name of Puritan holy war teachings. At the beginning of the First World War, British and German clerics both preached that this was a holy war. Since then, although the notion of holy war is often seen as profoundly mistaken, it continues in various ways such as violence toward abortion providers. Politicians continue to invoke the help of God in their wars and often talk about the sacrifices made by soldiers; the word "sacrifice" evokes religious connotations. Tribalism is one of the unconscious motivations for religious wars.

Religion and tribalism

The biologist E.O. Wilson sees tribalism as part of the dark underbelly of all religions. For Wilson, the religious violence emerging from tribalism is an outward expression of this "ancient instinct" that divides people into us and them. He believes that sectarian religion is "the central rationale for lethal tribalism…in particular, the conflict between those faithful to different myths" (2015, pp. 151 and 154). Tribalism allows one to see other groups as less valuable than one's own group. Unfortunately, tribalism has deep evolutionary roots in the human psyche. Wilson points out that *Homo Sapiens* is "hampered by a Paleolithic curse" of evolutionary adaptations that worked well when they developed among our hunter-gatherer ancestors but are now a hindrance (p. 176). Wilson's suggestions are based on the approach of evolutionary psychologists who believe that natural selection made it imperative that our early hominin ancestors would evolve to distrust strangers and stay within their own group for the sake of safety, at a time when competition for resources between groups made a life-or-death difference. We see a residue of this evolutionary trait in the phenomenon of stranger anxiety, the distress experienced by babies beginning toward the end of the first year of life in the presence of people they do not know. This form of anxiety may have evolved to ensure that children would not stray far from their own social group. This persistent component of human psychology now manifests itself as a component of xenophobia, racial hatred, and predator anxiety. Within groups, tribalism promotes human bonding, social cohesion, a sense of identity, and solidarity, but tribalism also plays an important role between groups in various kinds of prejudice and intolerance of difference. Tribalism also promotes mass-mindedness and allows the avoidance of individual responsibility when the group acts.

If we are certain that our religious group is chosen or saved but others are not, they are seen either as a threat or as less important or less virtuous than one's own group. This kind of narcissistic religious certainty fosters tribalism. It is also dangerous because it allows one's doubts and one's shadow material to be repressed, projected onto non-believers, and attacked externally instead of being acknowledged.

Splitting mechanisms in religion

One of the characteristics of religious orthodoxies and fundamentalisms is the phenomenon of splitting, usually into all-good and all-bad. There are various ways in which this defense appears. One is to insist that traditions other than one's own are completely wrong, with no redeeming features. One's own tradition has all the goodness. Other traditions may even be demonized. Any view other than one's own is oversimplified and discounted. This attitude has important adaptive value; it preserves one's own tradition as the only valid one, denies any doubt, reduces anxiety about one's own beliefs, and excludes acknowledging the possibility of error, thus fostering a feeling of safety and order. Splitting defenses protect the individual against thoughts and feelings that may dangerously conflict with each other. Splitting also seems to protect goodness from contamination with anything bad. Splitting into all-good and all-bad helps to make sense of confusing situations. However, splitting also reduces complexity by oversimplifying the situation, does not allow one to see the nuances of a situation, and leaves no possibility of seeing ambiguity or feeling ambivalence.

Splitting into all good and all bad is vividly noticeable in apocalyptic texts such as the book of Revelation. In this text, the followers of Jesus are radically split from evil people, a group which for this author includes the Jews.

The righteous will enter a heavenly Jerusalem while the others will suffer a range of sadistic punishments. Contemporary believers in apocalyptic fantasies still take Revelation literally as the prediction of an imminent End Times, perhaps because this kind of splitting is consonant with their own intrapsychic splits, and they can identify with the righteous and project their shadow onto non-believers while enjoying the fantasy of how non-believers will suffer. Another example of splitting is seen in the legend of the Antichrist (McGinn, 1994), who represents absolute evil in contrast to the all-good Christ.

The Jewish claim to be the chosen people is a form of splitting that automatically makes other nations not chosen and inevitably sets up sibling rivalry and envious comparison. The radical demonization of the Jews by Christians throughout history characterizes the kind of splitting that is accompanied by idealization of one pole of an all-good/all-bad split, in this case the elevation of Jesus himself, which necessitated the complete devaluation of any opposing view. Splitting is also seen in Christian theology's division between those who are saved and those who are condemned. Intense splitting is seen in Matthew 23: 15, where Jesus is reported to have said that scribes, Pharisees, and Jewish proselytes become "a child of hell." He accuses them of being "serpents" and "broods of vipers" (Matt. 33).

St. Paul tended to promote either-or splits, such as writing that because the Jews murdered Jesus and the prophets, they "displease God and oppose all men" (1 Thess. 2: 14–16). (The authorship of this letter is disputed.) Paul denied that circumcision is important (1 Cor. 7: 19; Gal. 6: 15; Acts 21: 21), an attitude calculated to cause a split with traditional Judaism. Splitting permeates the New Testament and the subsequent Christian tradition, which harshly criticizes those who did not accept the Gospel writers' insistence that Jesus Christ is the salvation of the world. Typical of this either-or attitude are verses such as "And there is salvation in no one else, for there is no other name under heaven given among men by which we must be saved" (Acts 4: 12) and "no one comes to the Father, but by me" (John 14: 6). Christian writers insisted that anyone who does not acknowledge Jesus is eternally condemned.

The early followers of Jesus were one of several Jewish sects in first-century Palestine, but as Christianity spread its adherents became more and more gentile. A deep-seated hostility eventually developed between these traditions, despite their shared ancestry, because the Jews refused to acknowledge Jesus as the Messiah. In part this division occurred because Christians changed the Jewish concept of the Messiah into an image that Jews could not recognize as anything like the description of the Messiah in their scriptures. Jesus did not fulfill any of these prophecies, such as the advent of universal peace and righteousness (Isaiah 2: 23–24: Micah 4: 1–3). Because of their rejection of Jesus, Jews were branded as incorrigible apostates. The idea arose that God had rejected them, and the covenant had been transferred to Christians who now substituted for the original people of Israel. In order to assert the supremacy of Christianity, Judaism had to be completely devalued, discounted, and no longer necessary (Ruether, 1974; Freudmann, 1994). St. John Chrysostom wrote that the synagogue is "a den of thieves...impure beasts...the Jews in shamelessness and greed surpass even pigs and goats...The Jews are possessed by demons" (quoted in Cook, 1983). These kinds of extreme comments are examples of primitive all-good all-bad splitting combined with shadow projection. A hateful event such as the Holocaust cannot be divorced from 2000 years of this kind of religiously based anti-Judaism within the Christian tradition, based on anti-Jewish comments in the New Testament and fostered by subsequent theologians.

The history of religion is replete with such splits, both within each tradition and between traditions. Sometimes, the splits within a tradition are particularly bitter, as when heretics such as Gnostics are demonized. Elaine Pagels has documented the ways in which the early splits developed between different groups of Christians. She notes that "Christians preached—and practiced—division on earth" (1996, p. 130). Splitting often leads to bloodshed; Martin Luther suggested that the believer should "bathe his hands in the blood of the bishops and the pope, who is the devil in disguise."

Glossolalia

Glossolalia, or speaking in tongues, is a phenomenon in which an individual involuntarily speaks an unknown, usually unintelligible language, with no discernable semantic content. These episodes are often understood as a divinely inspired form of prayer, or sometimes as a form of spirit possession. To enhance his authority, Paul talks about his ability to speak in "the tongues of men and of angels" (1 Cor. 1: 13). He sees glossolalia as one of the gifts of the spirit (1 Cor. 12–14) and he asserts the importance of this phenomenon. Indeed, he boasts that he spoke in tongues "more than you all" (1 Cor. 14: 18), although he thinks that "the one who prophesies is greater than the one who speaks in tongues" (1 Cor.14: 5). He was concerned that unbelievers would think that speaking in tongues was a sign of madness, and he wanted to relativize the practice. In the Church at Corinth this language was unintelligible and needed an interpreter (1 Cor. 14: 27). The practice caught on; in Acts 2: 1–13 it is reported that the disciples spoke in tongues when the Holy Spirit descended on them, and their listeners understood them. Speaking in tongues was associated with prophecy and was also understood (Acts 19: 6). It is noteworthy that Jesus did not speak in tongues, and the question of the validity of this practice is controversial, although it continues.

In his early work, Jung (CW 2, para. 143) saw glossolalia as a product of cryptomnesia. Later he saw it as a form of possession by non-ego levels of the unconscious (CW 11, para. 433, note 51) and it is still seen as the language of the unconscious. Its detractors see it as either dissociative, hysterical, self-aggrandizing, or as meaningless infantile babbling, but this dismissive attitude may be due to skeptical bias. Another possibility is that glossolalia is a way to cope with the narcissistic injury produced by challenges to the believer's tradition and values in the face of modern secular culture, allowing him to maintain a connection to the supernatural. John Castelein (1984) believes that glossolalia and the associated charismatic fellowship is therapeutic for believers, allowing them to restore narcissistic equilibrium and maintain their relationship to the supernatural. This is especially important if they feel abandoned by God "in a taunting, disbelieving world" (p. 57). Speaking in tongues is welcomed within certain religious groups, which greatly benefits the individual's self-esteem and reduces shame. Castelein points out that glossolalia can also be seen as a transitional phenomenon in Winnicott's sense.

Gerd Theissen (1987) offers a range of psychological and exegetical explanations for this phenomenon, ranging from behavioral theories that it is socially learned behavior to psychodynamic explanations in which it allows repressed impulses to emerge, or it is a regression to a childhood level of simply making primitive sounds. Theissen believes that when these unconscious utterances are translated, they can provide inspiration or direction for the community. Today this phenomenon occurs mainly among fundamentalist, charismatic Christian and Pentecostal groups, where it does not seem to be associated with psychopathology, although it may occur in a state of altered consciousness and heightened suggestibility and may seem to be self-aggrandizing, a mark of spiritual superiority. To the observer, it may seem to be largely hysterical, but for the subject, glossolalia seems to be a form of catharsis or an emotional outlet. It often occurs in the setting of a group meeting in which it is encouraged because it is seen as a manifestation of the Holy Spirit and a form of heavenly language, although it may also occur in private.

Religious hatred

Religions generate a great deal of emotional intensity, including hatred, which I understand to mean chronic rage accompanied by a wish to destroy that which is hated. There are many sources of hatred, including historical, social, and individual developmental factors, which have been explored by authors such as Acland (2018) and Corbett (2018). Religious hatred is often the result of years of political persecution, poverty, humiliation, and mistreatment by an occupying power, combined with the fact that some members of religiously based terrorist organizations have had hatred of a particular enemy instilled in them since childhood, and they are receptive to religious preaching that justifies killing enemies. They are then able to adopt a combined political and religious justification for their behavior. Their need for justice and revenge overrides ordinary moral constraints, allowing religious terrorists to kill innocent civilians without mercy. Moral justification for killing others is achieved by believing they are fighting evil oppressors, or by pointing out that the enemy's behavior is even worse than their own. Hatred of the enemy becomes part of group identity, with group pressures to participate in violent resistance. This process may occur among people who had an average childhood, but it is especially appealing to individuals who were chronically abused in childhood, leading to poorly contained aggression. These individuals are likely to be attracted to organizations and religious groups that allow them to channel their hatred and violence into socially approved targets who become the projected representatives of their own internal persecutors. Hatred is a powerful force within their personality. It is preferable to hate and feel strong rather than to feel helpless, passive, and weak; the pain of being oppressed is made more tolerable by actively hating the oppressor, which at least allows a symbolic sense of power. Hatred of an enemy also gives the individual a purpose and mission in life. Because hatred has an enlivening effect, it may develop an intoxicating or even addictive quality.

Projective mechanisms in religion

Projection is a defense mechanism that often results in religious prejudice. We saw this process when the white supremacists who marched in Charlottesville in 2017 shouted "Jews will not replace us." This was a major projection; in fact, replacement was exactly what Christian theologians had been trying to do to the Jews since the Church made adversaries of the Jews who did not accept Jesus. The Charlottesville racists may not have been familiar with the Christian theology of supersessionism, or replacement theology, on which their projection was based. This theology assumes that Christians have replaced and superseded Jews as the people of the covenant, as if Christians had become the new favorites of the divine father. In their Sunday schools, the Charlottesville marchers had probably been exposed to the many anti-Jewish sentiments in the Gospels, which manage to ignore the fact that Jesus was Jewish.[22] The notion of supersessionism may explain why many Christian leaders were silent during the Holocaust. There has been resistance to the idea of supersession in some Christian denominations.

The psychological underpinning of the need to be the replacement people has not been much discussed in Christian circles, because it would involve acknowledging primitive envy and sibling rivalry of the Jews' claim to have been originally chosen by Yhwh, and the wish to be special in their place. Envy can be assuaged or defended against by devaluing what we envy. By substituting faith in Jesus for adherence to the Torah, the giving of the Torah to the Jews was no longer important. By teaching that God's covenant was transferred to the Gentiles, one no longer has to be envious of those to whom it was first given. Instead of acknowledging these dynamics, Christian persecution of the Jews has been seen as a righteous punishment for their rejection of Jesus.[23] Justification of this hatred is found in descriptions of Jews in verses such as "You are of your father the devil" (John 8: 44). In the Gospel of John, the Jews are vilified as if they are entirely evil (8: 44). Needless to say, it is often protested that such verses have been taken out of context or they are interpolations by the early Church authorities, but nevertheless they are part of the canonical text, and they are significant sources of anti-Judaism.

Cognitive dissonance

Cognitive dissonance is an emotionally painful experience that occurs when a strongly held, important belief is disconfirmed by new evidence. It is then necessary to find ways to reduce or eliminate the dissonance by finding a way to reconcile the belief with the evidence. I assume this situation arose among Jesus' followers when he was executed, since the Jews of the time were expecting their messiah to be a victorious king, not someone ignominiously executed as if he were a criminal. Jesus' death was therefore an awkward problem for his followers, apparently showing that he was not a true messiah. To deal with the distress caused by the resulting cognitive dissonance, the crucifixion had to be rationalized and explained by suggesting that somehow it happened in accordance with the scriptures (1 Cor. 15: 3). Disappointment and cognitive dissonance were avoided in several other ways. Paul decided that Jesus' resurrection proved that he was righteous, so he must have been killed for the sins of others. When the fantasized Kingdom of God did not appear in the lifetime of Jesus' followers, as he had promised, its appearance was moved to some future, unknown date.[24] The fact that Jesus believed that the End Times were soon to arrive (Matt. 16: 28), and this hope was not realized, was rationalized with the notion of the Second Coming, based on material from Zechariah 14, which talks about the coming of a "day of the Lord." A range of explanations have developed to account for the failure of this prophecy, such as the idea that God's time scale is not the same as human time. This kind of rationalization is required to reduce the confusion and distress produced by cognitive dissonance.

It is very difficult to abandon emotionally important beliefs; witness the fact that movements that predicted Jesus' return, or those predicting the exact date of the End Times, sometimes did not immediately disband when nothing happened. These movements simply assumed they had miscalculated, and their expectations persisted. Such movements have occurred in all religions, throughout history. In 1533, a group of Anabaptists believed that the millennium was at hand. Many disposed of their possessions. When nothing happened at the predicted time, the group's religious fervor and proselytizing increased, apparently in the hope that increasing numbers of believers would sustain the possibility that the group's ideology is true, while helping to suppress doubt. In the mid-seventeenth century, amid intense messianic expectations, the false messiah Sabbatai Sevi gained a large following, and many Jews prepared for an imminent return to Jerusalem and the redemption of Israel. Many people sold their houses and possessions in preparation for this event. In fact, Sevi was arrested by Turkish authorities and imprisoned in Constantinople. Gershom Scholem (1973) points out that his failure was assumed to be an intentional strategy to assume the form of evil in order to kill it from within. His suffering was seen as a necessary aspect of his messiahship. Typically, new enthusiasm, proselytizing, and reports of miracles followed his failure and spread widely.

The disappointment was turned into a positive affirmation of faith, so the analogy with early Christianity is obvious. It is noteworthy that even after Sevi converted to Islam, the movement continued for a while before it collapsed. In the mid-nineteenth century, based on calculations from the book of Daniel, William Miller decided that the end of the world would occur in 1843. Thousands of people joined his movement. Again, increased conviction and enthusiasm followed the failure of the prophecy, which was assumed to be due to a calculation error. In the 1990s, a group of orthodox Jews, the followers of Rabbi Menachem Schneerson, believed he was the Messiah. Even after he died, messianic fervor did not die down; it was assumed he would be resurrected and lead the world to redemption (Heilman et al., 2012).

A group of social psychologists (Festinger et al., 1956) used the term cognitive dissonance to discuss the effects of failed prophecies. They described a group of UFO believers that included a woman who believed she was receiving messages from outer space (via automatic writing) that predicted a flood that would engulf much of the USA on December 21, 1954. A UFO would rescue survivors. When no flooding happened on that day, a message was received that God had prevented the flood because of the group. This was an example of how, when unequivocal evidence disproves a belief, the individual may become even more convinced of its truth and may even want to convert others. To avoid the psychological discomfort produced by cognitive dissonance, people may hold firmly to their beliefs in the face of disconfirmation, in a kind of defensive entrenchment.

Religious believers dislike the invocation of cognitive dissonance as an explanation for the persistence of religious beliefs that are disconfirmed by historical and scientific evidence. However, this phenomenon helps to explain how Jesus' followers coped with his execution, which seemed to disconfirm his messianic status. Skeptics believe that predictions by Jesus of his death (Mark 8: 27–33; 9: 30–32; 10: 33–34) may have been added later to cope with his followers' disappointment (e.g., Luke 24: 17 and 21). His death was treated as if it was intended to happen all along and was further rationalized by reference to scriptural passages such as the Suffering Servant of Isaiah 53: 8: "For he was cut off from the land of the living; for the transgression of my people he was punished." As well, the failure of the Kingdom of Heaven to arrive, which was expected to happen in the lifetime of Jesus' followers (Mark 9: 1, 14–25; Matt. 10: 23), also produced cognitive dissonance among Jesus' committed followers. This crisis made it important to find ways to reduce cognitive dissonance, as in reports of Jesus' post-crucifixion appearance, the story of the empty tomb, and the gradually increasing idealization of Jesus into a divine being. Jesus's humiliating death was reinterpreted and converted into a message of power through humility. (The process by which the early followers of Jesus dealt with their cognitive dissonance is further explored by Fernando Bermejo-Rubio, 2017.)

One of the sources of cognitive dissonance that affects some Christians today is the conflict between their political behavior and Jesus' values, which stress altruism and fellowship, in versus such as "Truly, I say to you, as you did it to one of the least of these my brethren, you did it to me" (Matt. 25: 40). These kinds of teachings conflict with conservative opposition to expenditure for social services and other attempts to be helpful to those in need. Liberal Christians may struggle with their need to reconcile their acceptance of homosexuality and abortion with biblical and Church teachings. According to Lee Ross et al. (2012), one of the ways Christians have alleviated this kind of dissonance is either to adjust their perception of Christian teachings or to adjust their perception of the political positions on compassion that Jesus would hold if he were alive today. That is, Christians project their own values and opinions onto Jesus and give different weight and priority to different aspects of his teachings, depending on how his teaching on particular issues correspond to their own views. Sometimes, cognitive dissonance is avoided by simply ignoring some of Jesus' teachings. Adherents to the prosperity gospel, which promises believers financial success, see poverty as a sin. Not only is this attitude not found in Jesus' teachings, it contrasts with comments such as "a man's life does not consist in the abundance of his possessions" (Luke 12: 15) and "it is easier for a camel to go through the eye of a needle than for a rich man to enter the kingdom of God" (Matt. 19: 24).

Some religious believers experience dissonance between biblical stories of creation and modern science. Believers have to find a way to reconcile this tension, such as by insisting that God was the background intelligence behind evolution, and God designed the laws of physics so that life on earth could exist.

The orthodox Jews who believe that the land of Israel was promised to them by God, whose faith is centered in the Jerusalem temple, have to deal with the cognitive dissonance produced by the fact that the land and the city are shared by other faiths and the site of the temple is occupied by a mosque. The contrast between the political reality and the Jerusalem of faith, prayer, and biblical promises is huge, leading to violent clashes. Consistent with what is known about the effects of cognitive dissonance, catastrophic events like the Holocaust may actually strengthen religious belief. Thus, orthodox Jews still believe in a just God who allowed millions of their family members and coreligionists to be slaughtered for no reason. The resulting "explanations" often require intellectual contortions, such as the idea that the Holocaust was a punishment for being unfaithful to the law, and the pious had to suffer with those responsible. (A range of alternative explanations is discussed in Corbett, 2021.)

One of the sources of both apocalyptic fantasies and belief in punishment and reward in the afterlife is the need to believe that divine justice will ultimately prevail, thus avoiding the cognitive dissonance produced by the inexplicable suffering of the innocent. Similarly, the idea of a messianic age also promises that eventually all will be well, so there is no need to be distressed about the failure of the many promises made by the prophets about a glorious future.

Sometimes, the distress produced by cognitive dissonance is felt as threatening and motivates defensive violence and religious extremism. Cognitive dissonance also drives the need for sophisticated theodicies, the attempts to justify God in the face of widespread, underserved suffering and the presence of radical evil, both of which God apparently either permits or cannot prevent.

Christian anti-Judaism

Because the Jews rejected Jesus' messianic claims, as early Christianity developed the Jews were increasingly demonized and accused of being agents of the Devil. This rivalry was incorporated into the Gospels (Crossan, 1995). In 70 CE, the Romans destroyed the temple in Jerusalem, and the early followers of Jesus saw this as proof that Judaism had been superseded. The hope for the future conversion of the Jews became a component of an apocalyptic vision connected to the Second Coming of Jesus. Over time, a negative view of Jews became incorporated into the Christian mythic view of history.

Accusations that the Jews killed Jesus appear in various parts of the New Testament (1 Thess. 2: 14–16; Acts 3: 12–15). Jesus' Parable of the Wicked Tenants is found in the Gospels of Mark (12: 1–12), Matthew, (21: 33–46), and Luke (20: 9–19). The story describes a man who lets out his vineyard to tenants who do not care for the land and beat and kill the owner's messengers and his son. The vineyard is then given to others, who will deliver its fruits. This story was used as an allegory for the transfer of divine grace from the Jews to the Christians, who become the new chosen people. Jewish guilt in the death of Jesus became part of Christian mythology and became necessary to the idea that Christianity had replaced and superseded Judaism.

The passion narratives (the stories of the suffering and death of Jesus) in the Gospels all suggest that the Jews are responsible for the death of Jesus. Matthew 27: 25 has the Jews saying: "His blood be upon us and on our children," meaning that they accept moral responsibility for Jesus' death, and this responsibility is extended to future generations. Even if the Church authorities realized that this comment can have referred only to the Jewish leaders present at Jesus' trial, rather than the entire population of Jewish people living in Israel at the time, the Church did nothing to dispel that illusion. In fact, the Jewish authorities who participated in the trial of Jesus were puppets of the Roman regime and did not represent the majority of the Jews of the time, many of whom were sympathetic to Jesus. However, Jewish corporate guilt for the death of Christ was repeated constantly in subsequent sermons, art, politics, and scholarly writing. Contemporary anti-Semites believe that Jews living today are guilty by association.

The Jews were said to be involved in a plot to kill Jesus (Matt. 26: 3–4) and were said to have a wicked nature (Matt. 23). Overt hatred of the Jews appears in the Gospel of John, where the Jews are reported to have handed over Jesus to be crucified (John 19: 13–17), and Jesus is said to have accused the Jews of being "children of the devil" (John 8: 44). In the Gospel of Matthew (23) the Jews are called hypocrites, snakes, and murderers of the prophets. Acts (13: 45) calls them jealous blasphemers, betrayers, and the like. These defamatory polemics have been and are used to justify continuing anti-Semitism (Ruether, 1974), but until the mid-twentieth century, some Christians used such verses to spread hatred and vilification of the Jews. It is difficult to reconcile the anti-Judaism of New Testament with the fact that Jesus was Jewish and so were his early followers.

Michael Cook (1983) believes that the anti-Judaism of the New Testament occurred because Christianity was trying to distinguish itself from its mother faith. The new tradition denigrated Judaism in response to Jewish challenges to Jesus' messiahship, which were based on the fact that he did not meet the descriptions of the messiah described by the Hebrew prophets. Cook believes that the Gospels' anti-Jewish material was a later development within Christianity's struggle for identity. However, Hyam Maccoby (1998) prefers the idea that anti-Semitism is not simply an outcome of religious rivalry but is an essential element in the Christian myth of redemption and the deification of Jesus, which he sees as the work of Paul. According to Maccoby, Paul believed that it was necessary to appease an angry God who had condemned humanity to hell. This required a divine, entirely innocent sacrifice. In this scheme, the Jews became cosmic villains and agents of evil because of their role in the death of Jesus. The story of Jewish corporate guilt helps to explain why much of the Christian world and many Christian theologians ignored the Holocaust while it was proceeding, although after the war some members of the World Council of Churches declared anti-Semitism sinful. However, not all Christian denominations renounced the idea of Jewish guilt in the death of Jesus, and some saw the persecution of the Jews as divine punishment for their rejection of Jesus. Renunciation of the "deicide" charge did not begin until the 1960s by the Episcopal Church and the Second Vatican Council. (A review of the history of Christian–Jewish relations is provided by von Kellenbach, 2020.)

Early Christians told the story of Jesus' trial in a way that diminished the role of Pilate and blamed the Jewish leaders for the execution of Jesus. Attention was diverted from the Romans' political accusations against Jesus. Pilate saw Jesus as a revolutionary political insurgent, but the Gospels try to depict Pilate as innocent of Jesus' death and merely an instrument of the Jews who used him to kill Jesus. This picture of Pilate is an invention. Contemporary sources, in the work of Josephus and Philo of Alexandria, described Pilate as prejudiced against the Jews, cruel, and oppressive (Wroe, 2000). However, subsequent Christian writers gradually softened Pilate's role and increasingly enlarged the role of the Jews, until, by the early fourth century, Christians had decided that all Jews deserved to be punished because of their ancestors' rejection of Jesus. This anti-Jewish attitude required an extraordinary level of denial, since Jesus himself was Jewish. The Church wanted to show that Jesus was the promised Messiah of the Jewish scriptures, which meant that the Jews who rejected him had to be discredited. The intensity of the subsequent calumny heaped on the Jews and Judaism reveals a desperate need to devalue and even exterminate the opposition in order to promote the Christian cause, at the same time suppressing Jesus' actual identity as reformer within Judaism. Centuries of denial of Jesus' Jewishness ignored the fact that Jesus was very concerned with details of Jewish law (Matt. 5: 17–20; Mark 2: 23–28; Luke 4: 16). Jesus largely confined his ministry to the Jewish community.

Anti-Judaism became second nature for subsequent Christian theologians. A consistent strand of Christian supersessionism colored Christianity's view of Judaism, to which was attributed a list of negative qualities such as legalism and hypocrisy. Christian theologians assumed that Jesus had somehow ended Judaism, which had existed only as a preparation for Jesus. The resulting institutionalized hatred led to centuries of Christian persecution, culminating in the Holocaust but still persisting.

The psychology of Christian anti-Judaism

Psychological factors played an important part in Christian theology that saw Jews as all-bad. This theology demonstrated splitting and the resulting polarized thinking, so that if Jesus was all good, his opponents must be all bad. Over time, rivalry between Christianity and Judaism led to extreme projective mechanisms, as in the medieval era when the Jews were scapegoated for problems such as plagues, poisoned wells, and famines. In the fourteenth century, the pope declared that the Black Death was sent by God to punish Christians for an unknown sin, which was eventually identified as tolerating the presence of Jews. Because of the power of splitting and projection, as Ostow (1996, p. 137) pointed out, "antisemitism doesn't require Jews," because the Jew of antisemitism is a mythic creation unrelated to actual Jews.

In the medieval era, paranoid fantasies developed, such as the notion of the blood libel, the idea (first reported in the twelfth century) that Jews murder gentile children to use their blood for baking unleavened bread at Passover, an idea that was revived by the Nazis. This is particularly ironic, in view of the Jewish prohibition about eating blood (Lev. 3: 17), which may have been due to the sense that since blood represents the life force or the essence of a living being, it belongs to God alone. Alan Dundes (1991) believes that the folkloric idea of the blood libel arose as a defense against guilt produced by the unconscious cannibalism involved in eating the Eucharistic host; the guilt is displaced onto a scapegoated group. Thus, instead of saying that Christians use the blood of a murdered victim for ritual purposes, the projected fantasy is that the Jews do so. The paradox here is that Jews are accused of eating blood, which is forbidden in their tradition, but Christians consume blood symbolically in the Eucharist, so that the Jews were imagined doing in reality what the Eucharist does in fantasy. Dundes believes that the blood libel legend has not died out. Magdalene Schultz (1986) pointed out that the blood libel occurs when societies with abusive child rearing practices become aware of a minority in their midst that treats its children kindly. Then, when a child dies, the abusive larger group disclaims responsibility and accuses the minority group of child murder. The dead child is then elevated to the status of a martyr, which atones for the parents' mistreatment of it. In the pogroms of the late nineteenth and early twentieth centuries, entire Jewish communities were annihilated in revenge for the death of a gentile child, indicating the level of impotent rage and need for a scapegoat that emerged. These kinds of accusations are very old; before Constantine, the Romans had charged the early Christians with ritually using the blood of non-Christians. The Christian preoccupation with blood was also seen in the medieval myth that Jewish men menstruated. Fantasies of the purity of blood lines dominated the Nazi ideology, in which Jews were seen as polluters.

A range of psychoanalytic interpretations of anti-Semitism has been postulated. An obvious candidate has been sibling rivalry because of religious precedence, since Jews claimed to have been first chosen by the Father God. Competition for God's favor is then a factor in anti-Judaism, and so is envy of the notion of the Jews being chosen. The experience of being chosen can be interpreted as a claim to superiority, so that an unconscious, narcissistically based struggle for dominance resulted. Anti-Semitism is often due to the projection of unintegrated shadow material onto Jews, as when they are accused of being money hungry, a problem that is obviously not confined to any particular ethnic group. However, shadow material is easier to deal with when it is projected and seen externally. Another factor is that the constant presence of Jews who rejected Christian claims about Christ made Christians uncomfortably doubtful about their own faith in him. Furthermore, psychoanalysts have postulated unconscious resentment at Jews for developing the Hebrew Bible's moral code, so to attack Jews is to attack the superego. Freud suggested that the Jews are resented because they transmitted a code of restrictive moral behavior, so hatred of the Jews is a disguised attack on the ethical demands of Christianity. It is after all difficult to meet the standards of compassion, forgiveness, and care for others that Jesus taught, much of which was directly modelled after teachings in the Hebrew Bible. But rather than attack Jesus for setting high standards of behavior, it is easier to attack the Jews in the guise of their not believing in Jesus' divinity. Other psychoanalytic explanations for anti-Judaism are outlandish; for example, the fear of Jews has been attributed to the belief that Jews wish to castrate others in order to retaliate for being circumcised. It is also true that circumcision seems to be part of the root of Jewish strangeness.

A continuing rather puzzling manifestation of anti-Judaism is its presence among Christian feminists and post-colonial scholars. Some of these writers, in the attempt to vindicate Christianity, have blamed Judaism for the introduction of patriarchy into the world (Melcher, 2003), as if Judaism alone is responsible for the oppression of women. These critics stress the tribal, ethnocentric, militaristic, and sexist aspects of the image of God in the Hebrew Bible, without always acknowledging the ways in which Christianity perpetuated a patriarchal prejudice against women.

The projection of human judgment onto God

The sinfulness of humanity and the consequent judgment of God are recurrent biblical themes. These often suggest the projection onto God of a rather primitive reward-punishment psychology, which presupposes that the relationship between humanity and divinity has a father-child or ruler-ruled quality. The prophetic tradition constantly focused on the judgment of Yhwh. Ezekiel 7: 7–8 threatened:

> Your doom has come to you...the time has come, the day is near...Now I will soon pour out my wrath upon you, and spend my anger against you, and judge you according to your ways; and I will punish you...

Because people were not living up to his standards, Yhwh will punish them in "furious anger and a flame of devouring fire" (Isaiah 30: 30).

The Hebrew Bible consistently attributed disasters such as the Babylonian Exile to divine punishment. The Israelites assumed that the nations who conquered them, such as the Assyrians, were agents of God. Yhwh would use a conquering army to inflict punishment on his wayward people. Their covenant with God applied only if they obeyed God's commandments (Deut. 28: 13–14), so their defeat and exile had to be rationalized by assuming it was the result of disobedience and the worship of other gods. The value of this interpretation of events was that it avoided cognitive dissonance, since defeat did not mean that the gods of the conquering nations were stronger than the God of Israel; it meant that Yhwh was still in charge. The Hebrew prophets also insisted that Yhwh's judgment on the enemies of his people will eventually bring a "day of vengeance, to avenge himself on his foes. The sword shall devour and be sated, and drink its fill of their blood" (Jeremiah, 46: 10). This imagery clearly represents the human need for revenge projected onto God.

The Hebrew prophets all complained that salvation cannot be achieved by sacrifices and traditional rituals. It required proper behavior on the part of the people and the direct action of Yhwh, which the prophets promised would eventually happen, leading to a future golden age of peace, a new Garden of Eden, and a new Covenant (Jer. 31: Ezek. 36: 24–35). At that time will arise a new, transformed type of person and a new heaven and earth. Speaking through the prophets, Yhwh promised eventual restitution, a messiah, and a magnificent future. However, the people continued to be oppressed, no messiah materialized, and their political difficulties continued. J. Harold Ellens (2007) suggests that one theological solution to God's failure to live up to his earlier promises to restore Israel to its former glory was to turn Jesus into Christ and then into God after his death. Because of this change in the image of God, instead of God failing to defeat his enemies he says he has no enemies and loves everyone indiscriminately. He incarnates in Jesus, expressing universal love, and he thereby changes his warlike character, thus revising the terms of the covenant and developing a new sacred drama. For this purpose, Jesus was mythologized in the decades after his death, or, as Jung described it, Jesus was covered in archetypal projections that completely obscured the historical person. Jesus' defeat and crucifixion were turned into a spiritual victory. Thus, the failure of God to live up to his earlier promises and covenant is defensively disguised by radically changing the tradition's image of God and by proclaiming a revised covenant. The necessity for a covenant seems to represent the need for a kind of theological insurance policy.

Notes

1 Here, I use the term in Freud's sense of moral masochism, which is not about deriving pleasure from pain and is not primarily a sexual phenomenon; it is about suffering for some greater good. Feminist scholars have pointed out that the term masochism can be misused with a gender bias, as if abused women bring on abuse themselves, thus blaming them for societal failures. However, eliminating the term or restricting it to sexual masochism has not diminished relational masochism or recurrent self-defeating behavior.
2 Paul complains that Satan gave him a thorn in his flesh (2 Cor. 12: 7), but the nature of that problem is unknown.
3 Some scholars believe there is no evidence for the Roman Catholic Church's claim that Peter had been Rome's first bishop (de Rosa, 1989). In this view, the real succession belonged not to Peter but to Jesus' family, the Ebionite-Nazarene dynasty, led by Jesus' brother James, which was in tension over doctrine with the group led by Paul. The Ebionites believed that Jesus was the messiah but not that he was a divine being. However, after the war with the Rome, the Pauline Church took over the leadership of the emerging church and claimed to be the true inheritor of the Apostles. The Church produced the necessary propaganda to justify this assertion (Schonfield, 2012) and conferred Peter's status onto him sometime after he died. In this skeptical view, there is no justification for believing that Peter was given "the keys of heaven and earth" or that his spiritual authority was transferred to subsequent bishops of Rome. The historical evidence for this sequence of events is obscure.
4 Frazer gives examples of child sacrifice among the Carthaginians, the Phoenicians, tribes of New South Wales, Africans, and some indigenous Native American groups.
5 This story has a variety of psychoanalytic interpretations, including the idea that Isaac had incestuous fantasies about his mother, Sarah, which explains Abraham's hostility toward Isaac. The biblical story disguises Abraham's filicidal rage.
6 The usual defensive interpretation is that his daughter was not sacrificed but had to remain a virgin.
7 There is a Talmudic story (*Sanhedrin* 89b) in which Satan goads God into testing Abraham, as he goaded God into testing Job. Both cases reveal an image of God willing to risk life to test human fidelity.
8 The motif of the father who tries to kill his son is found in the contemporary character of Darth Vader of *Star Wars*.

9 This is the kind of comment that makes us doubt that the Bible is the "word of God." It is more likely the attempt of the writers of the text to describe their image of God, which consists of human claims about God, which in turn are the projections of the writers' personal preferences onto God. Paul's approval of submission to authority is consistent with the authoritarian element in his personality. This characteristic also entered the mainstream of Christianity as it partnered with state power and a range of tyrants and autocrats.

10 These and the following examples are taken from Judy Wu Dominick's https://lifereconsidered.com/2020/02/12/how-some-of-the-early-church-fathers-views-on-women-affect-us-today/ accessed January 20, 2024.

"What is the difference whether it is in a wife or a mother, it is still Eve the temptress that we must beware of in any woman… I fail to see what use woman can be to man, if one excludes the function of bearing children." –Saint Augustine: *De genesi ad litteram, 9*, 5–9.

"Woman is a misbegotten man and has a faulty and defective nature in comparison to his. Therefore she is unsure in herself. What she cannot get, she seeks to obtain through lying and diabolical deceptions. And so, to put it briefly, one must be on one's guard with every woman, as if she were a poisonous snake and the horned devil. … Thus in evil and perverse doings woman is cleverer, that is, slyer, than man. Her feelings drive woman toward every evil, just as reason impels man toward all good." –Saint Albertus Magnus, Dominican theologian, thirteenth century: *Quaestiones super de animalibus XV q. 11.*

11 The apocryphal books of the Bible tell us about the beliefs of the society that produced them. In the *Protevangelium of James* (19–20), there is a story of a midwife who witnesses the birth of Jesus while "a bright cloud overshadowed the cave… A short time afterwards that light withdrew until the baby appeared, and it came out and took the breast of its mother, Mary." When the skeptical Salome insisted on testing Mary's virginity, her hand was consumed by fire and was healed only by touching the child. The glorification of Mary is reminiscent of the worship of Isis, who was important in ancient Egypt and the Hellenistic world. Parts of her story were transferred to Mary during the first century CE. Isis was the original *mater dolorosa*, mourning her son Horus and her husband Osiris.

12 I am assuming here that the wide geographical and historical range of stories about this mythological motif excludes its being simply the result of diffusion between cultures. It seems to be an archetypal pattern.

13 It is noteworthy that Islam also has detailed rules about purity, defilement, and the ritual need for purity.

14 However, in what is known as the Macbeth effect, based on Shakespeare's Lady Macbeth's attempt to wash her hands of guilt, there is a correlation between moral wrongdoing and the felt need for physical cleansing or between bodily purity and moral purity. Physical cleansing seems to alleviate the consequences of unethical behavior and reduces threats to one's self-image (Zhong & Liljenquist, 2006).

15 As well as referring to water, the Bible refers to the hyssop herb as a spiritual purification agent and protection; it was used to sprinkle the doorposts of homes with blood so that God would pass them by during the plague of the firstborn (Exod. 12: 22), and in a complicated ritual, this herb was used to cleanse individuals of leprosy (Lev. 14: 7). The Letter to the Hebrews (9: 18–22) mentions the tradition of sprinkling blood using hyssop, and this herb was later considered to be purifying and apotropaic, able to command spirits during exorcism.

16 https://aleteia.org/2017/01/09/christ-is-baptized-not-to-be-made-holy-by-the-water-but-to-make-the-water-holy/ accessed September 6, 2023.

17 Claude Daly described a menstruation complex in men as a source of castration anxiety, but it conflicted with Freud's understanding, so it has been largely ignored (Lupton, 1989).
18 The level of violence in these movies is unnecessary in terms of the story. Perhaps the gratuitous violence is intended to stir anger, a thirst for justice, revenge, or blood lust in the viewer.
19 The term "mana" is a Polynesian-Melanesian expression that attributes magic or sacred power and knowledge to special people, objects, or places. Jung (CW 7) thinks this phenomenon is due to the fascinating force of the collective unconscious with which charismatic individuals are in touch.
20 An emerging movement known as the New Apostolic Reformation believes that Christians must take control of social institutions such as education, government, media, and entertainment. This movement believes that since we are moving toward the End Times, spiritual warfare or even violence may be necessary to achieve this goal. Biblical forms of leadership, apostles and prophets, will then organize society.
21 Psychoanalysts see the tradition's attachment to the "land of milk and honey" as an attachment to mother.
22 Daniel Goldhagen (2003) lists forty anti-Semitic passages in Mark, eighty in Matthew, one hundred and thirty in John, and a hundred and forty in the Acts of the Apostles. Christian hatred of Jews has allied itself with many manifestations of anti-Semitism, including collaboration with the Nazi regime.
23 Envy is a very destructive emotion. It often occurs when one compares oneself with another person, one feels inferior or less than that person, and the gap between oneself and the envied person seems unbridgeable, so that one can never have that person's advantages. This often leads to hostility and even the wish to destroy the envied one.
24 Jesus may have been referring to a spiritual kingdom or a state of consciousness rather than a literal physical kingdom, but this was not the way his followers understood him.

Chapter 6

Religious narcissism and power dynamics in religion

The projection of the human need for power onto God

The Bible and the theistic traditions that emerged from it frequently assert the power of God, which they believe to be very important. This chapter explores the psychological sources of this assertion. I make the case that the attribution of power to an omnipotent God is based on the projection of the human needs for power and protection. The need to demonstrate power, the need to dominate others, and the need for authority are especially prominent among authoritarian leaders. During the biblical era, the cultural idea of human political hierarchies headed by powerful kings or potentates with absolute authority was projected onto the idea of a heavenly king and a celestial hierarchy. Like earthly kings, this heavenly king was assumed to be jealous of his power, in need of admiration, and intolerant of rivals.

Theistic religions such as Judaism and Christianity typically believe that God exhibits his power by intervening in the world, as shown in his ability to judge, forgive, or condemn and in his ability to create, destroy, or sustain reality in the way that he prefers. In the Bible, his powers are carried out in a manner that stresses his authority, his uniqueness, and his importance. However, the exact parameters of God's power have long been debated among theologians, such as by asking whether God has the power to act in a way that is incompatible with his own nature or whether he could lie or break his own promises. Theologians debate whether God creates reality directly or through mediating processes such as evolution, which may imply a limitation to his power. The exact nature of God's power, and in what way it is part of the essence of God, is therefore uncertain.

I suggest that to speak of God's power is merely an anthropomorphism. The attribution of power to a deity is the result of the human need for a protective deity. Process theologians have rejected the traditional notion of divine omnipotence because of the philosophical issues this attribute raises, such as the problem of evil. A loving God who is also omnipotent would be able to prevent evil, but evidently does not do so, and therefore may not be omnipotent. Process theologians therefore see God as persuasive but not coercive. The notion of

DOI: 10.4324/9781003537007-7

God's omnipotence also produces something of a logical problem for theologians, such as questions like "could God create a stone too heavy for him to lift?" or "could God lie?", because if God were able to do so, he would undermine his perfection, and if he cannot lie, he is not omnipotent. A further logical problem is that when God exerts power, he changes in the process of doing so, and change means he is not perfect as he is. If he changes, he is not eternal. To exert power, he must have desired to do something and again he is not perfect as he is. The other logical problem is that God cannot be both omnipotent and omniscient. If he is omniscient, he knows the future, and if he is omnipotent, he can change it, but if he changes it, he did not necessarily know it before he changed it. If he cannot change the future, he is not omnipotent. In other words, the traditional theistic image of God is incoherent in some ways.

Nevertheless, omnipotence is an essential attribute of God in the Abrahamic traditions. I suggest that the biblical examples of Yhwh's power are largely examples of the range of ways that human beings would like to exert power. In the Hebrew Bible, Yhwh's power is shown not only as creation but also as military conquest and defeat, the legislation of human behavior, the appearance of plagues and famines, the acquisition of wealth for the temple treasury, and Yhwh's insistence on condemning people who worshipped other deities. When human beings exert power, they usually do so for a reason, so Yhwh's activity is always assumed to have a reason, as if he has cognitive processes analogous to human thinking. These are meaningless projections onto Yhwh of human mental processes. Human beings prefer to find causes for natural disasters and military defeats and victories. Human beings relish the ability to have power over others and accumulate wealth. Consequently, I assume that these characteristics of divinity as they are represented in the Hebrew Bible are all the projection of elements of human psychology.

God is said to have created the world, and he is said to answer prayers and act in history. Yet these actions may not be the result of power in the ordinary human sense of this word; they may be expressions of divinity of an entirely different order than power as we know it. What looks to us like an action of God may simply be a manifestation of God's being rather than power-driven doing and willing in a human-like mode, which is a purely human projection onto divinity.

In biblical stories, the power of God is often stressed and demonstrated in his interaction with human beings, especially if his commandments are not respected. In the Bible, God's power may act for the benefit of humanity, or it is deployed to punish people or to express divine authority. Typical are verses such as "power belongs to God" (Psalm 62: 11). Or "Thine, O Lord, is the greatness, and the power, and the glory, and the victory, and the majesty; ... In thy hand are power and might" (1 Chronicles 29: 11–12). Jesus says that "hereafter you will see the Son of man seated at the right hand of Power and coming on the clouds of heaven" (Matt. 26: 64). At the same time, Jesus was teaching a religion of mercy and forgiveness. Perhaps he had to mention power because his public ministry created conflict with the religious authorities of his day.

Paul's Letter to the Romans stresses the power of God, perhaps because power was important to Paul himself, or his image of God was colored by the power-drenched image of Yhwh in the Hebrew Bible. Paul believed that God's power was shown by his raising Christ from the dead (10: 9). Paul refers to Jesus as the "Son of God in power" (Rom. 1: 4) and also writes that the Gospel is "the power of God" (Rom. 1: 16). He says that there is no excuse for not recognizing the "eternal power" of God (1: 20), power that God wants to "make known" (9: 22). He believes that human beings are "under the power of sin" (3: 9), which is so strong that only God's power, through Jesus, can oppose it. Paul encourages his followers to submit to the power of state authorities because he believed they have been given their power by God (Rom. 13: 1–7).

The theology of the Cross, in which God is said to have freely emptied himself of power and became powerless in order to identify with the human condition (Phil. 2: 5–11), is quite different from triumphalist images of God as a conquering monarch. The paradoxical view that God's power is "made perfect in weakness" (2 Cor. 12: 8–9) partly means that this power can best manifest itself during periods of human need. This idea also means that the power of God is not ordinary power but the power of being called by God, the power to suffer with the innocent, or the power of self-sacrifice. However, the importance of divinity manifesting itself in weakness is not stressed among Church hierarchies, which are justified because it seems that God created the universe in a hierarchical order. This attitude began with the early Church, which assumed that God modeled his creation on human kingdoms and governments. The hierarchical nature of the Christian Church, a chain of command with different ranks of the clergy, is an example of the human need for power and status that try to mimic an imaginary heavenly hierarchy.

Christians have often used overt power, or brute force, to impose their beliefs on others, leading to conversion by force (Ellerbe, 1995). In 380 CE, Emperor Theodosius made it illegal to disagree with Church doctrine. A series of subsequent Church councils established a uniform set of beliefs, and the mainstream Church became increasingly tyrannical in the enforcement of its ideology. One thinks of the Church's restriction and control of education and inquiry after the fall of the Roman Empire, followed by the medieval crusades, the Inquisition, the persecution of heretics, and the witch hunts. Such power-based enforcement of absolute truth claims accompanied by missionary zeal has been supported by threats of eternal damnation. Some Christians theologians have rejected the possibility that God or salvation can be found in any other tradition, based on the literal reading of scriptural statements such as "No one comes to the Father except through me" (John, 14: 6) and "Salvation is found in no one else" (Acts, 4: 12). These claims might be due to a conscious concern with saving souls, but unconsciously they seem to be psychologically motivated, driven by religious narcissism, the need to be superior to other traditions, and the need for certainty. To see oneself as an agent of God significantly enhances one's self-esteem. Sometimes, the attempt to convince others is a way to convince oneself, or it is a way to struggle with one's own doubt externally. As it became dominant, the Church rationalized its ruthless attempts at domination by insisting it spoke for God and that only its image of God is valid.

Erich Fromm (1950) describes two types of religion with different relationships to power. Authoritarian traditions insist on obedience and surrender to a transcendent power. Individual independence is denied, so that power and everything good within the person are projected onto God. The individual feels weak and insignificant but at least feels protected from demonic enemies. A future utopia is promised. Virtue is found in obedience and humility. This is essentially a repeat of infantile dependence, and it characterizes some forms of Church-based religion. In humanistic religions, rather than God being a symbol of power and domination, the individual is called to explore his relationship to God. The individual's own power and the power of his own reason are stressed. The individual can develop his own strength and not deny his own power. Virtue is found in self-realization and self-understanding. There are strands of both approaches in most religions.

Power and narcissism projected onto divinity

The psychodynamics of power

Jeremiah (32: 17) cries out: "It is thou who hast made the heavens and the earth by thy great power and by thy outstretched arm! Nothing is too hard for thee." This type of praise is typical of the projection of the human need for power onto the Bible's image of God, in a way that stresses divine dominion, majesty, and strength. My interest here is to explore why power is so important to human beings that it is a major aspect of all theistic images of God.

One obvious source of the projection of the human need for power onto divinity is the helplessness and vulnerability of childhood and the fact that parents inevitably do not meet all the child's needs for safety. As adults, we do not want to be failed again, so our image of God must include omnipotence and protection. It is easy to project parental power onto one's image of God. We can further understand the projected need for a powerful deity if we understand the major importance of the human need for power, which has both social and intrapsychic roots. Power may be a socially learned value, but there may also be an innate drive for power that is modified by socialization, as Alfred Adler suggested. He believed that the pursuit of a sense of power is the main motivating factor behind human behavior. Adler traced the origin of this desire to childhood, when the child compares himself with his parents and feels relatively weak and consequently inferior. His idea that the will to power is based on a neurotic feeling of inferiority contrasts with Nietzsche's belief that humans have an innate need to dominate their environment, which leads to a necessary will to power. The self-psychological approach sees ordinary childhood expressions of power as a function of self-expression and infantile grandiosity. In this view, the exercise of power may be enjoyed for its own sake as a way to enhance one's sense of self or the prestige of one's nation or cultural group. The use of power may be pleasurable, producing a sense of self-efficacy. However, the need for excessive control or power over others may also develop as a way to sustain or bolster a fragile sense of self. The need for power can also be a way to control one's own dangerousness, when one senses desires and aggression that are difficult to control. Power over others makes the vulnerable person feel less threatened and is often deployed to self-regulate and maintain narcissistic equilibrium. This strategy has only a temporary effect; in spite of their power, despotic leaders are often lonely, bored, and internally empty. These individuals also need power because they are incapable of acknowledging dependence on others. Instead, the acquisition of power over their environment and over other people produces a sense of safety, a dynamic that is noticeable in psychopathic individuals whose need for power arises because of the dangerous environment they suffered in childhood, when they were at the mercy of predatory parents. They need power and they need to win at all costs in order to feel safe.

The importance of power may have developmental origins because of the infantile omnipotence described by several theorists such as Freud (1909), who called it the "megalomania of infancy" (p. 234). Freud noted a kind of omnipotent fantasy in childhood, as in the case of a patient he named the Rat Man, who believed in the power of his magical thinking, which he believed could produce evil effects on his father (1909, p. 226[1]). Freud saw this idea as "a relic" of the Rat Man's infantile megalomania (Freud, 1913, p. 88[2]). Winnicott and Melanie Klein (1935) further developed the idea of infantile omnipotence, which refers to the idea that babies demand satisfaction, as if the baby feels it controls its mother or as if the world exists to serve the baby. Infantile omnipotence is partly related to the baby's inability to distinguish itself from the outer world. In normal development, the infant gradually realizes that the outer world is not under his control, so that over time infantile omnipotence is gradually tempered by reality. If this tempering fails to occur, persistent omnipotent defenses lead to enduring narcissistic inflation that denies the independence and autonomy of other people. This idea persists in authoritarian personalities who insist on power and entitlement, who try to enforce their ideology and bend the world to their will.

Some social scientists regard power as fundamentally important to societies, analogous to the way energy is fundamental in physics. Issues of power are often present in human relationships and in many interactions between people, institutions, and countries. Whether one possesses power or is oppressed by powerful others has a major influence on human behavior. Ideologies with an intoxicating mass appeal, such as fascism, may produce a kind of omnipotence in their adherents, leading to the abuse of power. One sees such a sense of omnipotence in leaders such as Hitler, and he seemed to be able to inspire this feeling in his henchmen. People are often drawn to such authoritarian leaders, "strongmen," whether political or religious, even when doing so threatens the individual's personal interests and autonomy. One of the classical ways to understand such submission is based on Ferenczi's (1933) notion of identification with the aggressor. He noticed that traumatized children become hypersensitive to what their abuser requires of them, in order to protect themselves from further abuse, even when this requires ignoring their own feelings. The child then compulsively complies with the wishes of the abuser and identifies with the abuser's perceptions and needs at the expense of the child's own needs. This mechanism may become an enduring pattern in adult relationships, leading to pathological accommodation to the needs of others. The threat of emotional abandonment and the need to meet the needs of a narcissistic parent are other sources of this dynamic. In politics, it is common to see the followers of a strongman both submit to him and identify with him, as if his power somehow enhances the follower. The strongman seems to embody order and certainty, so that people who feel cultural humiliation and dispossession are susceptible to the blandishments of a leader who seems to offer the restoration of a proper social order, restoring their own sense of specialness. The idealization of an authoritarian leader may become so intense that it overrides the followers' own sense of right and wrong, whereupon any harmful act he may commit is forgiven, ignored, or rationalized.

Narcissistic dynamics in religion

The narcissistic sense that one's own tradition is the only valid one is reflected in absolute truth claims such as "no salvation outside the church." The Roman Catholic Church tried to soften this attitude in the Second Vatican Council by saying it does not apply to people who do not know Christ through no fault of their own. However, the tradition that only baptism saves still persists. Comments such as "no one comes to the Father but by me" (John 14: 6) serve the purpose of excluding non-believers and developing an exclusive ingroup. Historically, this attitude has justified the Church's intolerance, revealing the violent power shadow of Christianity in contrast to its conscious teachings of love. Intolerance and murderous persecution of heretics and non-believers have been common features of religious traditions that try to suppress challenges to their authority. In the Christian tradition, St. Paul burned what he considered to be the wrong kind of books (Ac. 19: 19), and Constantine and later Christian authorities persecuted pagan priests. These were precursor steps to both the *Index of Forbidden Books*[3] in the sixteenth century and the medieval Inquisition, which led to the burning of heretics or those who proposed a cosmology of which the Church disapproved. All this Christian imperialism was part of the insistence that Christianity is the best and truest religion, which makes its adherents feel special and projects doubt onto other traditions.

Some of the triumphalism seen in the Hebrew Bible after Israel's victories in battle was a narcissistic display of the power of the victors' image of God.

An example was their exaltation over the drowning of the Egyptian army in Exodus 15. Victory in battle meant that their God was stronger than the gods of other nations, allowing the people to feel special and superior. The people or their chroniclers justified their own need for victory by assuming it was the divine will, giving a self-righteous quality to their violence. The assumption that their victory was the will of God allowed them to carry out a range of atrocities. The underlying narcissistic assumption was that they were an instrument of God's power.

Fundamentalists of all types have an uncanny capacity to know the will of God, which seems to coincide with their own will in a remarkable way. Some clergy manifest grandiose claims to speak for God or to know God's intentions, while other clergy develop a savior complex. J. Reid Meloy (1986) noted that being a clergyman may encourage grandiosity, and the concept of a call from God may enhance the individual's sense of specialness. Meloy also pointed out that dogmatic preaching, of the kind that avoids paradox or ambivalence, may be demanded by congregations. Religious leaders may be happy to collude with this process when it supports their own beliefs and their own grandiosity. The idealization of clergy may induce or emphasize narcissistic traits in their personalities that otherwise might not have developed.

Each theistic tradition claims to offer its adherents a unique connection to God that is not offered by other traditions. Each of the Abrahamic traditions insists on the truth and primacy of its own holy books. The wish to proselytize others is often driven by this kind of narcissistic insistence that one's own tradition is the best, in a kind of sibling rivalry for the divine father, a wish to be his favorite child, or a triumphant sense that one has been awarded that status by him. In these ways, religion can be used in the service of maintaining or enhancing the individual's self-esteem and supporting a fragile sense of self. One can easily use religion to feel superior and special. Both Judaism and Christianity have their own narcissistic view of their specialness; the Jews consider themselves to be chosen, while the Christians believe that they are God's elect or saved or that they are the new chosen people, superseding the Jews. The belief that one is chosen or saved may lead to a sense of entitlement, or to the sense that other religions are less worthy of divine favors, or even to the idea that other groups may be mistreated. God is then appropriated for the sake of proving the superiority of one's own tradition. Religion easily mixes with nationalism; orthodox Jews believe God gave their ancestors the land of Israel, and some Americans believe that God has a special relationship with the USA, an idea that goes back to the days of the Pilgrims.[4]

Belonging to a group of like-minded people such as a close-knit religious community promotes a type of self-enhancement and supplies a variety of other narcissistic needs. Being part of a religious congregation, surrounded by people with the same values and beliefs as oneself, produces a twinship or alter-ego relationship that supports the individual's sense of self. At the same time, group members are mirrored by each other, and they idealize the group's values, its heroes, its leaders, and its sacred texts. This kind of idealization has a soothing effect; it reduces anxiety by allowing the adherent to feel part of a larger source of power and wisdom, and it provides a sense of direction. In these ways, group membership consolidates and confirms the individual's identity. A common sense of mission and direction allows a feeling of belonging. These dynamics are all enhanced by the sense that God blesses the group's beliefs, in which case the individual can feel superior to non-believers. A charismatic, idealized group leader who can embody and focus the group's ideology helps to sustain the group identity. Unfortunately, the shadow side of these group phenomena is hostility to non-believers and the projection of negative traits onto other groups.

Divine–human narcissism in the Hebrew Bible

A commandment such as "You shall have no other gods before me…you shall not bow down to them or serve them; for I the Lord your God am a jealous God, visiting the iniquity of the fathers upon the children to the third and fourth generation" (Exod. 20: 3–5) reveals the human narcissistic need to be superior projected onto divinity, reinforced with a Mafia-style threat of violence to the children of those who disobey.

Yhwh says that the people of Israel were chosen to be his people out of all the peoples on earth (Deut. 7: 6–7). Did God actually choose ancient Israel, or did they choose themselves to be chosen? They were a nondescript, politically insignificant nation surrounded by more powerful empires. The idea of divine election, of being chosen, was a way of enhancing national self-esteem. They very much needed to be chosen by a powerful war God if they were to face the future. The only God who would be of value would be one who was prepared to act like tribal warlord. Being chosen and a holy people compensated for the Israelites' sense of insignificance, and prophetic promises of a great future gave consolation and hope for the future. To feel chosen would also justify the conquest of other groups by attributing it to a divine commandment. To be told that their nation is different, destined to bring salvation to the rest of the world, and that the world would eventually recognize their greatness made them important. By adopting their God's code of holiness, the people could participate in the holiness of their God and feel morally righteous.[5] Their claim of divine revelation at Mt. Sinai was a claim of exclusiveness; it was said to have occurred to a particular people at a particular time, once and for all, and most of the content was not intended for humanity in general. The drawback of being chosen was severe punishment if the people did not obey Yhwh's commandments. Punishments included plagues, famines, defeats in war, and the Babylonian Exile. To soften this blow, Jeremiah (31: 31–34) promised a new covenant after the exile. Isaiah (46: 10) rationalized the people's suffering by making it a process of testing and refinement by God. In order to explain the loss of the Jerusalem temple and to compensate for the resulting profound loss of national self-esteem, the idea developed that the Israelite God was invisible and ubiquitous, living in a transcendent realm rather than a physical building.

The Israelite captives were freed from exile in Babylon because Persian King Cyrus defeated the Babylonians. In an interesting appropriation of this event, speaking through Isaiah, Yhwh claimed that Cyrus was his "shepherd" and his "anointed" (Isaiah 44: 28; 45: 1). Cyrus is even reported to have said that Yhwh "charged me to build him a house at Jerusalem" (2 Chron. 36: 23), although Cyrus was actually a pagan polytheist who probably attributed his victory to Marduk, the god of the Babylonians.

The mystery of why God would choose a certain people seems inexplicable and is often explained as a divine mystery. The text says that God chose his people as an act of love (Deut. 7: 6–8) and he demonstrated this love by bringing them out of slavery in Egypt, apparently in order that they should know him (Ex. 6–7). In other words, he needed to be known or mirrored by his special people. Can we infer that he allowed them to be enslaved so that he could later show his power by freeing them? The theme of God freeing his people is repeated over and over again in the Hebrew Bible and is often given as a reason to justify various commandments such as keeping the Sabbath (Deut. 5: 15), as if being given freedom commits the people to obey their divine rescuer, ignoring the fact that he allowed them to be enslaved in the first place.

The idea of God "choosing" is an example of the projection of human family dynamics onto God, as if Yhwh were a personality who is more interested in some people than in others. Speaking of Yhwh, Jung points out that "Human beings were a matter of first-rate importance to him. He needed them as they needed him, urgently and personally" (CW 11, para. 568). It seems that God needs to possess the people (Psalm 135: 4) and make them a holy people (Deut. 7:6, Ex. 19: 6). The people are holy because God is holy (Lev. 21: 8), and he needs them to reflect his holiness. Psychoanalytic self-psychology would see God's need for this people as a mirror need, as if the divine personality needed to have his greatness reflected back to him. By singling out a particular people, God makes himself the most important deity for them. He acknowledges that he has chosen this people "For my own sake, for my own sake, I do it" (Isa. 48: 9–11), suggesting he realizes that he needs their mirroring. It is no accident that through the prophet Isaiah (45: 23) he insists that "To me every knee shall bow, every tongue shall swear." Here, he sounds like a typically grandiose potentate, clearly a projection of the behavior of human royalty onto the biblical image of God.

The narcissistic vulnerability of the biblical image of God is seen not only in his insistence that his people must not worship any other god but also in his rages and severe punishments when he is disobeyed. When his people are unfaithful, he ruthlessly kills them, as when he ordered the death of three thousand people after they worship a golden calf[6] (Exod. 32: 28). He kills twenty-four thousand men who consort with the priestesses of a Canaanite god (Num. 25: 1–9). Characteristic of narcissistically vulnerable people, and clearly a human projection, the biblical Yhwh is so sensitive to rejection that he likens disobedience to his commandments to adultery (Jer. 3: 6–9) or harlotry (Ezek. 16: 15; Hos. 4: 15).

Although it is often claimed that Yhwh's judgments are always just and in accord with the individual's deeds, (Jer. 25: 14), his punishments often seem radically disproportionate. He kills Aaron's two sons as a punishment for a mistake during a ritual sacrifice (Lev. 10: 1–3), in order to "show myself holy" and be glorified before the people. He threatens plagues, wild beasts, desolation, pestilence, military defeat, and cannibalism of the people's children if he is disobeyed (Lev. 26: 21–29). Through the prophet Elijah, he orders a three-year famine on King Ahab (1 Kings 17: 1) as a punishment for the worship of Baal, the Canaanite god. Blasphemy is such an affront to his self-image that it warrants the death penalty (Lev. 24: 16). Apparently, his self-esteem is so easily threatened that he cannot tolerate competition. Yhwh gets angry when David takes a census of the fighting men of the people (2 Sa. 24: 1–17), and 70,000 people are killed as a result—the reason is not given, but it may be that taking a census implied ownership or royal power, which was rightfully God's. This story has puzzled commentators because Yhwh told David to carry out the census, having been tempted by Satan according to 1 Chron. 21.

Yhwh is so anxious to display his power that, in a demonstration of his shadow, he "hardens the heart" of Pharaoh (Exod. 4: 21), to "get glory" for himself (Exod. 14:4), so that Pharaoh refuses to let the Israelites go free, resulting in the mass murder of Egyptian first-born children. In this behavior, Yhwh mirrors the behavior of Pharaoh, who had ordered the murder of Israelite baby boys at the beginning of the story (Ex. 1: 16). Moses attributes Pharaoh's refusal to his "stubbornness" (Exod. 13: 15), not realizing that Pharaoh had no choice. When Yhwh is angry, he sends plagues, earthquakes, famines, and invasions by other nations who act as his instrument. His narcissistic rage takes so long to calm down that he visits the sins of the fathers upon their children and upon their children's children. He promises Ezekiel that he will gather together the scattered people, not for their sake but to "vindicate the holiness of my great name" (Ezek. 36: 22–23) because it has not been properly respected—a further indication of his narcissistic vulnerability and need for mirroring. He says he afflicts people "for my own sake" because his name has been profaned (Isaiah 48: 10–11), and Psalm 106 (7–8) teaches that although the people did not appreciate him and rebelled, "he saved them for his name's sake/that he might make known his mighty power." The biblical Yhwh needs a constant supply of praise and prayers. The projection onto God of the human need for praise and a powerful reputation is obvious.

The emphasis on monotheism in the Hebrew Bible is striking, but there is no particular reason that monotheism is superior to polytheism. Monotheism seems to be a patriarchal development, since an omnipotent, totalitarian male sky-God gives some license to the idea of a father as head of the family, one supreme sovereign, and one pope who is the delegate of that God. Not surprisingly, polytheistic societies tend to be less authoritarian.

In short, the biblical image of God in the Hebrew Bible is colored by the projection of human narcissistic vulnerability and human narcissistic needs onto the

God-image. Although it is usually claimed that we cannot describe God in terms of human characteristics, throughout the Bible God is depicted as if "he" has qualities that are obviously human projections. These descriptions are so anthropomorphic that many of the ways God behaves would be pathological if they belonged to a human being. These characteristics are clearly the projection of elements of human psychology onto a God-image. The text describes the image of a deity who suffers from affective instability, moodiness, and narcissistic fragility that lead to lethal rage attacks. He suffers from envy of other gods, constantly insisting that he is the only deity worthy of worship. He can never be quite sure about the reliability of his people's connection to him, as if he has insecure attachment. He seems to need his people, as if he is lonely or suffers from abandonment anxiety. His insecurity is visible on many occasions, as when he allows terrible suffering to be inflicted on Job just to see if Job is truly faithful to him, in the process betraying his own lack of faithfulness and projecting his self-doubt onto his divine victim. Yhwh tries to force his people to love him, partly through threats and promises, as if he realizes that one cannot force love to occur. He can be impulsive, paranoid, and defensively inflated. He is prone to all-good and all-bad splitting, leading to large-scale, ruthless massacres, sometimes for minor offenses. As previously noted, the clinician will immediately see that this deity behaves like a human being with borderline personality disorder. Since this diagnosis is obviously meaningless in terms of the divine itself, we can again see the truth of Feuerbach's idea that the classical idea of God is based on the projection of human personality traits. However, the fact that human beings color their God-image with human traits does not mean that there is no God. It means that the biblical descriptions of God are relatively unsophisticated and consist largely of human projections and anthropomorphic fantasy. Perhaps it has been true that the only way to talk about God is by means of metaphor, symbol, and anthropomorphisms, but Jung's notion of the Self offers an alternative.

Yhwh's narcissistic vulnerability is seen in his demands for constant praise and exclusive worship. He constantly needs to be propitiated to deter his anger. However, external props to his self-esteem such as worship and sacrifice are never quite enough, and his self-doubt is constant. In an extraordinary parallel to Kohut's concept of the selfobject, Jung notes that Yhwh "fits a personality who can only convince himself that he exists through his relation to an object. Such dependence on the object is absolute when the subject is totally lacking in self-reflection and therefore has no insight into himself" (CW 11, para. 573). Or, in Kohut's terms, Yhwh needs constant mirroring from humanity. As Jung puts it, "he wants to be loved, honored, worshipped, and praised as just. He reacts irritably to every word that has the faintest suggestion of criticism" (CW 11, para. 604). This narcissistic problem is seen in Yhwh's demand for supremacy in the first of the Ten Commandments, which insists that "Thou shalt have no other gods before me." As the status of Yhwh's mythic image grew, in order to obey and placate him all "other gods" (sometimes goddesses) were repressed by his followers.

The parallels between Yhwh's narcissistic needs and those of humanity are striking. Yhwh demands submission, obedience, and a high standard of behavior from his people (Dt. 30: 16), but he never acknowledges that they may be resentful because of his demands. He reacts strongly to the way his people behave towards him, sometimes with attacks of murderous rage. He is also very sensitive to affronts to his prophets, as if they represent him; when in the name of God Elisha curses a group of children who make fun of him because he is bald, God sends two bears to attack 42 of them (2 Ki. 2: 23–24). Although Yhwh is said to know the future, in return for a guarantee of victory he allows Jephthah to promise to sacrifice whatever meets him when he returns home from battle. In the event, Jephthah has to sacrifice his only child (Jdg. 11: 28–40). In spite of the violent aspect of Yhwh's personality, which he repeatedly demonstrates, in an extraordinary act of denial by his devotees he is also said to be "slow to anger and filled with kindness and truth" (Ex. 34: 6–7) and also to be "merciful...and abounding in steadfast love" (Ps. 103: 8). However, his rage takes so long to calm down that he visits the sins of the fathers upon their children and their children's children (Ex. 34: 6–7). He has an amazing capacity to bear a long-standing grudge, as when he swears to eliminate the Amalekites "from generation to generation" (Ex. 17: 16) because they attacked the people of Israel on their way to Canaan. His rage does not die down; much later, God orders King Saul to continue to kill all the Amalekites, including women, children, and animals (1 Sa. 15 2–3). In spite of Yhwh's violence, in order to offer hope the text also promises that eventually he will bring about such peace that "The wolf shall lie down with the lamb" (Isa. 11: 6–8). The presence of such contradictory attributes are based on a splitting defense utilized to avoid cognitive dissonance.

The religious impulse has become entangled with human psychodynamics, leading to pathologies of narcissism, violence, and power among religionists. The relationship to God has self-serving elements even when it is based on love rather than a fear of punishment, since if one is loved, one is lovable, and if one loves, one typically hopes for love in return. The anti-narcissistic element in religion is largely due to its emphasis on selfless service to others and humility before God, but the fact that religious leaders claim to know what God wants suggests that the humbling effects of religion may be less potent than religion's potential for enhancing narcissism.

Religious narcissism in Christianity

The early Church became increasingly intolerant of deviation from official doctrine. Christianity developed a claim to superiority over all other traditions, as if Jesus were the final and highest form of revelation and the center of the religious universe. This form of religious narcissism was claimed by many subsequent Christian leaders. There is no conceivable way to prove such a claim, nor is there a way to invalidate the idea that other religions may allow their adherents to be close to God. The claim that Jesus' sacrifice redeems the sins of the whole world is a grandiose claim of the early Church; Jesus himself clearly believed that his ministry was restricted to his fellow Jews. The comment that "No one comes to the Father except through me" (Jn. 14: 6) was an attitude that continued in the Church's inflated insistence that there is no salvation outside the Church. From this point of view, the fact that untold numbers of human beings must have died unredeemed before Jesus appeared on earth is inexplicable. One cannot help wondering if traditionalists believe they are all in hell. The theologian Karl Rahner developed the somewhat condescending idea of "anonymous Christians," suggesting that non-Christian traditions might be vehicles of salvation arising out of the grace given by Christ. In his view, these individuals simply do not realize the real ground of their faith or what they really believe. Rahner realizes that this claim is presumptuous but sees it as "the source of the greatest humility both for himself and the Church" (Rahner, 1966, p. 134). To make this claim a source of humility rather than superiority requires a splitting defense, since it is clearly a grandiose claim. Christian attempts to proselytize are usually said to be based on conscious concern for the souls of non-believers, but these efforts sometimes have a defensive quality about them, as if they are warding off doubt that is personified by non-believers by asking them to join with the Christian's own beliefs in order to reassure the believer.

Paul's narcissistic needs

Paul did not simply transmit Jesus' teachings; he turned Jesus into the figure that Paul needed him to be to meet his own psychological needs. Jesus saw himself as a teacher and reformer of the Judaism of his time, but Paul greatly enlarged Jesus' image to the point that he saves all humanity. This seems to have been based on Paul's personal need for an idealized figure, someone who provides wisdom, soothing, and strength with which the self can merge and which it can aspire to emulate. Paul's rage at non-believers may have been in part a reaction to any threat to this intense need. A striking feature of his movement was his insistence on ideological control of his followers' beliefs.

Paul complains about the boastfulness of the Corinthians but realizes that he too is boasting (1 Cor. 9: 15; 2 Cor. 1: 12). Apparently, he wanted to demonstrate his leadership and his superiority to the other members of the Corinthian church, which was divided into different factions with their own leaders. Paul wanted members of the church to be submissive to him, but some of them were critical of him, or they compared him with the original twelve apostles (1 Cor. 4: 3–5; 9: 1–6). Terrance Callan (1990) has noted Paul's boastful, competitive attitude, his presentation of himself as a model for others, and his disdain for other leaders. Callan believes that these attitudes were typical of Paul's culture, so that no specific explanation of these character traits is required for Paul as an individual. In any case, according to Callan, after Paul became a follower of Jesus, he developed a new identity that was in conflict with his competitive character because he recognized his dependence on God, which restrained the excesses of his previous character. This analysis does not account for the extreme violence with which Paul rejected disagreement. Paul remained extremely intolerant of deviation from his teaching. He threatened vengeance on non-believers, to be inflicted by angels in "flaming fire" (2 Thess. 1: 7). He curses anyone who preaches a message different from his own (Gal. 1: 8–9), and he consigns non-believers to eternal damnation. This attitude begins a long tradition of Christian intolerance, exemplified by Mark 16: 16: "He who believes and is baptized will be saved, but he who does not believe will be condemned." The doctrine of hell and eternal punishment is one of the repellent aspects of Christian doctrine that has caused a great deal of fear and emotional suffering. It is incompatible with the notion of a loving God, but it has been taken seriously by many Christian theologians who have enjoyed debating what type of punishments await non-believers.

Some of Paul's writing reveals a character who is angry, masochistic, self-righteous, and intolerant of disagreement. He also shows pre-conscious awareness of his narcissistic traits when he reminds his followers of his effectiveness in 1 Thessalonians (2: 1–12), saying that although he is holy, righteous, and blameless, he is not looking for praise from people. He flatters his followers by telling them that God has chosen them (1: 4), calling them children of the light (5: 5), divinely elected and specially privileged, while rather patronizingly telling them that his relationship to them was like a nurse taking care of her children (2: 7). It is noteworthy that in several places Paul claims to have direct communications with Jesus, as when Paul says that he received the idea of communion directly from Jesus (1 Cor. 11: 23). He believes that what he was writing was "a command of the Lord" (1 Cor. 14: 37) and that the gospel he preached was given to him as a direct revelation of Jesus (Gal. 1: 11–12). Paul saw himself as a "chosen instrument" for this purpose, and his authority came directly from Christ. Not accidentally, in this way he became very important, or at least he could participate in Jesus' importance. His characterological tendency to authoritarianism is seen in that although he submits to the authority of Christ, he otherwise asserts his own authority and tries to control his followers. He insists on a hierarchy, at the head of which are the Apostles, of whom he believes he is one, followed by prophets, teachers, miracle workers, healers, guides, and those who speak in tongues (1 Cor. 12: 28).

Graham Shaw (1983) believes that Christian texts often assert authority in an attempt to consolidate power and manipulate the faithful. Shaw asks why the Church is "more effective in conveying guilt than communicating forgiveness" (p. viii). He shows that one of the roots of this problem is the way in which Paul exerted his authority by using eschatological anxiety about the future to manipulate his followers, combined with threats of divine judgment and punishment to control their behavior. He promises them ultimate salvation, peace, and joy, but often at the cost of necessary suffering or persecution, which he seems to think is a path to heaven. Shaw finds the same strategy in the Gospel of Mark (13), which also uses eschatological imagery and the threat of future judgment and hell to heighten anxiety (Mk 8: 38).

Notes

1 Freud, S. (1909). Notes upon a case of obsessional neurosis. *Standard Edition* 10.
2 Freud, S. (1923). Totem and Taboo. *Standard Edition* 13.
3 This index is a list of books that the Church authorities believed to be dangerous to the faith or morals of Roman Catholics. Its use was ended in 1966.
4 Some members of the Mormon Church believe that Jesus Christ rose from the dead following his crucifixion and came to America, which he designated the new Promised Land. Some Christian nationalists wish to make the USA a Christian country, using the Bible to dictate behavior and political decisions. This movement is often seen to be not only Christian in its values but also a religious disguise for conservative politics, which contravenes the clear constitutional separation of church and state.
5 There is a Talmudic idea that God threatened the people with death if they did not accept the Torah, by holding Mt. Sinai over their heads and threatening to bury them if they refused him (Tract. Sabbat. 88a). A question ensued about whether this coercion meant their agreement was not binding, but this was quickly dismissed.
6 The golden calf may have been a representation of El, the deity the people originally worshipped before Moses persuaded them to worship his preferred deity, Yhwh. The biblical text tries to reconcile the tension between these two divinities by having Yhwh state that he appeared to Abraham, Isaac, and Jacob as El rather than as Yhwh (Ex. 6: 2–3). The two deities gradually merged, with Yhwh absorbing the qualities of El, taking over his role of heavenly king as well as incorporating the attributes of Baal, the Canaanite storm god.

Chapter 7

Mental illness in biblical characters

This chapter discusses the question of whether our ability to detect mental illness in the behavior of the characters depicted in biblical stories is sufficient to either invalidate the religious message of the story or at least call it into question. It is important to know whether the fact that a person is mentally ill invalidates his spiritual claims, especially when such an individual retains self-awareness and is taken seriously by his contemporaries.

Traditional religious believers repudiate any psychological interpretations of biblical characters. Abraham Heschel (1962, p. 185) writes: "What we think is due to mental disorder may have been due to a higher spiritual order." He is concerned that the psychological approach to the behavior of a biblical character such as a prophet prejudges the individual by denying in advance that which it is supposed to explore. Heschel is concerned that "instead of elucidating the prophetic experience, it [psychology] has tried to explain it away." However, this is a misunderstanding, because the fact that a numinous encounter of any kind originates in the archetypal level of the psyche does not mean it is not real or that it is not spiritually significant.

Critics of a psychological approach to characters in biblical stories point out that we do not have enough access to these individuals to obtain a history that is detailed enough for a reliable diagnosis. Furthermore, the cultural differences between the biblical era and our own may be too great to make such a diagnosis meaningful. Nor is it clear that contemporary diagnostic criteria can be applied to people who lived at a very different time (Garfinkel, 1989). We do not know the extent to which behavior that seems abnormal to us may have been culturally acceptable. We do not know the effects of centuries of editing and transmission of the original text, which may have distorted the depiction of the personality in question. Therefore, the best the psychologist can do is to make informed inferences based on the textual descriptions. That is, we diagnose the literary rather than the historical figure, the character created by the text, which is the one that believers accept. In his study of Ezekiel, Garber (2004) refers to this approach as literary trauma theory. The resulting diagnoses are speculative and based on the psychologist's preferred model of the psyche.

A further proviso is that the psychologist has to acknowledge his or her transference to the story, which is partly based on the psychologist's religious background as well as the possible resonance between the story and the psychologist's own psychological structures. These factors are often significant enough to affect the psychologist's assessment. Needless to say, they also operate in the theologian's interpretation of the text.

Saul on the road to Damascus: Temporal lobe epilepsy?

Saul's experience on the road to Damascus was characterized by his seeing a blinding light, falling to the ground, and hearing the voice of Jesus saying "Saul, Saul, why do you persecute me?" Saul asked: "Who are you, Lord?" The voice replied: "I am Jesus, whom you are persecuting" (Acts 9: 3–6). Saul remained blind for three days and was unable to eat or drink. This episode, which is foundational for the Christian tradition, is sometimes thought to have had a neurological origin in temporal lobe epilepsy (TLE). Auditory and visual hallucinations and complex ideation are well-known features of this disorder. Religious experiences may occur during, immediately after, and between seizures. Individuals with this disorder sometimes experience hyper-religiosity or increased interest in religion between episodes. Temporary blindness is a rare but well-known concomitant of TLE.

There are some arguments against this diagnosis. Landsborough (1987) points out that Saul's experience of light and his falling down could have been epileptic, but the conversation with Jesus is too elaborate to be due to TLE. There are three different accounts of the road-to-Damascus story in Acts, in one of which other people travelling with Saul are also said to have seen the light without hearing the voice (Acts, 22: 9).

The content of the experience seems to have been engendered by Saul's preoccupation in the previous days. He had been struggling with a growing interest in the Jesus movement that conflicted with his persecution of Jesus' followers, as suggested by the report that Jesus said to him: "It hurts you to kick against the goads" (Acts 26: 14).[1] Saul had been moved by witnessing the martyrdom of Stephen and his quiet faith in the face of death. Emotionally important experiences are known to affect the manifestations of TLE, which may produce religious conversion or a permanent change in the individual's way of life, often leading to religious preoccupation (Dewhurst & Beard, 1970).

In Saul's culture, any sign of grand mal epilepsy was understood to indicate demonic influence, so he would not have been taken seriously if he had been obviously epileptic, but TLE may not produce visible motor effects. Furthermore, Saul's memory of the event is remarkably clear, which is not usual for seizure-induced events. If one does not accept this experience as an authentic numinous experience, another explanation might be a dissociative state or a hallucination while in a mild delirium due to a combination of heat, dehydration, and fatigue.

In favor of the diagnosis of TLE, Paul reports various other ecstatic visions. In his letter to the Church in Corinth, he describes a state in which he was "caught up to the third heaven...up to paradise and heard inexpressible things, things that no one is permitted to tell" (2 Cor. 12: 2). The experience was accompanied by the sense that did not know if he was in his body. He had a series of other visionary experiences described in the book of Acts (16: 9–10; 18: 9–10; 22: 17–21; 27; 23–24). Paul does have some features of the inter-ictal personality described in people with a controversial disorder known as the Geschwind syndrome, which is characterized by preoccupation with religious concerns, extensive writing on these matters in diaries and letters (hypergraphia), pedantic or circumstantial speech, reduced sexual activity, a "sticky" personality,[2] and aggression (Geschwind, 1983).

The important question is whether the content of Paul's spiritual experiences is invalidated if he had TLE, in which case his visions were purely personal, brain-induced phenomena. Alternatively, even if this was indeed an epileptic episode, the seizure may have served only to reduce normal brain activity sufficiently to remove any gate or filter to the spiritual dimension.

The mental state of the prophets

In the ancient Near East, the world was thought to be full of signs from the gods, and prophecy was an important channel for divine–human interaction and for discerning the will of the gods (Cryer, 1994). The biblical prophet was not simply someone who foretold the future; he was a kind of oracle who passes on the divine message or, in psychological language, someone who mediates between ego consciousness and the archetypal unconscious. Prophecy was an important aspect of both the Jewish biblical tradition and early Christianity, as we see in 1 Cor. 14 and 1 Thess. 5: 21.

The Hebrew prophets had an intense sense of mission but sometimes appeared reluctant to assume their mission by modestly saying that they do not speak well enough (Jer. 1: 6) or they are not fit to convey the divine message (Isa. 6:5) or, like Moses, by making statements such as "who am I to do this?" (Ex. 3: 11). The prophets were active during very uncertain times for their nation. They may have been trying to deal with their own anxiety and uncertainty about the future by projecting the way they imagined or hoped God would intervene. Their exhortations were delivered with special urgency and intensity. They typically began to speak by making an accusation intended to produce guilt or anxiety in their listeners. They threatened divine punishment but then offered some kind of comfort or alternative outcome if people changed their behavior.

We do not know exactly how the prophets of the Hebrew Bible received their messages, but they clearly felt they spoke for God. It is interesting to ask why they believed that their thoughts and feelings were divinely inspired. The prophets usually say that the word of God "came" to them (e.g., Jer 1: 4), making them speak in an inspired state of mind, allowing the prophet to disclaim personal responsibility for their message. The fact that such an experience arises from beyond the ego is suggested by the way in which Jeremiah was very shaken by his experience: "My heart is broken within me/all my bones shake...because of the Lord" (23: 9). This sounds like the effect of a constellated complex that overwhelms consciousness. Jeremiah pleaded with God to be rid of his prophetic duty. Sometimes, there is a clear description of possession, as in the case of King Saul: "The spirit of God came mightily upon him, and he prophesied" (1 Sam. 10: 10–13). Apparently, something like an autonomous complex overpowered Saul's ego, and he went into an altered state of consciousness. Some prophets, like Isaiah, experienced visions (Isaiah 6; 21–23; Zechariah 5; Jer.1: 11; Amos 7–9). Their experience may have been an active imagination in Jung's sense, a process that allows material from the mythopoetic level of the psyche to emerge into ego consciousness. Some prophecy occurs in the form of an audible external voice, as in the case of the author of Revelation (14: 13), who reports that "I heard a voice from heaven saying "Write this..."" The prophet may have had a flash of insight, a strong intuition, an inner conviction that was driven by a complex, or he experienced a thought that seemed distinct from the prophet's own thoughts. The experience may have occurred in a dissociative state, in a state of self-induced hypnosis, or as a dream or vision. The prophets may have been able to induce trance states in themselves, perhaps through self-hypnosis or meditative techniques. Or they had an unusual permeability to the autonomous level of the psyche, which was able to seize the attention of the prophets' ego.

Another possibility is suggested by Julian Jaynes's (1976) controversial idea of the bicameral mind. Jaynes believed that until about 1000 BCE the right hemisphere of the brain produced experiences that were coded as voices and perceived or interpreted by the left hemisphere to be the voice of gods. The Hebrew prophets were still experiencing reality in a partially bicameral manner. Jaynes suggested that because characters in the early prophetic books of the Hebrew Bible (e.g., Amos, circa 750 BCE) lacked self-consciousness about their own behavior, the voice of the gods, actually the products of the right hemisphere, took the place of such self-awareness. People seemed to be moved by the gods rather than their own initiative. Over time, as the left hemisphere became increasingly dominant, the voice of God gradually disappeared from the text of the Hebrew Bible. Because of historical and cultural changes and especially the development of writing, we no longer hear these voices, except in cases of schizophrenia, which Jaynes believes is a type of experience similar to hearing the voice of the gods in antiquity. Jaynes (p. 313) suggested that the Old Testament depicts "the story of the loss of the bicameral mind" as the gods of that period became silent. Jaynes thinks that the loss of our bicameral mind answers the question of why the gods have left us and why prophecy declined during post-exilic Judaism. Religion is then an expression of our thirst for the old bicameral experience that used to warn people and give advice.

The relationship between prophecy, mysticism, and insanity is an old question. It would be a mistake to assume that phenomena such as hearing the voice of God are invariably pathological; they often occur among contemporary Pentecostal groups, and their reports do not sound psychotic (Dein & Littlewood, 2007). There is a range of opinions about the prophets' mental state. It is difficult to assess whether the voices and visions that the prophets claim to have experienced as the voice of God were really pathological symptoms. Spiritual experiences do have some of the characteristics of mental illness, but these states are usually distinguishable (Jackson et al., 1997), and mentally ill people may have authentic spiritual experiences. In the prophets' descriptions, there is always a sense of something other than the ego affecting the person, which is interpreted in terms of the prophet's personal theology. An example is Jeremiah's experience of an inner prompting to visit a potter's workshop, which he attributed to the word of God coming to him (Jer. 18: 1–11). As Jeremiah watched the potter re-work spoiled clay until the potter was satisfied, Jeremiah realized that this was an analogy for the way in which God can break down and rebuild a nation. He then understood the reason for his earlier urge to visit the potter.

At times, the prophets' experiences concern the future, as in case of Amos' visions about the future of Israel, in which God threatens punitive destruction (Amos 7: 1–17). Second Isaiah was a prophet of salvation who expected the return from exile to be highly successful. Notably, however, most prophecies of a positive future for the prophets' people failed to materialize. Subsequent generations had to reinterpret these failed prophecies to avoid too much cognitive dissonance. A similar phenomenon occurred when the Second Coming of Jesus failed to materialize, so that explanations were necessary, such as the necessity for other events to happen first (Matt. 24: 14; 2 Thess. 2: 3).

Sometimes, the prophet's visionary state is very complex, as in the vision of Ezekiel, discussed below, or that of Isaiah 6: 1–10: "I saw the Lord sitting upon a throne...above him stood the seraphim; each had six wings...and the foundations of the thresholds shook." Then one of the angels touched his lips with a burning coal, telling him this would take away his guilt. He then hears the voice of God. This may have been an active imagination or a state of possession.

Heschel (1962) rejects any attempt to reduce the prophetic experience to some kind of disorder. He wants to take at face value the prophets' claim that they speak for God, and he insists that the prophetic consciousness has to be understood on its own terms, in part because we have no access to what happened to them and so we cannot analyze it. We have only their verbal accounts. Heschel believes that the prophets had an empathic connection with God's feelings. The prophet's emotional life was assimilated into the divine emotions, so the prophet identifies with and feels God's feelings, which are affected by human behavior. The prophets urgently wanted to communicate God's feelings to their contemporaries. The very dubious, anthropomorphic assumption here is that God has feelings that are at least analogous to human feelings, and the prophet is guided by what God feels. This raises the obvious question of whether the prophets were simply attributing human emotions to God, but Heschel believes that "The prophets had to use anthropomorphic language in order to convey His nonanthropomorphic Being" (p. 56). Heschel (1955) believes that God seeks humanity, which is seen as a partner in creation, and God somehow needs human recognition. The urgency of the prophets' exhortations expresses that need. This sounds like a child's wish to be sought after and wanted by a parent.[3]

Heschel does not escape the criticism that his God-image is colored by the projected qualities of human psychology. He believes that the prophets experience God as a "feeling of subjective presence" (p. 266), and he assumes that this confirms the existence of God—he refers to this existence as a "presupposition" (1962, p. 46). However, having felt this inner presence, the prophets could attribute it only to their inherited idea of God. Jung would attribute this experience to pressure from the archetypal or non-ego levels of the psyche.

The moral strictures of the prophets were largely directed against the people of Israel, urging them to be faithful to their God. It is not clear that prophetic exhortations were intended to be universally applicable. Heschel avoids the skeptical issue of whether the prophecies of particular events were inserted by redactors at a date later than the events they depict.

Heschel is at pains to disagree with the theory that prophecy was the result of psychosis or a deranged nervous system. He believes it is foolhardy to attempt to make such a diagnosis of people who lived so long ago on the basis of literary material. He feels that the psychological approach errs in its prejudgment: "it has denied in advance that which it is supposed to explore" (p. 187), trying to explain away the prophetic experience rather than elucidate it. He believes this to be a reductive approach to prophecy that makes it "too irrelevant to justify the effort of analysis" (p. 189). The prophets developed moral and social ideas of great importance, and at least some were listened to by their contemporaries, which Heschel believes would have been unlikely if they had appeared to be seriously disturbed.

Heschel objects to the idea that prophetic inspiration begins in the imagination or in the unconscious or that it is based on the prophet's personal psychology; he insists that the essence of the prophetic consciousness is that it is transcendent. However, Heschel ignores the fact that numinous experience of the objective psyche feels like—and is—the experience of a level of consciousness that is transcendent to the ego. Numinous imagery feels quite different from personal material, which is why the prophets felt they were in contact with divine otherness or the voice of God.

Heschel describes the prophet as one who can move into a "mysterious realm" and be able to return to consensual reality and apply what he has seen to the ordinary world, in contrast to the psychotic who cannot easily return to ordinary reality. This is a restatement of the idea that the mystic swims in the same deep waters (of the unconscious) in which the psychotic drowns.[4]

For Jungian psychology, these waters, Heshel's mysterious realm, are the objective psyche. It is true that some individuals experience this level transiently and re-emerge for the better. The fact that we call these episodes psychotic, and see them as due to illness, is only a modern prejudice; they can also be seen as the psyche's attempt at self-healing or even as prophetic states (Perry, 2011). At the time of the prophets, the spirit of the age dictated that such states might reveal the will of the gods. The shamans of many cultures have the same ability to move between ego consciousness and the spiritual dimension of the psyche.

Heschel notes that William James and other writers believed that spiritual experience arises from the unconscious, but Heschel believes that this idea would stamp the prophets as "deceived deceivers" (p. 201) and would not explain the mystery because the notion of the unconscious is too "wide and vague." In contrast, Jung's idea is that the numinous imagery that arises from the archetypal unconscious is indistinguishable from the experience of the divine. From this point of view, the prophets were not being deceptive; they were unusually permeable to the archetypal unconscious.

The personality of the prophet is sometimes very distinct, such as in the case of Jeremiah, who shares his depression, anguish, and struggles.[5] He was unhappy about his role as a prophet, saying things like "Cursed be the day on which I was born!" (20:14). He is often referred to as a prophet of doom, and he seems to have been tortured by his ministry: "I have become a laughingstock all the day; everyone mocks me" (20: 7). Jeremiah believed he had been destined from the womb to be a prophet (1: 5). He said he did not know how to speak because of his youth (1: 6), but Yhwh "touched his mouth," putting words into it, until he felt God's word as a "burning fire" in his heart. He sometimes felt abandoned by God: "I sat alone, because thy hand was upon me" (15: 17). He was often lonely, hopeless, and afraid, even though God promised to make him "a fortified wall of bronze" and reassured him that "they will not prevail over you" (15: 20). His anguish and depression are very clear: "Woe is me, my mother, that you bore me, a man of strife and contention to the whole land! I have not lent, not have I borrowed, yet all of them curse me" (15: 10). He goes on: "Why is my pain unceasing, my wound incurable, refusing to be healed?" (15: 18). He felt surrounded by people who plotted against him (18: 18), and even his family turned against him. Of course, he asked God: "Why does the way of the wicked prosper? / Why do all those who are treacherous thrive?" (12: 1). He felt deceived by God (20: 7), who seemed to put him in an impossible position. At times, he identifies with the sins of the people: "we have sinned against thee" (14: 7), but he is also filled with "the wrath of the Lord" (6: 11), as if God's anger is his own. His attributes his angry imprecations toward the people as God's anger, but they seem to be expressions of his own rage that is attributed to God. He sounds as if he has an introjective depression and a harsh superego, which he experiences as the critical voice of God. He projects the harshness of his inner critic onto his image of God, as if God's anger is directed at both the people and Jeremiah himself.

Most interpreters of this book speak of a dialog between Yhwh and Jeremiah. An alternative to this literal sense of Jeremiah's experience is to see it as an internal dialog with non-ego levels of the unconscious, as a series of active imaginations in Jung's sense of that term. That is, Jeremiah's prophecies actually emerge from his own dialog with the unconscious projected onto Yhwh. Jeremiah attributed the emergence of this material as inspired communication from Yhwh because it seemed autonomous and other than his ego, which is characteristic of material that emerges during active imagination. The only possible interpretation available to Jeremiah was in terms of his cultic background. Merkur (2004) sees Jeremiah as primarily engaged in profound reveries that are analogous to lucid dreams. He believes that Jeremiah's experiences of prophecy were demonstrably different than auto-hypnotic phenomena, hallucinations, obsessions, conversion symptoms, and the like. Merkur sees Jeremiah's prophecies as wish-fulfilling.

Ezekiel

The book of Ezekiel has had a significant effect on the Jewish and Christian traditions. The book is often dated to the sixth century BCE, but it is sometimes thought to have been edited hundreds of years after Ezekiel's death, so the text cannot reliably be attributed to the historical figure himself. Any "diagnosis" is therefore restricted to the description in the text and does not necessarily describe a specific man.

The possibility of mental illness has often been raised in the case of Ezekiel because he exhibited bizarre behavior and frequently claimed to hear the voice of God. In one of his visions (Ezek. chapters 1 and 10), he saw a great cloud of light with lightening flashing within it. In the cloud were what looked like four figures with human forms, each with four faces and four wings. The noise of their beating wings was like the sound of an army. Each had the face of a man, a lion, a bull, and an eagle. There was a wheel beside each figure, and the rims of the wheels were full of eyes. Whenever the beings moved, the wheels moved with them. Over them was an expanse of crystal, and above that was something resembling a throne with a figure that had the appearance of a man but was surrounded by fire and radiance. It appeared to Ezekiel to be the glory of the Lord, so he fell on his face. A voice told him to speak the word of God to the rebellious people of Israel, even if they refused to listen to him. He was given a scroll (perhaps describing his commission) and told to eat it, and it tasted as sweet as honey (3: 3). In the subsequent tradition, his vision was seen as the descent of God on a throne or in a chariot, surrounded by angels, and it became a source of inspiration in the Jewish mystical tradition. Perhaps this was either a numinous dream or an elaborate pareidolia in a cloud formation, reminiscent of people who saw the face of Satan in the dust cloud billowing out of the World Trade Center when it collapsed. It has also been suggested that Ezekiel saw a UFO. The vision is amplified in detail by Edinger (1986), who sees it as an experience of the Self in the form of a gigantic mandala. Jung (CW 11, para. 665) suggested that because of the human form on the throne, Ezekiel grasped "in a symbol, the fact that Yahweh was drawing closer to man."

Ezekiel has often been seen as psychotic. He experienced command hallucinations. He was told by God to "eat this scroll that I give to you and fill your stomach with it" (3: 3). He was told to shave his head (5: 1), dig a hole in a wall, and carry baggage through it (12: 5). He sometimes tries not to listen to these voices. At one point, he was told to lie motionless on his left side for 390 days and then on his right side for 40 days with the sensation of bands around him. One of the few conditions in which this might occur is catatonia, but the textual description may be some kind of allegory rather than a literal event. Ezekiel also had intermittent episodes of mutism (3: 22–26; 24: 25–27: 33: 21), whose duration is not clear. He was told to cook his food using feces baked into barley (4: 12). All this is suggestive of schizophrenia, although the evidence for this diagnosis is not definite and has been debated. One proponent of this diagnosis was Edwin Broome (1946), who sees Ezekiel as a paranoid schizophrenic exhibiting periods of catatonic stupor. This diagnosis would explain his feelings of being persecuted, his hallucinations, his mutism, and his lying motionless for long periods. However, Broome does not believe this diagnosis disqualifies Ezekiel's religious contribution to the world. Broome's paper has never been adequately refuted, although it has been criticized for treating Ezekiel as if he were a contemporary, ignoring the meaning of his behavior and speech in their historical context and the possibility that the text has been radically edited. This is a valid criticism, but at the same time, the text is regarded as theologically valuable enough to be in the biblical canon. Based on the received text, we cannot answer the question of whether Ezekiel was receiving authentic divine revelations. It is important to remember that even if he was psychotic, his experience of divinity may have been genuine.

George Stein (2009, 2010) offered evidence that Ezekiel exhibited catatonia and first-rank symptoms of schizophrenia, such as thought insertion, the sensation that one's thoughts are not one's own. In 38: 10, we read: "Thus says the Lord God: On that day thoughts will come into your mind and you will devise an evil scheme." Passivity experiences, or the feeling that one's body is being controlled by an outside will, are suggested by "the Spirit entered into me and set me upon my feet; and I heard him speaking to me" (2: 2). The possibility that he heard voices talking about him is also suggested by "your people are talking together about you by the walls and at the doors of the houses" (33: 30). However, all these verses can be interpreted in ways that are not pathological, as Stein acknowledges. Ezekiel (37) reported that in a visionary state he witnessed the coming to life of a valley of dry bones. This may have been a hallucination, or it may have been meant allegorically to indicate the resurrection of his people. The fact that on one occasion Ezekiel was bound with cords to prevent him leaving his home (Ezek. 3: 24–26) may have been the result of his being restrained because he was seen to be disturbed.

An alternative diagnosis of TLE was suggested by Eric Altschuler (2002). As well as Ezekiel's visionary episodes, Altschuler believes that Ezekiel demonstrates the characteristics of the inter-ictal personality described by Geschwind (1983). In support of this diagnosis, Altschuler points out that Ezekiel was obsessively concerned about the minute details of the blueprint of the temple (40–42) and with the implications of religion for daily life. He also displays repetitive hypergraphia—the book is the fourth longest in the Bible, only 3% shorter than all of Genesis. Altschuler believes that Ezekiel's prophecies are "aggressive and pedantic" (p. 562), and he has a "sticky" personality, shown by his taking the reader on an obsessively detailed tour of the temple. He is known to have had multiple fainting or falling episodes (1: 28; 3: 23;43: 34). Altschuler prefers the diagnosis of TLE because he believes that it is unlikely that an individual with schizophrenia would have been able to maintain his ministry.

Ezekiel is famous for his vituperative rage, sadistic fantasies, and obscene sexual slurs that he puts into the mouth of Yhwh, thus avoiding personal responsibility. This is especially seen in chapter 23: 19–20, where he compares the people of Israel to harlots whose paramours had genitals the size of donkeys and emissions like those of horses. Ezekiel shows a great deal of rage toward women. He harshly criticizes, in great detail, various women he believes to be harlots. This material has been interpreted by David Halperin (1993), who applies Freudian theory to the book of Ezekiel, although his approach also uses historical and philological sources. Halperin offers support for earlier work suggesting that Ezekiel was schizophrenic. Halperin believes that Ezekiel was dominated by a pathological loathing and dread of female sexuality that are symbolized by his vision of the temple polluted by idolatry, and by talking of Israel and Jerusalem as promiscuous wives. Halperin believes that Ezekiel's mother sacrificed him, allowing him to be sexually abused by her lover or husband. Halperin sees Ezekiel's periodic paralysis and his impulse to eat food cooked with human excrement as the result of memories of childhood neglect at the hands of this dominant male, which helps to explain the cruelty and savagery of Ezekiel's image of God. Halperin's approach suffers from the usual difficulty in trying to recover an accurate description of the man from a text that has been multiply edited. He demonstrates the well-known danger that the writer may project his own preconceptions onto the material and make the text fit his theory. However, Ezekiel's language is so extreme, so contemptuous of women, and so violent that it demands some kind of psychological explanation, and it is inevitable that this will be biased in terms of a certain theory. Ezekiel's behavior has always been something of an embarrassment to orthodox believers, and theological commentators are ambivalent about him. Some see him as a major spiritual figure. H. Wheeler Robinson (1948) acknowledges Ezekiel's psychological peculiarities but suggests that this may have been the medium through which Ezekiel contacted God. Robinson believes that the very notion of psychopathology does not pertain to the spiritual realm.

However, this is not so; the presence of psychopathology and a fragile ego may make the individual particularly permeable to the transpersonal level of the psyche.

Dereck Daschke (1999) believes that Ezekiel suffered from post-traumatic stress disorder as a result of the trauma of the Babylonian Exile. Daschke also sees Ezekiel as suffering from prolonged mourning, melancholia, and overwhelming heartsickness or homelessness. Daschke points out that Ezekiel was a priest who had been forcibly torn away from his own land and his temple, then exiled in a strange country that worshipped strange gods. Ezekiel assumed that the defeat of his nation was a punishment for the failure of Israel to abide by their convent with God and their worship of other gods such as Tammuz (Ezek. 6: 9; 8: 14). This was the only way he could make sense of the catastrophic defeat his nation had suffered. Daschke believes that the vision of the divine chariot gave Ezekiel what he most needed, an experience of the God who had apparently not defended his temple. Daschke sees Ezekiel's vision of a restored temple as an attempt at self-healing, the development of a new worldview, and an idealized expectation of the future.

David Garber also looks at Ezekiel in terms of trauma theory. In Garber's (2004) review of the literature on the effects of trauma on a society, he notes the frequent reports of intrusive hallucinations and dreams among survivors of trauma. These phenomena are also seen in survivors' written testimonies to the trauma, which are often repetitive, trying to talk about what is impossible to describe. Ezekiel's community was trying to come to terms theologically with the loss of their temple and homeland, in the process blaming itself for the calamity, and Garber (p. 224) sees "both levels of communal and individual trauma" in Ezekiel. However, though clearly relevant, trauma theory would not account for some of Ezekiel's more bizarre behavior.

Ezekiel's community took him seriously in spite of his bizarre behavior, and the book was canonized in post-exilic Judaism. Whatever his mental state, his preaching must have resonated with the trauma of the Babylonian Exile following the fall of Jerusalem. It is not clear that Ezekiel's contemporaries saw him as mentally ill, at least not all the time, and it is possible that his behavior was only a dramatic attempt to get people to listen to him. Perhaps his extreme (by our standards) attitude to women resonated with the prevalent cultural misogyny. Believers may therefore argue that the psychopathology in the book does not diminish its religious value.

The response of the prophet's contemporaries depended on whether they believed he had a special connection to God. Some prophets conveyed the idea that they could intercede with God when evil threatened. Even today, whenever there is a serious social crisis, modern evangelists and preachers make similar promises or threats based on their claim to know what God wants and how God is feeling, which tend to coincide with their own interpretations of the Bible. However, their societal context no longer gives them the authority of the biblical prophets.

Mental illness and the casting out of demons

Jesus' healings in the Bible often involved his casting out of demons or evil spirits (e.g., Matt. 28–32; 9: 32). He also seems to have believed in the reality of Satan (Jn 8: 44), who is reported to have tempted Jesus (Matt. 4: 1–11). Jesus' followers believed that his name gave them power over demons (Lk. 10: 1; 17–20). The New Testament is replete with examples of Satan tempting people to sin (e.g., Luke 22: 31; Acts 5: 1–3; 1 Timothy 1:20). Christians were warned that "Your enemy the devil prowls around like a roaring lion looking for someone to devour" (1 Peter 5: 8) and "the whole world is in the power of the evil one" (1 Jn 5: 19).

Reports of possession by demons were fairly common at the time of the early Church. Traditionally, the Devil was described using features of pagan fertility gods such as Pan, who was depicted with horns, a tail, or hooves. In the Middle Ages and during the Reformation era, the mythology of Satanism and witchcraft further developed, including the idea that a satanic conspiracy was trying to destroy Christianity. The notion of possession by demons was a standard explanation for mental illness. Demons were thought to enter the body and control it. At this time, demonic possession was said to be more common among women than men, so that skeptics suggest that the phenomenon was a way of asserting women's limited social power. Demonic possession was goal-directed. It allowed the expression of blasphemy, the venting of frustration and aggression, and sexual behavior that otherwise was forbidden but could be attributed to the demon rather than the individual. Nuns possessed in this way gained attention and even respect, so epidemics of possession periodically swept through medieval religious communities (Spanos, 1996). In the twentieth century, accusations of Satan worship and ritual satanic abuse of children revived. An increase in reports of demonic possession occurred at the same time.

In terms of modern diagnostic criteria, the states of demonic possession described in the Bible may have been psychotic, hysterical conversion disorders, a manifestation of dissociative identity disorder, complex epileptic seizures, or the result of possession by a powerful unconscious complex. Modern psychology dismisses the existence of demons or demonic oppression, but states of possession are still reported in some religious subcultures (Gallagher, 2009). So too are exorcisms, sometimes known as deliverance, a faith-based form of mental health treatment among Pentecostal and other charismatic Christian groups (Mercer, 2013) who believe that the world is affected by supernatural agents of both Satan and God. Some of these groups describe the situation in terms of spiritual warfare. Explanations of mental illness in terms of demonic possession may be unhelpful if they discourage secular treatment. A small number of Roman Catholic clergy perform exorcisms, having first excluded cases of physical or mental illness. These clergy recognize possession using various criteria, such as the possessed person's ability to speak a hitherto-unknown language, the ability to see future or hidden events, hatred of sacred objects such as holy water or a crucifix, or revulsion to prayer. Possessed people are said to exhibit bizarre bodily and facial postures, scatological language, cursing and blaspheming, violence, changes in the voice, displays of unusual strength, and lasting personality changes. Some of these behaviors seemed to be shaped by the social expectations of the group in which they occur, which can be learned from hearing reports of possession and from the group's clergy. Belief in demonic possession can lead to very violent exorcisms that have led to death. (Demonic possession and the direct experience of demons are described by Corbett, 2018.)

Freud (1923) described a (seventeenth century) case in which a man alleged he made a bargain with the devil, whom Freud believed represented a substitute for the man's ambivalent relationship with his father, who had recently died. Freud believed that phenomena referred to as demonic are derived from the projection of repressed impulses. Modern psychoanalysts believe that destructive parts of the psyche are externalized by projecting them either onto other people or onto mythological figures such as Satan. Gavin Ivey (1993) sees the developmental nucleus of the experience of demonic possession as the internalization of a pathogenic parental object, living inside the individual as a kind of subpersonality, what Jung calls a complex. The dynamic of Satan worship might be due to a preference for identifying with such an internalized, sadistic bad object rather than feeling like a helpless victim. Then, the vulnerable parts of the self are projected onto others, and "satanic" deviant behavior, including destructive rage and hatred, is normalized by group involvement. Needless to say, critics of the psychodynamic approach see notions such as complexes and internal bad objects as mythological in their own right.

Notes

1 Goads were used to force oxen in a particular direction. The metaphor means that Saul had been trying to resist divine will and struggling against his attraction to Jesus.
2 Psychological stickiness refers to the individual's constant ruminating on one topic combined with obsessional preoccupations about possible future catastrophes.
3 Heschel's idea is in stark contrast to Maimonides' notion of an absolutely transcendent God who is independent of humanity.
4 Heschel denies the similarity between mysticism and prophecy; he believes that the Hebrew Prophets were unique.
5 The story of Jeremiah is often said to have been written about 600 BCE. It may be a later ideological composition composed of multiple redactions, but here I am describing the personality of the prophet as depicted in the canonical text.

Chapter 8

The psychodynamics of religions' emphasis on sin

In the Bible, the word "sin" is typically used to mean that the individual is guilty of a deviation from a religious, moral, or ethical code.[1] Religions specify what constitutes a sin in terms of their own doctrine and dogma. Typically, sin is considered to be a form of rebellion against God's law, to which the traditions all believe they have privileged access, and all want to uphold. God is often seen to be personally involved in punishing sin.

Sin is often a problem created by religious traditions themselves, when they define normal behavior and feelings (especially sexual) as forbidden. They then offer their own forms of solution, thus creating both the illness and its remedy. Christian theology sees human nature as intrinsically sinful and has tended to treat our instinctual nature and the body as a potential enemy. In his seminars on Nietzsche's *Thus Spake Zarathustra*, Jung writes that the redemption of the body has been lacking in Christianity, where the body has "always been depreciated" (1998, p. 193). Jung pointed out that the contemporary individual has heard more than enough about sin and guilt "and wants rather to know how he is to reconcile himself with his own nature" (CW 11, para. 523). Becoming a Christian does not automatically deal with shadow material, in spite of St. Paul's idea that one then becomes a new creation (2 Cor. 5: 17). Some Christians project shadow material onto people whose sexual behavior they believe to be forbidden by the Bible, such as gay people. This produces a well-known problem; the repressed shadow becomes stronger and more dangerous in the individual's unconscious.

The subjective sense of being sinful is closely related to feelings of shame or guilt. My thesis in this chapter is that the guilt and shame that originate in parental criticism during childhood can easily be appropriated in the service of religious notions of sinfulness. There is often a parental quality to religious ideas about sin, as if obedience to the divine parent ensures his protection and love, whereas his anger and punishment follow disobedience. A parental complex is also reflected in the need to work to obtain God's favor by good behavior, although belief in the idea of predestination[2] may cause some anxiety in this respect, since in this view God may ordain an outcome over which one has no control.

DOI: 10.4324/9781003537007-9

Christian theological notions of sin

The notion of sin is central to Christian theology. If it is true that Jesus came into the world to save humanity from sin, it is important to understand the way the tradition understands sin. This is usually behavior that is thought to disrupt one's connection to God, or it is produced by disobedience to God. Sin is taken very seriously; Ephesians 2: 1–5 and Colossians 2: 13 suggest that being sinful produces a kind of spiritual death. The Christian tradition has often used raw power and violence to enforce its own definition of sin, in order to maintain submission to ecclesiastical authority.[3]

According to the doctrine of original sin, human beings are born sinful even if we are unconscious of any malfeasance, because of the behavior of Adam in the Garden of Eden. The textual basis for this idea is found in Romans 5: 12–14, where Paul says, "sin came into the world through one man" and "one man's trespass led to condemnation for all men" (Romans 5: 18–19). That is, for Paul and subsequent developers of the idea of original sin, humanity's sinful nature is not simply a matter of the individual's behavior; it is the result of Adam's disobedience, which has continued to affect all subsequent generations. It seems incredible that the behavior of one of humanity's mythic ancestors could be believed to be responsible for the ongoing sinfulness of the whole human race.

Paul believed not merely that sin was something he did but that sin "dwells within me…in my flesh" (Rom. 7: 17–18). That is, he felt as if sin is in his body. He saw sin as a power that enslaved him or held him captive (Rom. 7: 23). He writes that no one is righteous (Rom. 3: 10). To the psychologist, this sounds as if he felt chronically bad and guilty in a way that is characteristic of an introjective depression and a punitive superego. This dynamic is generalized and projected into his theology by insisting that all human beings are all guilty before God. We can therefore see the great importance to him of the idea that forgiveness is offered through Jesus Christ (Rom. 8: 3–4), an idea that softens his harsh conscience and self-criticism. This dynamic operates in Christians who are attracted to the tradition for just this reason. They unconsciously project a tyrannical parent onto their image of God, who they imagine loves them but is also constantly criticizing them. They are relieved by the notion that forgiveness and redemption are possible.

In the interpretation of Romans 5: 12–14 by St. Augustine, sin is again traced back to the disobedience of Adam and Eve, which he too saw as a historical event.[4] According to Augustine, the soul becomes tainted by entering a body. Because of the Fall of Adam, his sin is transmitted sexually to subsequent generations, so human beings are all conceived and born in sin, which means there is a universal need for salvation. We inherit the sin of our remote ancestors. The fatal flaw in human nature is pride, which was one of the reasons that Adam and Eve sinned. Traditional Christianity insists that because human beings are intrinsically sinful, the only way to be in right relationship to

God is through belief in Christ. He takes on the burden of human sin and eliminates it by being a sacrificial victim on behalf of humanity.

It is worth mentioning the alternative to Augustine's view of Adam and Eve proposed by the second-century Bishop Irenaeus, who suggested that their behavior was simply due to child-like immaturity. The Greek Church Fathers held a similar view. The British monk Pelagius had the heretical view that human beings have the potential to live in accord with God by their own efforts, without the need for the grace offered by Christ. However, Augustine's view remained the dominant opinion.

For some (not all) theologians, Paul's passages in Romans support the idea that human beings have an inborn defect that makes them disposed to sin. Sin is somehow at the root of human nature, which we cannot improve without divine intervention. In some Christian denominations, the doctrine of original sin leads to the necessity for infant baptism.

Sin in the Hebrew Bible

The Jewish tradition did not develop an idea of original sin, although in the Hebrew Bible the idea of intrinsic sinfulness is found in places such as Psalm 51: 5 ("Behold, I was brought forth in iniquity/ and in sin did my mother conceive me") and also in the idea that "every inclination of the thoughts of the human heart was only evil all the time" (Gen. 6: 5). In the Hebrew bible, sin implies behavior that disobeys the laws of the covenant or the cultic rules. This behavior alienates the individual from God. Sin may be due to failure to properly adhere to a ritual practice such as the Levitical dietary laws or temple sacrifices (Lev. 4–5), failure in one's duty to God (Ezra 9:6), or other kinds of transgression of a taboo such as the worship of idols (2 Chron. 24: 18). Once threatened, the bond to God had to be reestablished through temple sacrifice.

In the Hebrew Bible, sin is typically attributed to a "stubborn and wicked heart" (Jer. 5: 23), meaning characterologically ingrained disobedience. Perhaps such phrases are one of the sources of Paul's emphasis on innate human sinfulness. The biblical Yhwh is very concerned that people obey his commandments, often with extreme punishment for disobedience, suggesting that disobedience is a narcissistic injury to his grandiosity.[5] In an extraordinary display of collective punishment for sin, Joshua 7 describes a case in which not only is a guilty man burned and stoned to death but his family and flocks were also killed. The transmission of guilt is carried to the third and fourth generation (Exod. 20: 5). The Hebrew Prophets and the Psalms constantly stress the sins of the people and the psychological burden it inflicts (Isa. 59: 9–15; 64: 5–6; Jer. 14: 7; Psa. 38; Psa. 32: 3–5). However, later rabbinic Judaism has no doctrine of vicarious atonement analogous to the Christian notion of Jesus as a substitute sacrifice; in Judaism, a sin has to be expiated by individual atonement and repentance. This tradition denies the notion of permanent spiritual corruption transmitted by Adam and only admits the existence of an evil inclination in tension with free will.

Developmental psychodynamics of guilt and shame

Theological strictures repeated often enough become incorporated into the individual's conscience and seamlessly blend with shame and guilt dynamics that originated in childhood.[6] The idea that we are prone to sin takes advantage of the feelings of guilt or shame that are produced when a child contravenes a parental instruction. It may feel that parental love is conditional on the child's behavior being in accord with parental values. Harsh parental judgment makes children feel guilty or ashamed, and this dynamic is easily transferred to the notion that an angry Father God is watching and judging one's behavior. Guilt and shame are evoked when a child is subject to abuse, devaluation, humiliation, devaluation, or threats of parental withdrawal.

Shame, the sense that one is defective in some way, is often a response to parental failure to respond to the child's feelings in an attuned, appreciative manner. Shame occurs when a child is constantly told that he or she is no good or if the parent gives the message that the child is unwanted or his or needs are too much. Chronic failure to respond in an attuned way to the child leads to a fragile sense of self and a painful sense of internal emptiness. Intense, persistent, guilt-inducing parental criticism that is internalized leads to a punitive superego, producing constant internal criticism, the sense that whatever one does is not good enough. Some people suffer from a combination of shame and guilt, which is a particularly painful state of mind in which awareness of a misdeed is generalized into negative feelings about oneself. Individuals who experienced these childhood dynamics are particularly prone to resonate with theological notions that he or she is intrinsically sinful in some way.[7] Unfortunately, some branches of Christianity insist on making people feel chronically guilty. There is a vicious and even ruthless quality to this theology that is completely incompatible with Christian teachings of love and forgiveness.

Christian religious traditions that insist on the individual's innate sinfulness resonate deeply with sectors of the psyche that retain memories of guilt and shame from childhood, which provide fertile soil for theological ideas such as original sin and the need for redemption. Jewish ritual laws become deeply ingrained family and community expectations, leading to guilt or shame if they are not followed carefully. Because of these dynamics, religious people in general tend to be particularly prone to guilt (Luyten et al., 1998).

In several religious traditions, sexuality is a major source of feelings of guilt or shame and accusations of sinfulness. Religions typically insist on limiting sexual expression, sometimes in ways that ignore human biology and normal sexual feelings, producing a further set of reasons to feel guilty, ashamed, or "sinful." Telling people not to be angry (Matt. 5: 22) and to not even think lustful thoughts (Matt. 5: 28) is an unhealthy prescription for the repression of emotion that ignores the fact that these feelings are natural and arise involuntarily. These teachings ignore the important distinction between feelings and action.

Many biblical passages forbid sexual immorality (1 Cor. 5: 9–11; 6: 9–10; Heb. 13:4), but the nature of immorality is defined by the tradition. Insistence on biblical standards of sexual morality often produces guilt about not living up to these standards, so that guilt may occur among religious people because of normal sexual thoughts and fantasies (Daniluk & Browne, 2008). Premarital chastity and sexual "purity," understood in the traditions' own terms, are greatly valued (Rae, 2018). In some religious families, any deviations from the tradition's standards are a major source of guilt or shame, often leading to sexual anxiety and reduced sexual enjoyment. Sexual guilt and shame may become deeply internalized during childhood and adolescence (Mayers et al., 2003), producing developmental damage to the sense of self, still seen in psychotherapy with current or erstwhile members of religious groups with rigid standards of sexuality. The "purity" messages of evangelical churches have told women that they provoke men's lust, an accusation that has had a harmful effect on women when they are regarded as sexually dangerous to men (Klein, 2018) and blamed for men's inability to control themselves.

It is often true that there is an association between religious participation and emotional well-being, but when religions instill unnecessary guilt and shame by claiming that normal behavior, thoughts, or feelings are sinful, religions cause considerable emotional harm. An extreme form of this problem is seen in obsessive-compulsive individuals who become scrupulously adherent to religious principles, leading to excessive prayer, extreme self-denial, frequent confession, and minute attention to the details of religious rituals. This condition is driven by intense anxiety about being sinful or about angering God (Olatunji et al., 2007). Many psychotherapists are familiar with individuals from fundamentalist backgrounds who are tormented by fears that they will go to hell because of their thoughts and actions. In these individuals, the word "sin" is almost synonymous with "evil." Such self-accusation is often based on nothing more than fundamentalist interpretations of biblical standards of behavior.

In general, what religious traditions refer to as sin is any behavior that the tradition believes would be disapproved of by God. Penance and some kind of ritual atonement are then necessary to reestablish the connection to God, and since the tradition prescribes the required form of atonement, the individual is effectively controlled by the institution. This dynamic also takes advantage of human attachment and selfobject needs. When a figure such as Jesus has become an important selfobject, the threat of the loss of connection to him because of guilt or shame may cause considerable distress.

The moral standards of a tradition are often imposed by a hierarchy or by senior members of the institution who may even represent themselves as speaking for God. Then, in an extraordinary projection of their own hubris, the hierarchy may accuse the congregant of sinfulness due to excessive pride.

Religious traditions often insist that theirs is the only way to be reconciled with God. Erich Fromm (1955) pointed out that having made their congregations feel sinful, the hierarchy or priesthood then offers pardon and expiation for the guilt feelings that the tradition itself has engendered. This is an important type of spiritual abuse that may cause lifelong distress. This process is especially true of forms of fundamentalism that stress divine judgment rather than love, usually accompanied by the insistence that their own tradition is the only valid one. Fundamentalism is partly a reaction to a conscious or unconscious sense that the grip of a traditional belief system is loosening, so these beliefs must be held onto ever more tightly. This is especially important when a tradition serves to provide a source of structure, identity, certainty, and safety that otherwise would be lacking. Fundamentalist insistence on a set of dogmatic beliefs is often a way to deal with emotional vulnerability. It reflects psychological rigidity and defends against doubt. Fundamentalism is also a way to cope with the grief produced by the loss of the authority of the traditional God-image and a response to doubts about Christianity in the larger community, which sometimes gives rise to the exaggerated claim that the tradition is under attack. It is easier to see the attack coming from others than to acknowledge one's own subjective doubts.

One of the problems faced by Christian missionaries was that the people they contacted did not realize they were intrinsically sinful. They had to be convinced of this and of their need for a savior. This was necessary because the missionaries (and some contemporary Christians) believe that anyone who, having heard about Jesus, does not accept him as their personal savior will go to hell. This kind of dogmatism requires splitting humanity into all good and all bad. Convincing others to join in one's beliefs serves to defend against personal doubt.

Today, one mainly hears the word sin in religious circles rather than in secular culture, where sin is no longer seen as an intrinsic part of human nature. Much behavior that was once considered sinful is now regarded as normal, and even real evil is understood to have many psychological and social explanations and cannot be dismissed as innate (Corbett, 2018). The notion that sin resulting from the disobedience of a mythic ancestor has been transmitted to subsequent generations is an example of the literalization and historicization of a myth, which has been used to justify the need for atonement and the necessity for Church involvement to achieve forgiveness.

Theories of atonement

The central claim of Christianity is that Jesus' death redeemed human beings by atoning for their sins and reconciling people with God, somehow resetting the relationship between God and humanity that Adam and Eve had disrupted.

Much debate has centered on how this is achieved, why such atonement is necessary, and whether atonement could have been brought about in some other way.

The early Christian theory of atonement suggested that Christ's death paid a ransom to the powers of evil, which had been holding humanity in thrall. Humanity had become estranged from God as a result of sin. (This idea was developed by Origen, a third-century Christian theologian.) The patristic tradition believed that Christ's death defeated the powers of evil. Perhaps because this assertion clearly did not materialize in practice, later theologians such as Anselm (1033–1109 CE) and John Calvin (1509–1564) developed a satisfaction theory, in which Christ voluntarily took on punishment for the sins of humanity to satisfy God's anger, because human sin incurs a debt that humanity could never repay. A suitable substitute had to be found. Only Christ's death could provide adequate restitution. For Anselm, divine honor had been injured, and justice and satisfaction demand that atonement be made, because universal order rests on the maintenance of divine honor, and God had been offended. The projective nature of this idea, as if God has "honor" at stake, hardly needs comment; divinity is not a human potentate who needs to protect his dignity.

Anselm believed that humanity would be saved if they believed in Jesus. It is worth pausing to note the mythic context in which Anselm developed his idea. In his *Cur Deus Homo* (Why God became man), Anselm wrote that Adam and Eve were placed in the Garden of Eden entirely sinless with the purpose of resisting the persuasion of the devil, resistance that would honor God. Since they failed, they dishonored God, thus incurring a debt, and it is sinful to not give God what is owed to him. This produces a situation of cosmic imbalance, so that all people are born into debt. That is, for Anselm, as for St. Paul and Augustine, the notion of original sin is built on a mythic basis that requires taking the Garden of Eden story literally.

The satisfaction theory of atonement was refined by Thomas Aquinas (1225–1274), who also believed that Christ's death acted as a sacrificial propitiation on behalf of sinners. His theory improved on the earlier idea that the devil justly enslaves sinners and Christ's passion was the ransom paid to buy their freedom. Aquinas believed that the devil holds sinners unjustly, and the price to redeem them from bondage is paid to God rather than to the devil. For Aquinas, there is no injustice in God's allowing the devil to cause sinners to suffer when they deserve it, as a punishment. This is an obvious anthropomorphism, as if God is so sensitive that he needs to be paid a price to compensate him for offenses committed against him. Aquinas' idea also requires literal belief in the Devil. It is noteworthy that in Aquinas' account, infants who die unbaptized are excluded from heaven. (Needless to say, the sacraments of the Church are essential to prevent this.) The satisfaction theory was dominant from the eleventh century until the Enlightenment. Later theologians (such as Gustaf Aulén in the 1930s) reinterpreted the notion that Jesus paid a ransom in terms of the Christus Victor (Christ the Victor) theory, which sees Christ as a triumphant rescuer of humanity from the powers of evil. This was an alternative to the notion of vicarious satisfaction and also to the moral influence theory, which had been developed in the twelfth century by Abelard, who saw Christ as an example of self-sacrificial obedience to God.[8]

In whatever way it is understood, the doctrine of atonement is at the heart of Christian theology, but it is controversial because of its archaic nature in which an innocent man receives the punishment due to the guilty, making God sound barbaric. It does not make sense for a loving Creator to show his mercy toward humanity by allowing the agonizing death of an innocent. Accordingly, some theologians have abandoned the penal theory of atonement because it seems contradictory to imagine a loving God who demands such a sacrifice, and the idea that the creator of the entire universe requires a single human sacrifice makes no sense. Traditional views of the atonement can be seen to justify brute force and submission to authority, with damaging consequences for victims of abuse who are told to suffer in silence. Atonement theory has been criticized on the grounds that it tends to justify the abuse of women and legitimates child abuse by implying that obedience to Church authorities should not be challenged.

The doctrine of atonement has a judicial quality about it. In defense of this doctrine, traditionalists point out that Christ's sacrifice was not a punishment but an offering or gift of love intended to restore humanity's connection to God that had been severed by Adam's sin. Nevertheless, the fact remains that rather than being truly forgiving, God requires a child sacrifice to restore this connection. This Christian idea of bloody retribution for disobedience and sin continues an earlier theme in the Hebrew Bible, in which God often demands lethal retribution if he is disobeyed, which is why Paul insists that "the wages of sin is death" (Rom. 6: 23). He believed that the blood of Christ saves us from the wrath of God (Rom. 5: 9), just as Hebrews (9: 22) insists that "without the shedding of blood there is no forgiveness of sins." Paul's image of God includes the fact that he is potentially dangerous, presumably related to Yhwh's punitive attitude to being disobeyed, seen in many instances in the Hebrew Bible. This attitude displays the projection of a punitive, all-powerful father image onto Yhwh, who (as Jung pointed out) is a disguised form of the superego. This dynamic is often combined with the projection of the human need for revenge and justice onto Yhwh.

Christ's sacrifice can be seen as an example of the scapegoat motif, which suggests that vicarious punishment has an atoning effect for one's own disobedience. The idea of the scapegoat is therefore a form of magical thinking, as if transferring one's own guilt onto another individual or animal somehow vicariously benefits oneself or the larger community. However, in the eighteenth century, philosopher Immanuel Kant pointed out that any debt incurred by sin is not like a financial debt; it cannot be transferred and is entirely personal. Only the sinner can bear it and no innocent person can assume it on the sinner's behalf (Quinn, 1986). For Kant, vicarious atonement is an unfathomable mystery.

The idea that Jesus is a scapegoat for humanity is still central to Christian thinking, but to many people, it seems to contradict the notion of personal responsibility by allowing Jesus to carry the individual's shadow. The idea that Jesus had to die for the sins of humanity also contradicts the idea that God is moral and loving, since if he is omniscient, he could have found a way to forgive humanity without a brutal sacrifice. Substitutionary atonement has been widely criticized for several other reasons, not least because it depends on the idea of original sin, which may instill a sense of worthlessness or helplessness in people, who then become easier to dominate. The doctrine is obviously unfair since punishment cannot rationally be transferred from a guilty person to an innocent person. A further problem with this doctrine is that some people do not feel sinful or guilty, so this ideology does not resonate with them.

The notion of intrinsic sin and the need for atonement also implies that silent suffering is virtuous, that God is close when we suffer, that suffering is redemptive or salvific, that violence is justified, and that we should love our oppressors because, somehow, we deserve to suffer (Carlson-Brown & Bohn, 1989; Brock & Parker, 2001). Notably, substitutionary atonement does not deal with the human proclivity to continue to sin and does not deal with individual guilt or personal shadow material. Nor does it deal with social evils. However, some defenders of this doctrine believe that penal substitutionary atonement has cosmic as well as individual significance. This remarkably inflated, mythic view assumes that the whole cosmos is in a fallen state because of Adam.

Notes

1 Numbers 5 is a typical biblical list of sinful behavior.
2 Predestination is the doctrine that God has already determined the fate of the individual's soul. God choses who will or will not be saved.
3 The human moral sense is easily coopted by mass movements and political ideologies such as Nazism or violent religious fundamentalism. When one's conscience has been subverted by such an ideology, the religious persecution of heretics or other evils may be perpetrated with a clear conscience or even in obedience to one's conscience.
4 This is not an idea that is compatible with evolutionary theory or modern paleoanthropology, unless the whole human race descended from one Mesopotamian ancestral couple, and Adam's and Eve's rebelliousness was transmitted epigenetically.
5 Charitably, one could see Yhwh's insistence on obedience as the result of pressure by the Self to differentiate itself within human consciousness. However, this would not account for the biblical stories of the devastating punishments that followed disobedience.
6 Here, I understand shame to be a negative evaluation of the self, such that the person feels so damaged or defective that his whole personhood feels bad. Shame occurs when one fails to live up to the expectations of one's ego ideal, the image of oneself one would like to be, or the way one would like to be seen by others. Guilt is not about a defect in the self but about specific behavior, either a misdeed that violated the standards of one's superego or regret about something that was not done that

should have been done. Even imagined actions, or actions we only consider performing, may produce guilt or shame. Guilt may induce a need for reparation, atonement, or confession and may be disproportionate, especially in obsessional people.

7 I currently have a patient whose mother often told her that she could "see the Devil in her eyes." It has been difficult for the patient to see her mother's projection onto her.

8 Peter Abelard was Anselm's contemporary. Abelard rejected the idea that God required a payment to forgive humanity's sins. He argued that if God has already decided to redeem humanity, Christ's crucifixion is not necessary. For Abelard, the cross is a demonstration of God's love for humanity. The crucifixion has also been seen not as necessary for objective reasons such as atonement but in purely subjective terms, affecting the way the believer relates to God when she contemplates the cross.

Chapter 9

The biblical portrayal of Jesus

The charisma of the Jesus of the Gospels

My interest here is to understand how Jesus made such a powerful psychological impression on his followers that they radically changed their lives to be with him, sometimes giving up their families and occupations to do so. They must have had considerable faith in him. To understand his followers' devotion to Jesus, it is tempting to apply contemporary psychological theory to the Gospel's descriptions of him. However, a caveat is in order. It is by now a truism that when people attempt to describe the life and personality of Jesus, the writer's own needs and personality radically color the resulting portrait. Albert Schweitzer (1981) reviewed many of the nineteenth-century attempts to describe the historical Jesus and demonstrated the writers' biases, which were colored by their personal beliefs, their own psychology, and their own biographies. Schweitzer noted that people who searched for the historical Jesus tended to project what they were looking for into the Gospel texts. Schweitzer says of such writers that they breathe into their image of Jesus "all the hate or all the love" of which they are capable (p. 10), indicating the intensity of feeling that this figure induces. Because the Gospels leave so many details unanswered, the story of Jesus is rife with opportunities for transference projections and theological superimpositions onto it. In the end, the image of Jesus held by an individual writer is often the projection of an image of his or her idealized self.

Since Schweitzer, there have been more than forty written portrayals of the historical Jesus (Weaver, 1999), all rooted in particular traditions. These interpretations, combined with what little can be known about him from historical research, are invariably colored by the writer's personal religious commitments and conscious and unconscious feelings about this subject. The resulting portraits are often historical fictions. Most authors look at Jesus through the lens of their faith, beliefs, and a long-established tradition (discussed by Corbett, 2021, and Miller, 1997). The contemporary psychologist wonders about factors such as the developmental effects of being illegitimate in Jesus' society, his estrangement from his mother and family, his conflict with religious authorities, the origin of his intense sense of mission, and the question of whether he

DOI: 10.4324/9781003537007-10

saw himself as the expected Messiah as the Gospels claim. However, there is not enough information in the Gospels to be definitive about these factors, and as Jung pointed out (CW 11, para. 228), our image of the historical Jesus is completely overwhelmed by the archetypal projections onto him as a Godman, savior, redeemer, and healer.

Psychological understanding of the Gospels is complicated by the fact that there is a huge cultural and historical gap between first-century CE Israel and our own time, so it is difficult for us to imagine what it was like to live at that time and place. Translation is another problem. It is not always clear that the original meaning of Jesus' words have been transmitted correctly.[1] The language we use influences how we think about and perceive reality. Language is often used metaphorically, and different cultures use different metaphors which may be difficult to translate or impossible to understand outside their original cultural context. Jesus spoke Aramaic and probably understood Hebrew and perhaps some Greek, which was the original language of the New Testament. The Bible was rendered into Latin in the late fourth century and eventually into vernacular languages during the Reformation. The meaning of some of the words used in the original Greek text of the New Testament is debatable, so that many of today's popular translations of the New Testament (there are hundreds of them in English alone) are clearly interpretations based on the translator's personal preferences. Sometimes, the translator modernizes Jesus while making it seem as if he made statements he was unlikely to have made. In addition, two thousand years of theological speculation and superimposition onto what Jesus said have made it difficult to know much beyond the Christ of faith, who has completely obscured the historical Jesus, whose very existence is still occasionally debated (Doherty, 2005). The Gospels were written between forty and one hundred years after Jesus' death, by people who did not know him personally, partly with the intention of proving that he had been the Messiah. The Gospels were written not as history but to convey the writers' beliefs and to evangelize. For example, the Gospel of John (20: 31) overtly states that "these are written that you may believe that Jesus is the Messiah, the Son of God." The controversial Jesus Seminar tried to separate the historical figure from these kinds of superimpositions onto him by getting rid of St. Paul's elaborations of the story of Jesus, by eliminating the text's apocalyptic imagery and Jesus' messianic claims, and by removing anything attributable to faith alone (Funk, 1997).

Jesus and the psychology of idealization and charisma

It is reasonable to assume that Jesus was a charismatic personality, given the way he attracted devoted followers. Charismatic authority is characteristic of leaders of religious movements.[2] The nature of the charismatic bond between the leader and his followers has been studied a great deal but is incompletely understood. A range of theories are summarized here that seem to be relevant to Jesus' charismatic authority. Charisma usually requires unusual qualities and abilities on the part of the leader that set him apart from ordinary people. These abilities are sometimes considered to be of a supernatural kind (Weber & Eisenstadt, 1968). The charismatic religious leader seems to emanate a connection to the sacred, which may be attributable to his sense of connection to the Self. He also demonstrates and claims spiritual authority. He is self-confident and insists he speaks the truth, even if doing so contradicts or transgresses received practices and traditional religious authority. He is a visionary, able to articulate his followers' unspoken wishes, aggression, strivings, ego ideals, and hopes for the future. Weber noted that periods of social turmoil and distress create the conditions for the emergence of such charismatic leaders (Castelnonovo et al., 2017). In these situations, the charismatic leader seems to make sense of what is otherwise incomprehensible or chaotic. To follow a charismatic leader may be an alternative to feeling helpless. Often, such leaders have superior rhetorical skills and portray themselves in a heroic role. Some followers identify with the leader's goals and values, seeing in him a symbol of their own concerns. They may try to bask in his glory, and when they are with him, they may display abilities beyond the ordinary that are otherwise unavailable to them. These characteristics foster an idealizing transference to such a leader, while some followers see the charismatic leader as a protective, ideal father.

Followers often make considerable sacrifices to be with a charismatic leader, but the follower may not realize he is being drawn into the leader's concerns even to the extent that the follower's personal concerns are forgotten. At the extreme, devoted followers will abide by the leader's claims even if his assertions disagree with the evidence of their own senses. Being with a charismatic individual is stimulating and exciting and makes the individual feel important, special, and seen. It may be difficult for the follower to articulate exactly what makes the charismatic leader so attractive, because charisma appeals not to his mind but to his feelings. Interestingly, charismatic people sometimes say that they do not know the source of their effect on other people, but they say that when they speak, "something comes over me," as if they feel possessed by an outside force. Charisma is the result of a co-created interpersonal field between the leader and his followers; it is not only a quality of the leader himself. Charismatic authority is therefore quite different from bureaucratic authority.

It is worth noting that charismatic people may sometimes be malign figures, such as Adolf Hitler, and they may have a dark or deceitful shadow side. Sometimes, because of an underlying sense of omnipotence that is magnified by the followers' idealization, charismatic people have a self-destructive potential due to a tendency to ignore the limits of reality and a disregard for social constraints.[3] This potential may be relevant to the way in which Jesus did not try to avoid arrest by the Roman authorities, perhaps hoping that a miraculous event would save him.

Kohut (1978) points out that a charismatic personality who becomes an idealized leader usually suffered a dysfunctional childhood. Kohut shows that charismatic leaders are identified with the archaic, grandiose self of infancy, every child's innate need to feel special. Based partly on Kohut's work, Len Oates (1997, 2010) has further described the developmental psychology of charismatic leaders. Both Kohut and Oates see charismatic prophets as trying to recreate a childhood pattern in which the child's mother idealized the child, and the world seems to revolve around the infant.[4] When this illusion is inevitably dispelled, the developing charismatic personality, instead of trying to adapt to the world and in the process allowing his grandiosity to be tempered, tries to make the world conform to his wishes by exercising a mesmerizing influence on others and by striving for mastery. Charismatic people therefore exhibit infantile grandiosity that has not been adequately tempered by reality as it usually is, nor has it been integrated within the rest of the personality.[5] Charismatic leaders often idealize themselves, but also have a tremendous need for continuous affirmation from others to support their grandiosity. This affirmation affirms the leader's unshakable self-righteousness and self-confidence. As a result, he expresses opinions with total certainty in a way that convinces others of the correctness of his ideas (Winer et al., 1984). He feels that his perceptions and ideas are a basis for how others ought to live. The leader's self-confidence and energy attract followers, but the leader often has little regard for their feelings. The leader's self-assuredness makes the individual particularly attractive during times of crisis, when he is able to maintain hope. He becomes an admired, omnipotent selfobject endowed with magical powers who can defend against the helplessness of his followers, who carry the leader's own split off, projected helplessness.

Aberbach (1995) points out that the intensity of his followers' admiration allows the leader to recover the love and wholeness that he lost early in life. Aberbach stresses the importance in the charismatic character of early loss of affectional bonds in childhood, leading to unresolved grief, which makes the leader seek a new identity by finding wholeness and love by creating a "prosthetic relationship" with the outer world. That is, the leader replaces the lost early maternal love with the public's love. The charismatic individual needs to exert charismatic authority over others in order to feel loved. He has an intense need for the admiration of others, and he needs the gratification produced by being the center of his followers' need to idealize him. However, charismatic figures often see their followers as narcissistic extensions of themselves and not as individuals in their own right.

Many followers project onto the charismatic leader their need for an idealized selfobject (Kohut, 1978). According to the Gospel accounts, Jesus was greatly idealized. Here, we face a dilemma. Idealization means an exaggeration of a person's attributes and abilities such that he or she is seen as perfect, strong, special, wise, and even more than human. Qualities of omniscience may be projected onto such a figure. People with unmet needs for an idealizable selfobject are drawn to charismatic leaders who project strength. This kind of idealizing transference is likely to occur in the presence of unrequited longings for such a figure that was not present in childhood. For the skeptic, therefore, the leader's charisma is not necessarily due to a divine gift but the result of the leader's need for mirroring combined with a developmental deficit in the leader's followers, leading to their projection of specialness onto the idealized leader. In Jungian terms, idealization is due to the search for a god, the projection of the Self onto the leader. However, people who see Jesus as literally the incarnate divinity will insist that he actually did have exalted qualities and it is no exaggeration and not simply a matter of idealization to describe him in such elevated terms. In this view, he was deserving of veneration, worship, and awe. A more skeptical reading sees him purely as the subject of an idealizing transference, which means that he met his followers' need for a wise, strong, and unfailing selfobject who can soothe their anxieties, uplift and inspire them, and give them a new sense of direction in life. They no longer feel helpless when under his influence; he empowers them to perform actions they did not realize they were capable of.

Kohut (ibid.) noted a distinction between two types of charismatic personalities: the messianic individual who identifies with an idealized superego and charismatic leaders who identify with a grandiose self. Using this distinction, Oates distinguishes messianic prophets who invoke a transcendent divinity beyond themselves and charismatic prophets who affirm their own spiritual sovereignty. He believes that Jesus belongs to the former group.

The mana personality

An alternative formulation is to see Jesus as a mana personality, a term on which Weber drew in his work on charisma. This Melanesian word describes an extraordinary, magical, mystical, or sacred power that seems to emanate from some individuals, especially figures such as shamans and tribal chieftains. Mana seems to be a form of charisma that appears to give the individual a higher state of consciousness and superior wisdom. These individuals are often fascinating to their followers, leading to archetypal projections onto them. It seems that such individuals are in close touch with the objective psyche, which imbues them with a kind of magnetism. According to Jung (CW 7), this represents an archetypal phase of the individuation process, preceding deeper engagement with the Self. Jung believes it is necessary to overcome this stage because of the risk that when such individuals become inflated, they may develop a savior complex and feel they have a special mission ordained by divine providence. Political leaders such as Hitler exhibit this phenomenon.

Using the examples of Mormonism, Alcoholics Anonymous, and *A Course in Miracles*, Ann Taves (2016) describes the ways in which a charismatic founding figure who possesses unusual abilities, surrounded by a group of collaborators and believers, has led to new religious movements or spiritual paths. She believes that this combination leads to the sense of a guiding presence and new revelations as the founding figure acquires new knowledge that the group attributes to a spiritual source. Taves shows how groups form social identities around such figures and try to keep alive the memory of the founding events.

The image of Jesus in the Gospel stories

It has been difficult to establish how much of the Gospel reports of Jesus' behavior is authentic and how much is a later insertion into the text or the result of changes made by copyists. The Gospels mainly show their authors' opinions about Jesus and not necessarily Jesus' opinions about himself. The Gospel of John reports that he "called God his own Father, making himself equal with God" (5: 18), but when asked at his trial about this, he replied in a non-committal way: "You say that I am" (Luke 22: 70). Whether Jesus thought of himself as a divine being, having existed with God from the beginning of creation, as the Gospel of John claims, is a theological or mythological enhancement of his image that cannot be found in the earlier synoptic texts (Mathew, Mark, and Luke). In the earlier Gospels, it is clear that Jesus was limited to the knowledge and attitudes of his era (e.g., in terms of his beliefs in demons).

Many critics have pointed out that the Gospel stories are more theological texts than they are historical or biographical accounts. The Gospels reflect the beliefs and hopes of the early Christian community. Skeptics believe that early Christians fabricated details of Jesus' life to make doctrinal points. In this view, the Gospel stories are colored by the theology of the authors or the early Church, such as by trying to make the story of Jesus consistent with messianic prophecies of the Hebrew Bible. When one tries to evaluate the historical truth of the Gospels, much depends on whether one believes that the Gospel of John or the Synoptic Gospels are more reliable. The stories about Jesus within these two traditions cannot be harmonized, and there are inconsistencies within and between the three synoptic accounts. For example, Luke 14: 26 insists that no one can be Jesus' disciple unless he hates his father and mother, while Matthew 19: 19 repeats the commandment to honor one's father and mother. In Matthew 7: 1, Jesus tells us not to judge, but he refers to his opponents as dogs and pigs in Matthew 7: 6. Some of these inconsistencies are based on the Gospel authors' personal belief about Jesus. These authors were not aiming for historical accuracy; they were trying to persuade different audiences. The fact that changes to Jesus' actual remarks were made is seen, for example, when Jesus categorically forbids divorce in the Gospel of Mark but allows it in cases of adultery, according to Matthew, showing a readiness to change Jesus' teachings according to local needs.

The Jesus of the Gospel of John is different from the picture found in the synoptic Gospels, and these views of him are different from the description of him in the letters of Paul. These differences have never been well explained, at least to skeptical readers who are not willing to accept the accuracy of conflicting Gospel accounts at face value, as if they could be authoritative even when they contradict each other. The non-specialist can find commentaries on the Gospels by qualified scholars who arrive at very different conclusions about the validity of these texts. There simply is not enough evidence to be sure who is correct. The only thing the authors have in common is loyalty to Jesus. Given the Bible's internal irreconcilable inconsistencies, only fundamentalists are willing to insist that the whole text is the word of God.

The problem of trying to discern Jesus' personality is exacerbated by the fact that some of the stories about him seem to be inventions of the early Church. In Christian writing, Jesus was increasingly idealized, and his image was hugely exaggerated, eventually to the point of contradicting Jesus' own words. Thus, in the Chalcedonian creed of 451 CE, which tried to explain how Jesus could be both man and God incarnate, he is described as "perfect in Godhead and perfect in manhood, truly God and truly man" (Bindley, 1950, p. 234). However, in the Gospels, Jesus pointed to God as distinct from himself, saying, for example, "Why do you call me good? No one is good but God alone" (Mark 10: 18).

Some of Jesus' reported harshness toward people who did not listen to him makes one suspicious of claims that these passages are authentic statements of his and not later interpolations. He curses the Pharisees (Luke 11: 42–52), condemns to Hades those who do not believe in him (Luke, 10: 15), and insists that those who are not with him are against him (Luke 11: 23). It is hard to imagine him saying "If anyone comes to me and does not hate his own father and mother and wife and children and brothers and sisters, yes, and even his own life, he cannot be my disciple" (Luke 14: 26), even if this hyperbole is only a way to point out the high cost of being his follower or that this must take priority over the rest of one's life.

Over time, the image of Jesus evolved from being an iterant teacher, healer, reformer of Judaism, and perhaps an apocalyptic prophet to the status of Messiah. Over time, projections of the Self onto him escalated, until after his death he was elevated to the status of the Son of God and eventually God himself.[6] He later became a Pantocrator, or world ruler, and King of Kings. Christianity became a religion about Jesus himself and not only about his actual teachings. Unfortunately, he has not been sufficiently acknowledged as an example of the discovery of the inner divine.

In the Gospel of John (14: 6), Jesus says "I am the way and the truth and the life. No one comes to the Father except through me." The implications of this remark are staggering. It means that all other religious traditions (thousands of them) are not viable approaches to God and that the only way to know God is through Jesus. There are no criteria of the truth of this statement, except in the statement itself, which is only an assertion. Later writers within the early Church clearly put words into Jesus' mouth as a form of propaganda, such as the instruction to "make disciples of all nations" (Matt. 28: 19), which it is unlikely Jesus would have said because he primarily wanted to reform his own tradition and shows no sign that he wanted to begin an entirely new religion or minister to non-Jews.

In the synoptic Gospels, Jesus is evasive about his identity; he never directly said he was God incarnate, although his startling statements that he is Lord of the Sabbath (Mk. 2: 27–28) and he can forgive sin (Mk. 2: 5–12) are often said to imply the knowledge that he was God. The eventual Christian theological image of Jesus as both a messianic and a divine figure was a construction based on a forced interpretation of the Hebrew Bible's prophetic texts combined with material from the Gospel of John, as when the disciple Thomas addressed Jesus as "My Lord and my God" (John 20: 28). However, it is not at all clear from the synoptic Gospels that Jesus thought of himself as God, and it seems unlikely that these writers would not have mentioned that Jesus referred to himself as God if he had clearly done so. I believe he was God-realized in the nondual sense of the Eastern religious traditions, in a way that was a great deal more advanced than his peers. This means he had experienced the Upanishadic "Thou art That," the sense of being one with divinity. This is admittedly a speculation based on some of his comments that can be understood in a non-dual sense.[7] Jesus sometimes talks about himself as the Son of Man, but it is not clear what he meant by this term. In the Hebrew Bible this phrase usually referred to a human being, except in the book of Daniel (7: 13–14), where it refers to a figure who is led into the presence of God and given authority and power. In the Gospel of Mark (8: 38) when Jesus uses this term about a figure "coming in glory" he may have been talking about someone else. Matthew 10: 23 refers to this figure but its meaning here is debatable, although in Matthew 17: 9 Jesus seems to use this term to refer to himself.

Opinions differ on the timing of Jesus becoming a divine figure. The Gospel of Mark identifies the baptism of Jesus as the critical moment, while Matthew and Luke believe he was divine at birth. John says that the divine Logos was present from the beginning of creation and "became flesh" in the form of Jesus. Jesus' divinity was proclaimed at the Council of Nicaea (325 CE), where he was officially declared to be "true God of true God." However, Jesus would not have recognized himself in some of the complexities of later Christian theology. For example, the Creed of Chalcedon (451 CE) says that "our Lord Jesus Christ himself taught us" about his two natures, but I have not been able to find that idea in Jesus' actual teachings. Unless he did have a personal sense of God-realization as discussed above, he would not have understood the Christian notion that he was both God and man, which is antithetical to his Jewish concept of God and was not expressed in Jesus' public teaching. Given his assertion in Matthew 5:17–18 that he had not come to abolish the law or the prophets, and "not an iota, not a dot will pass from the law," I suspect he would have been distressed by the idea that the Jews had somehow become superseded from their covenantal agreement with Yhwh. He simply rejected an overly literal reading of Jewish law in a way that angered its orthodox adherents. The later Christian emphasis on redemption of the world through Jesus' blood, combined with the idea of a God who demands the killing of his son, would have been entirely alien to Jesus' Jewish background.

It is not clear that Jesus regarded himself as the messiah throughout most of his ministry, although In Mark 14: 61–62 he is reported to have acknowledged this to the high priest. The fact that he rode into Jerusalem on a donkey, as predicted by the prophet Zechariah (9: 9), also suggests that he did acknowledge this status eventually, although he did not do so in the expected manner. At the time, the Jewish people were occupied and oppressed by Rome, and they expected to be rescued by a divinely sent messiah as the prophets promised. The people assumed that the messiah would be a political or military leader, which Jesus was not. The title "Christ" is the Greek equivalent of the Hebrew "Messiah," and was used to describe Jesus by the early Church and by Paul, who changed Jesus' status from an itinerant preacher and reformer to a heavenly being. The situation changed from Jesus as the bearer of the divine message to Jesus himself as the message. Over time, Jesus the teacher from Nazareth who was preaching the Kingdom of God became the Son of God, a representative of God, and eventually identical with God. The gulf between Jesus of Nazareth and the Christ of theology has not been bridged to everyone's satisfaction.

There is a striking, often completely incompatible, difference in behavior and attitude between Yhwh, the punitive, aggressive man of war of the Hebrew Bible, and the forgiving Jesus, said to be a Prince of Peace. However, a part of the evolving Christian agenda was the appropriation and re-interpretation of the Hebrew Bible to find a way to make it relevant to Jesus. Accordingly, the prophetic books of the Hebrew Bible were reinterpreted as if they referred to Jesus, even though none of the prophecies that were said to accompany the age of the Messiah actually materialized. In order to prove that Jesus was a son of the Davidic line of kingship, which the Jewish tradition believed would produce a messiah, Bethlehem had to be Jesus' birthplace as predicted by the prophet Micah (5: 2). His followers such as Simon Peter told him he was the messiah (Matt. 16: 16), and this seems to have been the claim that got him in trouble with the High Priest (Matt. 26: 63). The Jewish religious leaders, who probably saw Jesus simply as a false Messiah, were concerned that any messianic claim would be understood by the Romans in political terms and would be seen as a sectarian rebellion, which would have led to a violent Roman reaction. Jesus may therefore have been offered to the Romans as a scapegoat to avoid a bloody retribution. Another possibility is that the Romans saw Jesus as a political threat, but the Gospel writers did not want their Messiah to appear as a political figure, so they displaced Roman responsibility for his death onto the Jews. There are skeptical biblical scholars who believe that the story of the trial before the Sanhedrin (the Jewish religious court) is fictional because the reported details do not accord with the Jewish legal customs of the time. (Ranke-Heinemann [1994] discusses the issues involved.)

Jesus' assertions did not materialize; the End Times and the Kingdom of God did not appear. The Romans continued to afflict his people, who divided into those who believed in him and those who did not. Jesus' failure to overthrow the Romans and his ignominious death might have led to his becoming a footnote in history, had it not been for the subsequent enlargement of his image by Paul, who developed an image of Jesus quite unrelated to Judaism. The transformation of Jesus' image into the God to whom Jesus also prayed was imposed on him by the Gospel of John, where Jesus says, "He who has seen me has seen the Father" (John 14: 9) and "I and the Father are one" (ibid., 10: 30). Later theologians developed this idea in a way that imposed a mythic image onto him and his mother.

The Roman Church modeled itself on a hierarchical human kingdom with increasingly man-made doctrines and dogmas developed as a result of a series of Church councils, beginning with the Council of Nicaea in 325 CE. Each subsequent generation adjusted its view of Jesus according to the demands of the historical situation in which his followers found themselves. This process continues today with the appropriation of Jesus to support political positions.[8]

Jesus as avatar

The Christian idea of Jesus as an incarnation of divinity is related to a similar idea in the Hindu tradition, in which a deity or a portion of a deity can take on the form of a human being and live a human lifetime as the avatar of a god. In Hindu mythology these figures always retain awareness of their divine identity. There are some important differences between the Hindu and Christian notions, such as the fact that the Hindu concept is cyclical, so that avatars return more than once, and the law of karma would preclude one person paying for the sins of others (Seth, 2002). The unique feature of the Christian notion is that the Incarnation is said to have happened just once, at a particular place and time in history, and not in the cyclical manner of the Hindu tradition.

Avatars in the Hindu tradition act as a bridge between the remote Absolute and the human level. Both Hindu philosophers and Christian theologians had to explain the metaphysical paradox of an eternal, infinite God squeezing into a temporal human being. In Hinduism this problem was sometimes resolved by assuming that the body of the avatar is made of a pure kind of matter, and his human qualities are only appearances. Christianity took the more cumbersome metaphysical position of a hypostatic union, the idea that Christ's human and divine natures are combined, as if he has two natures and two minds at the same time. It is a perplexing problem to imagine how his divine will, his human will, his human mind, and his divine mind coexisted.

Paul's image of Jesus

Paul was steeped in both traditional Jewish law and Hellenistic culture. He tried to integrate Greek thought with the revelation in the Hebrew Bible and with his own spiritual experiences. He had the problem of asserting his apostolic authority despite the fact that he had not met Jesus personally and was not one of the twelve original apostles. Paul believed that he was called by Jesus while in his mother's womb, and he implies that this was somehow a more important form of apostolate than that of Jesus' earthly disciples. He also believed that his constant suffering in the service of Christ helped to demonstrate the authenticity of his apostolate, and he showed: "The signs of a true apostle...with signs and wonders and mighty works" (2 Cor. 12: 12). Paul believed that Jesus chose him to be his messenger in his visionary experience on the road to Damascus (Acts 9: 3–4), and he claimed to have received his teachings as a direct revelation from Jesus himself (Gal. 1: 11). He says that the divine office "was given to me...to make the word of God fully known" (Col. 1: 25). Much depends on the validity of such claims.

There is no evidence from the Gospels that Jesus intended to be the founder of the tradition that was begun by St. Paul, and for several reasons it is doubtful that Jesus would have approved of Paul's theological elaboration of Jesus' identity. Jesus may not have approved of Paul's mission to the Gentiles, since Jesus specifically told his disciples: "Go nowhere among the Gentiles" (Matt. 10: 5) and: "I was sent only to the lost sheep of the house of Israel" (Matt. 15: 24). It is clear from these statements that Jesus believed that he was primarily a reformer of the Jewish tradition. Based on these comments, he did not come to save the world but only to minister to his own people. Jesus would have been uncomfortable with Paul's repudiation of important aspects of Jewish law such as circumcision, since, in contrast to Paul, rather than wanting to abolish Jewish law, Jesus said that "till heaven and earth pass away, not an iota, not a dot, will pass from the law until all is accomplished" (Matt. 5: 18). There is no evidence from his teaching that he thought he was a universal savior. That idea was an invention of Paul.

Paul believed that Jesus "was appointed the Son of God in power by his resurrection" (Rom. 1: 4). In various places Paul clearly distinguishes between Jesus and God the Father (e.g., 1 Cor. 8: 6; Gal. 1: 1–2), although some theologians believe that Paul saw Jesus as the Yhwh of the Hebrew Bible, partly based on Paul's descriptions of Jesus as "the image of the invisible God" (Col. 1: 15–16). However, the Jewish tradition forbids making any image of God, and Jesus clearly distinguishes himself from God the Father. In Mark 10: 18, Jesus points out that no one is good except God, and in John 14: 28 he says that "the Father is greater than I." It therefore seems unlikely that he really said: "All authority in heaven and on earth has been given to me" (Matt. 28: 18), which sounds like a later grandiose image of him projected back into the text by the early Church, which invented this kind of material. This inflation of Jesus' image during the later Roman Empire was a part of the expansion of Christianity as it became increasingly involved with state power and militarism.

Paul's letters began to be written about 53 CE, and it is possible that the Gospel tradition, written between about 70–110 CE, expressed some of Paul's ideas. However, it is not clear how much Paul knew of Jesus' actual teachings. Paul certainly heard stories and beliefs about Jesus, and from his letters it seems that he knew about the crucifixion, the resurrection, and the last supper. We see his knowledge of Jesus' teachings repeated in Romans 12: 9–21.

However, not all of Paul's claims about Jesus are derived from Jesus' actual behavior and sayings. Paul does not quote Jesus' actual words very much, because the risen Christ was more important to Paul than the earthly Jesus. Paul reinterpreted Mosaic law, such as pointing out that circumcision should be a matter of the heart, a spiritual rather than a literal physical process (Rom. 2: 25–29). Trying to free himself from Mosaic law in general, he devised various strategies. He pointed out that being "led by the Spirit" and living by the Spirit is more important than literal adherence to the law, and he radically contrasted the "works of the flesh," various forms of immorality and negative emotions, with the "fruit of the Spirit," which he saw as love and goodness (Gal. 5: 18–23). He sees love as the greatest divine gift, as seen in his enduring paean to love (1 Cor. 13: 1–13). He also believed that the law was only necessary until Christ came, but then faith took precedence over the law (Gal. 3: 23–27). Hugh Schonfield (2012) points out that what Jesus actually taught is quite different from the teachings of the later Church, which was founded on the teachings of Paul. Hardly any of Paul's theology is found in the teachings of Jesus.

How did the word spread?

Gerd Theissen's *Shadow of the Galilean* describes in the form of a novel how stories and rumors about Jesus may have spread. In a similar vein, James Dunn (2005) also points out that knowledge of Jesus was initially transmitted by word of mouth, beginning about 30–50 CE, since literacy at the time was very limited. Dunn therefore believes that too much emphasis has been placed on the literary tradition. In his view, we have to consider the Jesus who made the initial impact on his disciples and the way they remembered and spoke of him. They lived in an oral culture, and Dunn thinks their faith carefully preserved their memories of Jesus. The oral tradition affected the subsequent writing of the Synoptic Gospels, which are the only way we can know anything about Jesus. The differences between the Gospels may be due to the characteristics of oral transmission, but Dunn evaluates the oral tradition positively, and it may well be accurate, but doubts about the accuracy of oral transmission over the subsequent decades color the reliability of the Gospel accounts.

Philosophical and psychological aspects of the trinity

The trinity is one of several Christian doctrines that are philosophically complex and difficult to understand. Therefore, they are often described as mysteries that are adhered to based only on faith.

The trinity tries to describe the ontological nature of God. The trinity is said to consist of one divine essence or substance (Gk. *ousia*) but three persons or hypostases,[9] each of which is equally the one God. It is not clear what the word "person" means in this context. It may mean some kind of distinctiveness within an underlying unity, without implying three different consciousnesses. Human personhood may be nothing like the divine persons of the trinity, which many people believe to be radically unknowable. The word "person" may not have the same meaning today as it had in the fourth century when the idea was conceived. Rather than referring to a self or to individuality in the modern sense, in the ancient usage of the word a "persona" was a role being played. Perhaps the three persons are intended to represent centers of intentionality or uniqueness or internal communion within an underlying unity, or they express different ways in which God relates to the world. Or the three persons refer to relationships that depend on each other for their meaning, just as one cannot have a son without a father. No hierarchy is implied.

The idea of the trinity arose partly in response to the fact that early Christianity consisted of a range of theological opinions. The doctrine was an attempt to hold together different Christian experiences and views of God. In particular, the trinity tries to address the problem of the relationship of the Yhwh of the Hebrew Bible to the divinity of Jesus, while remaining monotheistic. The problem is partly that Jesus prays to the Father but is also identified as divine himself and one with the Father (Jn. 1: 1; 10: 1). An additional puzzle was to incorporate into the tradition's image of God the spirit that descended on the disciples at Pentecost (Acts 2). Jesus, Yhwh, and the Pentecostal spirit seem to be so different that it was difficult to see them as manifestations of the one God, but there was a psychological and theological need to unify them. Other problems were how to account for a God who was paradoxically transcendent but also near and immanent in Christ, and how God could act relationally but also preserve his independence of anything outside himself, an attribute known as his aseity.

The trinity is not found in the Bible in any obvious way, so its presence has to be inferred from what scripture says about God's appearances (Feinberg, 2005), as when Abraham encountered three visitors at the oaks of Mamre (Gen. 8: 1–6), which to early Christian exegetes had the quality of a theophany. The nature of these visitors is much disputed, and many contemporary writers have abandoned the idea that they refer to the Christian trinity.

The Council of Nicaea (325 CE) developed the notion of the trinity to address the problem of how God the Father, Jesus, and the Holy Spirit could be the same God. The Council wanted to uphold traditional monotheism while at the same time talking about the divinity of Jesus and the work of the Holy Spirit. This Council did not want to subordinate Jesus and the Holy Spirit to the Father, and they wanted to maintain the idea of three persons without producing three different divinities. The paradox is that the persons meet in the trinity but do not merge or dissolve into each other. This issue continued to be debated for several decades until the Council of Constantinople in 380 CE decided the matter, finally confirming the Holy Spirit as a part of the Godhead.

The competing notion, known as the Arian heresy, was that Jesus was not of the same nature as God the father, but he was a being created by God for the redemption of the world. Arius (250–336 CE) believed that Christ must have had a finite nature, because if Jesus was begotten by God the Father, Jesus did not exist before that event and so did not have equal divinity. This idea was opposed by Bishop Athanasius (293–373 CE), who insisted that the begetting of the Word by the Father was an eternal relationship and not an ordinary temporal event. For Athanasius only a fully divine Christ could save the world. Jesus therefore had to be of the same nature as God, coequal, and eternal, while Arius continued to insist that their natures were only similar. He therefore acknowledged a hierarchy in which they are not equal. Arius was condemned, but this bitter controversy continued for decades, until the Athanasian argument was eventually reaffirmed at the Council of Constantinople in 381 CE.

Another heresy that was rejected was the idea that the Father, Son, and Holy Spirit are three different modes of the same God or three ways that God revealed himself, rather than the mainstream view of three persons within the Godhead, each of whom had existed individually from eternity, distinct but equally the Godhead. The nature of the relationship between the three persons is said to be incomprehensible. Officially the trinity consists of three distinct identities or subjects within an underlying divine unity, with no distinction in their essence. Exactly how they are related to or differentiated from each other remains unclear. The trinity was in part an attempt to reconcile the idea that Jesus was both divine and human using the formulation that he was of "the same essence as the Father."

The Trinity was a way of dealing with some anxiety about how to make Jesus the same as the Yhwh of the Hebrew Bible, who became God the Father in the Trinity, even though these figures seem very different in their properties. The question of whether the trinity is foreshadowed in the Hebrew Scriptures, or whether it can be inferred from New Testament teaching, is controversial. Matthew 28: 19–20 has Jesus telling the disciples to baptize people "in the name of the Father, and of the Son, and of the Holy Spirit," but most authorities see this as a later interpolation into the text.

The trinity raises questions such as whether it contains three different centers of consciousness or subjectivity, or even three different wills, and whether they might clash or interfere with each other. Complex problems of identity arise here, combined with a tangle of logical problems produced by the question of how the three persons of the trinity could have the same identity since according to Christian doctrine they have different properties. For example, the Son became incarnate and was crucified and died, but God the Father cannot die. A further problem is the complaint of feminists that the androcentric names of the first and second persons of the trinity perpetuate a male image of God and thus an oppressive patriarchal system. Feminists would prefer to use neutral names. Feminists have also complained that the "Fatherhood" of the Judeo-Christian image of God implies that male power and authority is divinely ordained. Similarly, they argue that the implication of the idea that Jesus is the Word made flesh is that only males are fitting vehicles of divine revelation. However, it is possible to see words like "Father" as only analogies or metaphors, just as we don't know what it is for God to be a "Son." These masculine nouns do not necessarily imply that God has a biological sex. Traditionalists resist any change in terminology, pointing to Jesus' frequent use of the word "Father," as if God has chosen this name for himself, acknowledging that divine fatherhood is not comparable with biological human fatherhood. However, at the level of homiletics, liturgy, and hymnology, it is difficult to remove the culturally embedded masculine connotations of the words father and son, especially combined with the incessant use of masculine pronouns to speak of God. Their combined effects may be particularly powerful at the unconscious level. As a result, the collusion between the patriarchy and Christianity is still with us. Resentment at the patriarchy in general may contribute to the decline of religious traditions seen to be patriarchal. (The gender debate in relation to the trinity is reviewed by McWhinnie, 2017.)

There are various traditional models of the trinity that try to explain its complexity. St. Augustine favored the "psychological" model. It suggests that just as the human personality is a unity that consists of diverse aspects, including the mind, the heart, and the will, so the Godhead has three aspects. Another analogy is that the mind, its knowledge of itself, and its love of itself are inseparable. Objections to this model include the point that it is too close to the heretical idea that the Father, Son, and Holy Spirit are different modes of God rather than three distinct persons. Thirteenth-century theologian Bonaventure saw the Holy Spirit as the bond that joins Father and Son but also as the fruit of their union (Dourley, 1975). The "social" model of the trinity sees the three persons in a in a relational dance. Or the trinity is a divine society whose members are fully personal and in a loving relationship with each other. For some theologians, this model comes too close to be postulating three gods.

The metaphysical implications of the trinity are still of interest to theologians. Two of the major modern approaches are described by Alistair McGrath (2022). One view considers the doctrine to be an intellectual construct, an epistemic framework that coordinates multiple insights about the nature of God. Another view sees the trinity as a statement about the ontological reality of God, or about the actual nature of God, which is the predominant view among Christian theologians today. McGrath believes that these approaches are not incompatible. The fact that books and scholarly articles on the trinity continue to appear (e.g., Bourgeault, 2013), with different ways to understand it, suggests that the doctrine still causes some unease and needs clarification. A part of the reason for this discomfort is that the doctrine of the Trinity smacks of polytheism to many skeptics, and it is often accused of being irrational, but the intellectual difficulties involved in the idea of three persons and one God are often covered up by demands for greater faith. I suspect that Jesus would have been mystified by the idea of the trinity, typical of the abyss between the theological portrait of Jesus and his own sayings about himself in the synoptic Gospels.

A Jungian view of the trinity suggests that the underlying *ousia* that is the divine essence of the three persons refers to the Self, which may manifest itself in a range of archetypal processes such as Father, Son, and Holy Spirit, but also in many other ways including the feminine aspects of divinity.

Jung's account of the psychological aspects of the trinity

According to Jung's account, he had become interested in the trinity because it expressed a paradoxical "oneness that was simultaneously a threeness" (1963, pp. 52–53). His minister father had been unable to explain this symbol, telling the young Jung that it had to be accepted on faith. This was a pivotal moment for him that revealed the gap between belief in dogma and direct experience of the sacred. Jung felt that this gap seriously hurt his father, and it seems to have awakened in Jung a determination to understand the trinity. His father's experience was one of the sources of Jung's conclusions that the Christian myth no longer meets the spiritual needs of contemporary people, and belief in doctrine is no substitute for direct numinous experience.

Jung tries to understand the trinity psychologically rather than theologically. For him, the trinity not only refers to a metaphysical reality; it also reveals a psychological process. Jung wants to elicit the psychological meaning underlying the doctrine. He was aware that such an attempt to discuss Christian symbols psychologically might be objectionable to traditional believers, even as he tried to avoid any infringement on the religious value of these symbols. He referred to his approach as "an undertaking of audacity" (CW 11, para. 171). However, he thought it would be even more dangerous to make Christian symbols "inaccessible to thoughtful understanding by being banished to a sphere of sacrosanct unintelligibility" (CW 11 para. 170). He sees this kind of symbolism as an archetypal, irreducible expression of the psyche. Such symbols act as bridges, allowing the unconscious to become conscious, allowing the Self to realize itself within the empirical personality.

Jung begins his essay on the dogma of the trinity (CW 11) by noting a range of mythological trinitarian divinities. As well as the Christian trinity, trinitarian divinities are found in Plato's *Timaeus*, the philosophy of Pythagoras, and in Hindu, Buddhist, Babylonian, Egyptian, and Greek mythologies. This widespread manifestation is not surprising if the trinity is an archetypal symbol. This means that the Christian trinity and its manifestations in other religions all share a common origin in the deepest levels of the psyche. Jung assumes a universal level of meaning underneath the various surface levels of manifestation of this archetypal image, whose specific appearance is colored by local traditions. He believes this meaning extends "far beyond the confines of Christianity" (CW 11, para. 294). The symbolic approach treats the trinity symbol as if it were a dream image that requires amplification (ibid., para. 269).

Jung believed that the controversial idea of the homoousios, the idea that the three persons are of the same substance, is important from a psychological point of view because the trinity represents "the progressive transformation of one and the same substance, namely the psyche as a whole" (CW 11, para. 289). According to Jung, as a psychological symbol the trinity denotes a process of the evolution of consciousness. Each of the three persons represents a specific stage in a process of "conscious realization continuing over the centuries" (ibid., para. 288). The first stage of the trinity, referred to as the world of the Father, symbolizes a time of humanity's original oneness with the nature, without separation, critical judgment, differentiated consciousness, or moral conflict. This is a stage of pleromatic wholeness or unity out of which everything arises. This child-like stage of humanity was lost because of the irreversible increase in human consciousness, leading to the second stage of the Son (the development of the ego), which represents a period of conflict, critical reason, reflection, and differentiation, combined with a longing for redemption and for a return to the state of perfection in which man was one with the Father (ibid., paras. 201 and *passim*). Jung sees the spirit as the healing and reconciling power that unites opposites and is itself realized in those united opposites. This last stage of this process resolves the conflict, differentiates, and then unites the opposites, and restores the lost unity of Father and Son, which he also sees as Christian symbols for the unconscious and consciousness. Psychologically, this final stage means the ego's recognition of the unconscious and the development of the ego-Self axis, which is necessary for the unconscious to become conscious. As a result of human attention to this work, "God becomes manifest in the human act of reflection" (CW 11, para. 238). It is notable that Jung does not deny the Christian notion that the trinity represents the nature of the divine, as if the trinity were only a representation of "the personification of psychic processes in three roles" (CW 11, para. 289), but he shows that these processes exist within the symbol. However, the relationship between these different levels of meaning, both metaphysical and psychological, is uncertain. Jung realizes that to amplify the archetypal ground of such imagery is not to explain its nature or to exhaust its meaning (ibid., para. 295).

The theme of wholeness or completeness is central to Jung's psychology. Based on the way the unconscious expresses wholeness in his patients' dreams, Jung believed that the unconscious typically images divinity (the totality, or the Self) using fourfold, that is quaternary, symbolism. He therefore tended to see trinitarian images as incomplete symbols of wholeness (CW 12, para. 31; CW 9, ii, para. 351), as if something is missing or left out of symbols of three-ness. Somewhat inconsistently however, Jung also implies that the trinity is a different type of symbol of wholeness than the quaternity, and the trinitarian developmental process described above may not need a fourth. Typically, however, although the trinity is itself an archetypal symbol, Jung usually stresses that the trinity requires completion, either by the addition of the dark side of God, or by the body and matter, or by the feminine. Without these elements, the trinity as a sacred symbol denies the archetypal reality of evil or the dark side of divinity, does not include the material origin of all that is, and denies the sacrality of the feminine.[10] (Here, he does not consider the importance of Mariology in the Roman Catholic tradition.) Jung believed that these factors had been split off or repressed in Christianity as if divinity is only good, only spirit, and only masculine. Hence too the devaluation of the body and matter in traditional Christianity. Jung veers between including one or other of these factors as the missing fourth. He believed that Christianity has been too one-sided in its deification of masculinity, spirit, and goodness, and such one-sidedness is "deleterious to health" (para. 286). In Jung's myth, the sacredness of the body, matter, and the feminine must be affirmed instead of being excluded, and evil must be recognized as an element within divinity. Overall, therefore, he sees the trinity as an early stage in the evolution of human consciousness. Again, based on his observation of his patients' dream material, Jung believed that a mythology is emerging that would imagine deity as a more inclusive quaternity rather than a trinity (CW 11, para. 63).

Edinger (1964) suggests that the quaternity is a structural, static, eternal expression of the totality of the psyche. It conveys stability and rest. In contrast, the trinity expresses totality in its dynamic, developmental, temporal aspects, implying movement and growth. The symbol of three often means the restoration on a higher level of the original unity of the one that had divided into two. Edinger therefore sees the trinitarian divinities of world mythologies as deities in process as opposed to deities who represent fixed structures or goals attained.

The Incarnation

The classical Christian statement about the Incarnation was decided by the Council of Chalcedon of 451 CE, after a long period of dispute about what statements about Christ were or were not permissible. The council asserted that Jesus was one hypostasis (underlying reality) who had two natures, human and divine, which came together in a single person. The properties of both natures were preserved. That is, Jesus was of the same substance as the Father and also the same as human beings in his personhood, except that he was sinless. The divine nature has properties such as omniscience and omnipotence, while the human nature has ordinary human properties. The Incarnation was therefore an attempted solution to the problem of how the immortal God could also be fully physically human, how two natures and the divine and human minds can be unified, or how a purely spiritual God could become material. Over time, the notion of the Incarnation developed into the status of a revelation.

To avoid invoking miracles such as the Incarnation, this doctrine has been challenged by liberal theologians such as John Hick (1977), who believed that the Incarnation cannot be understood literally. For him it is a mythological or symbolic way of describing the importance of Jesus. Hick sees the Incarnation not as a historical fact but as a metaphorical way of expressing the church's sense of salvation received through Jesus. Hick thinks that the idea that Jesus is both fully man and fully God is unintelligible, incoherent, or self-contradictory because the properties of God and those of humanity are incompatible. Hick believes that more than one Christology is possible, and several have developed with equal validity. His ideas gave rise to considerable controversy because he denies the Incarnation in the literal sense of the word, but Hick believed that belief in ideas such as the Incarnation or the Virgin Birth are not essential to being a Christian. He pointed out that although Jesus was an outstanding religious authority, he was not unique in this respect. He can be compared to others such as the Buddha, who also had great spiritual power and authority. Frances Young's essay in Hick's book suggests that the notion of God incarnate is "read into" the Pauline letters and other New Testament documents but is not found within them (ibid., p. 22).

Because of the logical problems involved in explaining how one person (the Son) could have two natures, both human and divine, in recent decades a variety of models and metaphysical justifications have been developed to defend the validity of the idea of the Incarnation in response to its skeptical critics (Marmodoro & Hill, 2011). These models had to avoid at least two heresies; Nestorianism, the idea that the human and the divine were actually two distinct persons, and Monophytism, the claim that the Son had only one, divine nature.

The typical response to the point that humanity and God have incompatible properties is that ordinary logic does not apply to this situation; the Incarnation is a mystery. However, attempts to explain the Incarnation by recourse to divine mystery, paradox, or the limitations of human reason are not satisfying. They do not solve problems such as the tension between divine omniscience and the limitations of Jesus' personal knowledge. For example, in Mark 13: 32, talking about when the Son of Man will come, Jesus says, "about that day or hour no one knows, not even the angels in heaven, nor the Son, but only the Father." Divinity is said to be omniscient, omnipotent, and eternal, but Jesus did not appear to have these qualities. That is, in his human nature Jesus was limited but in his divine nature he was not, thus raising difficult questions about the relationship between these natures. The kenotic (self-emptying) theory suggests that when the Son became incarnate, he voluntarily shed some divine attributes such as omniscience and omnipotence, but he remained divine while sharing the human condition. The argument here is whether that would be compatible with divine glory or whether it weakens the idea of divinity or makes Jesus not fully human.

Another suggestion is that during his Incarnation as a man, Christ had not only two natures but two consciousnesses or two minds, one divine and one human. Perhaps the divine consciousness existed within Jesus' unconscious, an idea that is consistent with the notion that the archetypal or transpersonal level of the psyche coexists with the personal level, in all human beings. Another view suggests that the divine mind extended itself into Jesus to carry out some of its activities. In contrast, some contemporary philosophers still defend the literal or metaphysical reading of the Chalcedonian dogma of hypostatic union (Dobrzeniecki, 2021). The compositional view of the Incarnation suggests that the Son of the trinitarian God added to himself a complex of body and soul to become the incarnate Christ. A less popular view is that Christ took on the full set of human attributes and properties except that his divine nature took the place of a soul.

Psychological approaches to the Incarnation

The psychological value of the doctrine of the Incarnation is partly that Christians believe that by becoming human God can empathize with human difficulties, much more so than would have been possible if he had remained in the realm of pure spirit, because by incarnating God experienced human suffering and death. The Incarnation therefore means that God becomes close to humanity, suffers with us, and understands human life from within. Christianity proclaims that God's sacrifice was carried out as a result of his love for humanity, given at so great a cost and in spite of our fallen nature.

Jung believed that the Incarnation is not unique to Jesus. In Jung's model, incarnation refers to a psychological process that occurs in all human beings as the unconscious gradually becomes conscious within the empirical personality. During the individuation process, the unconscious progressively embodies its potentials as they are developed and lived out during the course of the individual's life (CW 11, paras. 658, 693, 749) in a universal process of maturation. "That is to say, what happens in the life of Christ happens always and everywhere" (CW 11, para. 146). Because the relationship between consciousness and the unconscious is a dialectic, Jung believes that this is a process of mutual redemption in which the unconscious differentiates the opposites within itself as they emerge into the ego, which *pari passu* expands and relativizes the ego. For Jung, the process of the incarnation of the transpersonal levels of the unconscious into human consciousness allows divinity to become conscious of itself, which is Jung's mythic notion for the reason that conscious human beings were created (CW 11, para. 642). As he puts it, "God becomes manifest in the human act of reflection" (para. 238), or human beings act as a reflecting consciousness for the divine. This is a radically different view than the Christian notion that creation occurs out of the fullness of divine goodness. Jung's view is also very different from the theological ideas that the Incarnation in Christ was necessary to deal with Adam's disobedience in the Garden of Eden. Because the unconscious is a part of human interiority, and the human level of the psyche comingles with its transpersonal levels, Jung posits a process of continuous contact between divinity and humanity, which is therefore not unique to the figure of Christ. (CW 11, para. 105). This is not a position that traditional Christianity would accept since Jung's view denies the Christian concept of divine otherness.

The resurrection

The Gospel story of the resurrection

The story of the resurrection, the miracle that Jesus rose from the dead, is central to Christianity. Jesus' resurrection is said to be a model or prototype that promises eternal life to his followers. Traditional Christians take the story of the resurrection at face value, but there has been much debate about whether resurrection refers to an actual historical event (Crossan and Wright, 2006), or whether it was nothing more than a belief of the disciples. One can also see this theme symbolically, as a spiritual rather than physical resurrection, which to many moderns seems impossible. It can also be seen to refer to the continuation of some form of consciousness after death.

Paul's main evidence for the resurrection is that after the crucifixion Jesus appeared to Cephas (Peter) and the other disciples but also to "more than five hundred of the brothers and sisters…then to James…and to me also" (1Cor. 15: 5–10). The resurrection is so important to Paul that, "if Christ has not been raised, our preaching is useless and so is your faith…if Christ has not been raised, your faith is futile" (1 Cor. 15: 14–17). That is, everything depends on the truth of the resurrection. Perhaps Paul made this strong statement because there were people in Corinth who doubted its reality (1 Cor. 15: 12). They may have mirrored his own doubt, which he tried to suppress by insisting that many others believed the resurrection happened. He was also trying to bolster his own apostolic authority by claiming to have been one of those who saw the resurrected Jesus. The Gospel stories of the resurrection had not yet been written, and it is not known if Paul knew of the tradition of the empty tomb, which for believing Christians implies a physical resurrection, although that is not the only possible explanation for the missing body. Paul probably knew of the idea of resurrection from examples in the Hebrew Bible of people reported to be resurrected from the dead, such as the story of the Valley of Dry Bones in Ezekiel and the statement in the book of Daniel (12: 2) that "many of those who sleep in the dust of the earth shall awake." The motif also appeared in the Hebrew Bible when Elijah brought back to life the son of Zarephath (1 Kings 17: 7–16) long before Jesus raised Lazarus.

Some scholars believe that Paul implies that resurrected bodies are purely spiritual, because he says that the body begins physically but is "raised a spiritual body" (1 Cor. 15: 44). However, because Paul also writes that "the trumpet will sound, the dead will be raised imperishable" (1 Cor. 15: 52), other authors insist that he conceived of the resurrection as a raising of the physical body. This became the church's preferred understanding, and physical resurrection became an article of faith for many Christians.

Matthew 27: 52 suggests the resurrection of the physical body: "the tombs broke open. The bodies of many holy people who had died were raised to life." According to the Gospel story, after the resurrection Jesus could walk and talk with his disciples, who could identify him because of nail marks and the scar on his side. Although they initially did not recognize him, he was able to speak to them (Lk. 24: 25) on the road to Emmaus, all of which sounds as if he had a physical body. The story in the Gospel of John that Thomas was able to physically inspect Jesus' wounds seems to be an addition of the later Church. The Gospel of John describes him as physically resurrected and having several conversations with the disciples. He was, however, also able to appear, disappear, and move through locked doors (Lk 24: 31, 36; Jn 20:19, 26), which sounds more like a spiritual body.

John Crossan (2012) and David Tacey (2015) see the stories of Jesus' postcrucifixion appearances as mythic narratives or as parables. Symbolically, the story on the road to Emmaus refers to the way in which spiritual reality may appear but not be recognized. However, typical of the tradition's resistance to symbolic and metaphoric understanding, this story was understood to have been a physical meeting, according to which Jesus was able to eat with the disciples to prove his physical reality. By transmitting the story in this literal way, the mythic connotation of the story is lost.

Resurrection implies some kind of continuation of consciousness after death, but this idea involves several philosophical problems, including the very nature of personhood and identity. In Christian tradition, the soul will be rejoined with its resurrected or glorified body at the time of the eschaton, or at Jesus' Second Coming, although if the soul is immortal this reunion seems unnecessary, and it raises the problem of the dualism of body and soul. Questions also arise about the identity of the resurrected individual, such as whether he or she will be a duplicate of the original body or an entirely new creation. Resurrection may refer to the appearance of a spiritual principle that maintains the identity of the person, or to an angelic existence, but Jung believes that to early Christians the resurrection had to be "a concrete, materialistic event to be seen by the eyes and touched by the hands" (CW 18, para. 1574).

Skeptics believe that the story of the resurrection was contrived and is grounded on nothing more than the disappearance of Jesus' body from the tomb and suspect accounts of his postmortem appearances. Many of his followers must have been enormously disappointed by his execution, which seemed to disprove the possibility that he was the Messiah. The problem is then to explain how a defeated group evolved into such a confident movement. Believers attribute this change to visionary experiences of Jesus after his death, which may have been typical bereavement experiences (described below), which are fairly common. A skeptical possibility is that, to avoid too much cognitive dissonance, Jesus' immediate followers managed to see the resurrection as proof that he had indeed been the Messiah, and they turned his defeat on the cross into a triumph. Disconfirmation was turned into positive evidence. As part of this process of reversal, when Jesus' mission seemed to have failed because he was executed, to deal with the disappointment he was gradually elevated to the Son of God and the Incarnation of God.

Because of the conceptual problems raised by the idea of resurrection, liberal Christians have tried to downplay its importance, focusing mainly on Jesus as a moral exemplar, because they doubt the historicity of the resurrection story. Its truth is a matter of faith that cannot be decided on the basis of the Gospels. Skeptics believe that since dead people do not become alive, the story of the resurrection is a construction of early Christians combined with a myth-making process of some kind, either as a conscious deception or as an attempt to cope with Jesus' followers' disappointment at his death. Making the situation even more confusing is the fact that the Gospel accounts of the empty tomb offer discrepant stories.[11]

Psychological approaches to the story of the resurrection

For the skeptical psychologist it seems that the story of the resurrection arose as an attempt to soften the blow of Jesus' death, which probably caused his followers considerable emotional trauma. The question is whether the post-crucifixion appearances of Jesus had a purely psychological basis, a way to cope with his followers' crushed hopes and their intense need to believe he was still with them. However, it is not clear from the text whether his postmortem appearances were spiritual, physical, parapsychological, dream-like, hallucinatory, or otherwise purely subjective. Jesus' postmortem appearances can be understood as the kind of event that is common among bereaved people during periods of intense grief (Castelnovo et al., 2015). His followers may have experienced him after death in a dream, as a sense of his presence, or in a waking vision. Bereavement encounters commonly include the ability to see and talk to the deceased person. Whether one regards these experiences as hallucinations or as visits from the deceased is a matter of one's belief system. It is easy to imagine how such reports would become exaggerated with constant retelling over time. Jung (CW 10, para. 597) described the kind of "visionary rumors" that occur during periods of collective tension, giving rise to phenomena such as the angelic vision of the soldiers at Mons in the First World War. Belief in resurrection was well established in the Judaism of Jesus' time, and the heightened emotional tension among his followers after his death may have predisposed them to have this kind of experience. Traditional believers see this psychological approach as reductionist, as if it denies the factual or literal nature of these experiences. However, given Jung's insistence on the reality of the psyche, these kinds of visionary experiences are encounters with something real and cannot be dismissed as purely defensive.

Brooke Hopkins (1989) believes that the appeal and power of the resurrection story have never been adequately explained in psychological terms. She suggests that the destructiveness of the crucifixion combined with the fact that Jesus was able to survive this attack by resurrecting, and subsequently loved the world that had tried to destroy him, can be understood through a Winnicottian lens as part of the capacity to use objects.[12] This term describes the infant's experience of mother's survival after the infant's destructive impulses toward her. This process allows the infant to experience its objects as separate from itself and at the same time as reliable and constant. Hopkins sees the power of the resurrection story in the fact that it reflects the developmental process by which the object survives being attacked and does not retaliate, which transforms it into a genuine object of love. She believes that the story of the resurrection reenacts this developmental pattern of destruction/survival/ rebirth of the loved object. The resurrection represents Jesus' survival of destructive attacks, and his lack of retaliation represents his continuous love even of those who tried to destroy him. Each time the believer takes the sacrament, he acknowledges his destructiveness in eating it and expresses his faith that the love-object survives and continues to love.

The archetypal nature of the resurrection story is suggested by the fact that this motif is seen in many mythologies, at least as early as the Egyptian story of Osiris, who also resurrected after death. An Akkadian poem tells the story of the death and resurrection of the goddess Ishtar. The death and resurrection of the vegetation god Attis was celebrated yearly. He reappeared at the vernal equinox, an appearance that according to Frazer (1919) was understood by his followers to be a promise that they too would be raised from the grave. Frazer also notes several examples of the resurrection motif among tribal initiation ceremonies and rites of passage around the world.

The psychology of the wish for continuity after death

The Nicene Creed states: "We look for the resurrection of the dead and the life of the world to come...I believe in ...the resurrection of the body, and life everlasting." The psychologically potent mythic image of the resurrection of the dead at some future time of God's choosing can be seen to be a way to cope with the prospect of death, which has always been a mystery that seems to reverse creation. The mythic notion of resurrection offers hope for the continuation of some kind of existence after death, partially alleviating death anxiety or even overcoming death in some sense. For some believers, this possibility offers the comforting prospect of reunion with loved ones, and life after death seems to offer the possibility of reward, retribution, and justice when these seem to have been unavailable during life. Many Christians who believe that God loves them find it hard to imagine that he would suddenly allow them to cease to exist altogether and their relationship with him would summarily end with death.

The need for some kind of continuity after death is so widespread among disparate cultures that it seems to be an archetypal component of human psychology, part of the human need to find meaning in life. The notion of resurrection can also be seen as an example of what Ernest Becker (1973) has referred to as religion's denial of death. The fact that the popular concept of life after death includes a paradisiacal existence makes it seem that the idea is defensive, and the fact that Christianity consigns large numbers of people to hell merely sounds like revenge and exclusivism. We can imagine moral and spiritual development after death, but the notion of the ongoing postmortem development of the soul is speculative and raises its own bevy of questions. The question of some kind of postmortem survival is a little easier if we do not adhere to a materialist theory of the psyche, since if the psyche is truly independent of the brain, which seems to be the case in near-death or other out of body experiences, it is plausible to imagine it survives the death of the body.

Notes

1 How did the Aramaic-speaking Jesus converse with the Latin-speaking Pontius Pilate?
2 The word "charisma" is derived from the Greek "*charis*," meaning a gift or favor.
3 Charismatic politicians sometimes have a secret life of illicit activity such as infidelity, financial deceptions, or other ethical violations. The dark side of the charismatic religious leader becomes evident when these individuals are caught in some kind of unethical behavior.
4 Oates describes a series of stages in the personal development of such individuals. These are early narcissism, a period of incubation, a sense of mission, and often a decline and fall. However, there is insufficient information about the childhood of Jesus to know if this sequence applies to him.
5 Kohut believes that when a child is frustrated by being forced to prematurely take over the functions of his parental selfobjects because of their failure to meet his needs, he takes on a selfobject role for the parent, and in the process, he develops an insatiable need for recognition. If the parent inflates the child's grandiosity and sense of power rather than tempering it in a phase-appropriate way, the individual may grow up feeling that ordinary limits do not apply to him. This feeling can fuel originality and achievement but can also be a source of grandiosity.
6 The tendency to keep enhancing Jesus' image continues, as seen in Teilhard de Chardin's notion of the Cosmic Christ.
7 For example, his comment in Matthew 25: 40: "as you did it to one of the least of these my brethren, you did it to me" suggests a deep understanding that the Self is the same in all of us. Also, "I and the Father are one" (John 10: 30) reflects a non-dual understanding, and so does his comment in the Gospel of Thomas, verse 77: "Split a piece of wood; I am there. Lift up the stone, and you will find me there.".
8 I'm referring to Christian Democratic parties in Europe that promote religious values. Hungarian Prime Minister Viktor Orbán champions Christianity, and so does Giorgia Meloni in Italy. Many on the American Right combine Christian worship with their political activities.
9 The word *ousia* refers to an essence or nature, while the word hypostasis refers to a fundamental entity. The *ousia* is the underlying essential unity of the three hypostases.
10 I should note here the mistaken impression of some feminist critics of Jung that he equates the feminine with matter and evil. This is not the case; it simply happens that these are the elements of creation left out of the trinity.
11 Matthew 28, Mark 16, Luke 24, John 20–21.

12 The psychoanalytic use of the word "object" here refers to people. It is a remnant of Freud's use of the term to indicate a person who is an object of one's drives. Winnicott (1969) describes how mother, the original object, is at the same time both an object of love but also a danger to the baby because of its projected aggression onto the mother, which may make her seem hostile. Because the mother survives the baby's anger at her and remains empathic and loving to the baby, the baby's anxiety and guilt feelings about its destructiveness are transformed into reparative behavior. The baby then achieves a sense of the reliability of mother's love and the capacity for concern. The mother's survival is key to this process. The process repeats itself in later relationships.

References

Aberbach, D. (1995). Charisma and attachment theory: A cross-disciplinary interpretation. *International Journal of Psychoanalysis, 76,* 845–855.
Acland, A. F. (2018). *Religious hatred and human conflict: Psychodynamic approaches to insight and intervention.* Routledge.
Altschuler, E.L. (2002). Did Ezekiel have temporal lobe epilepsy? *Archives of General Psychiatry 59,* 561–562.
Anthony, N. (2020). Menstrual Taboos: religious Practices that Violate Women's Human Rights. *International Human Rights Law Review, 9*(2), 291–323.
Bakan, D. (1971). *Disease, pain, and sacrifice.* Beacon Press.
Bataille, G. (1991). *The accursed share.* ZoneBooks.
Becker, E. (1973). *The denial of death.* Free Press.
Becking, E. (2009). David between ideology and evidence. In B. Becking & L. L. Grabbe (Eds.), *Between evidence and ideology: Essays on the history of ancient Israel* (pp. 1–44). Brill.
Beltz, W. (1975). *God and the gods: Myths of the Bible.* Penguin Books.
Benedetti, F., Mayberg, H., Wager, T, Stohler, C, & Zubieta, J. (2005). Neurobiological mechanisms of the placebo effect. *The Journal of Neuroscience, 25*(45), 10390–10402.
Bergmann, M. (1992). *In the shadow of Moloch: The sacrifice of children and its impact on Western religions.* Columbia University Press.
Bermejo-Rubio, F. (2017. The process of Jesus' deification and cognitive dissonance theory. *Numen 64,* 119–152.
Bettelheim, B. (1962). *Symbolic wounds: Puberty rites and the envious male.* Collier Books.
Bindley, T.H. (1950). *The Oecumenical documents of the faith.* Methuen.
Blumenthal, D.R. (1993). *Facing the abusing God: A theology of protest.* John Knox Press.
Bollas, C. (1999). *The mystery of things.* Routledge.
Bord, C., & Bord, J. (1985). *Sacred waters: Holy wells and water lore in Britain and Ireland.* Granada Press.
Bourgeault, C. (2013). *The Holy Trinity and the law of three.* Shambhala.
Brennan, T. (1997). Social evil. *Social research, 64*(2), 211–234.
Brock, N.R. & Parker, R. (2001). *Proverbs of ashes: Violence, redemptive suffering and the search for what saves us.* Beacon Press.
Brooke, H. (1989). Jesus and object use: A Winnicottian account of the resurrection myth. *International Review of Psycho-Analysis, 16,* 93–100.

Broome, E. C. (1946). Ezekiel's abnormal personality. *Journal of Biblical Literature*, *65*(3), 277–292.

Brueggemann, W. (1997). *Theology of the Old Testament: Testimony, dispute, advocacy.* Fortress Press.

Buber, M. (1952). *Eclipse of God: Studies in the relation between religion and philosophy.* Harper & Row.

Bultmann, R. (1960). *Primitive Christianity in its contemporary setting.* Collins.

Bushart, H.L., Craig, J.R. & Barnes, M. (1998). *Soldiers of God: White supremacists and their holy war for America.* Kensington.

Callan, T. (1990). *Psychological perspectives on the life of Paul: an application of the method of Gerd Theissen.* Edwin Mellen Press.

Campbell, J. (1964). *The masks of God: Occidental mythology.* Penguin Books.

Campbell, J. (1986). *The inner reaches of outer space.* Alfred van der Marck Editions.

Campbell, J. (1991). *The power of myth.* Doubleday.

Campbell, J. (2001). *Thou art that: Transforming religious metaphors.* New World Library.

Capps, D. (1995). *The child's song: The religious abuse of children.* Westminster John Knox Press.

Capps, D., & Carlin, N. (2009). Methuselah and company: A case of male envy of female longevity. *Pastoral Psychology*, *58*(2), 107–126.

Caputi, J. (1988). *The age of sex crime.* Bowling Green State University Press.

Carlson-Brown, J. & Bohn, C.R. (Eds.). (1989). *Christianity, patriarchy, and abuse: A feminist critique.* Pilgrim Press.

Castelein, J.D. (1984). Glossolalia and the psychology of the self and narcissism. *Journal of Religion and Health*, *23*(1), 47–62.

Castelnovo, A., Cavallotti, S., Gambini, O., & D'Agostino, A. (2015). Post-bereavement hallucinatory experiences: A critical overview of population and clinical studies. *Journal of Affective Disorders*, *186*, 266–274.

Castelnovo, O., Popper, M., & Koren, D. (2017). The innate code of charisma. *Leadership Quarterly*, *28*, 543–554.

Chamberlain, B. H. (2010). *Aino Folk-Tales.* Nabu Press.

Cook, M. J. (1983). Anti-Judaism in the New Testament. *Union Seminary Quarterly Review*, *38*(2), 125–137.

Copan, P. (2011). *Is God a moral monster? Making sense of the Old Testament God.* Baker Books.

Corbett, L. (2015). *The soul in anguish: Psychotherapeutic approaches to suffering.* Chiron Publications.

Corbett, L. (2018). *Understanding evil: A psychotherapist's guide.* Routledge.

Corbett, L. (2020). *Psyche and the sacred.* Routledge.

Corbett, L. (2021). *The God-Image: From antiquity to Jung.* Chiron Publications.

Corbett, L. (2023). *Jung's philosophy, controversies, quantum mechanics, and the self.* Routledge.

Creed, B. (1993). *The monstrous-feminine: Film, feminism, psychoanalysis.* Routledge.

Crenshaw, J.L. (1984). *A whirlpool of torment.* Fortress Press.

Crossan, J.D. (1995). *Who Killed Jesus? Exposing the Roots of Antisemitism in the Gospel Story of the Death of Jesus.* Harper San Francisco.

Crossan, J.D. (2012). *The power of parable: How fiction by Jesus became fiction about Jesus.* HarperOne.

Crossan, J.D., & Wright, N.T. (2006). *The resurrection of Jesus*. Fortress Press.
Cryer, F.H. (1994). *Divination in ancient Israel and its Near Eastern environment: a sociohistorical investigation*. Sheffield Academic Press.
Cupitt, D. (2001). *Taking Leave of God* (Second ed.). SCM Press.
Daniluk, J. C., & Browne, N. (2008). Traditional religious doctrine and women's spirituality: Reconciling the contradictions. *Women & Therapy*, *31*(1), 129–142.
Daschke, D.M. (1999). Desolate among them: Loss, fantasy, and recovery in the book of Ezekiel. *American Imago*, *56*(2), 105–132.
De Rosa, P. (1989). *Vicars of Christ*. Corgi Books.
de Vos, G. A., & Suarez-Orozco, M. M. (1987). Sacrifice and the experience of power. *Journal of Psychoanalytic Anthropology*, *10*(4), 309–340.
Dein, S., & Littlewood, R. (2007). The Voice of God. *Anthropology & Medicine*, *14*(2), 213–228.
Dever, W.G. (2006). The Western cultural tradition is at risk. *Biblical Archeological Review*, *32*(2), 26.
Dever, W. G. (2017). From the Bible to the levant and beyond. *Near Eastern Archaeology*, *80*(3), 148–153.
Dewhurst, K., & Beard, A.W. (1970). Sudden Religious conversions in temporal lobe epilepsy. *British Journal of Psychiatry*, *117*, 497–507.
Dobrzeniecki, M. (2021). The metaphysics of the incarnation in contemporary analytic philosophy of religion. *Verbum Vitae 39*(2), 571–587.
Dobson, J. (1996). *The new dare to discipline*. Tyndale House.
Doherty, E. (2005). *The Jesus puzzle: Did Christianity begin with a mythical Christ?* Age of Reason Publications.
Douglas, M. (1966). *Purity and danger: An analysis of concepts of pollution and taboo*. Routledge.
Dourley, J. (1975). *Paul Tillich and Bonaventure: An evaluation of Paul Tillich's claim to stand in the Augustinian-Franciscan tradition*. E.J. Brill.
Dreifuss, G., & Riemer, J. (1995). *Abraham, the man and the symbol: A Jungian interpretation of the biblical story*. Chiron.
Dundes, A. (1991). *The blood libel legend: A casebook in anti-Semitic folklore* (pp. 336–360). University of Wisconsin Press.
Dundes, A. (1993). *Folklore matters*. University of Tennessee Press.
Dunn, J.D.G. (2005). *A new perspective on Jesus: What the quest for the historical Jesus missed*. Baker Academic.
Edinger, E. (1972). *Ego and archetype*. Penguin Books.
Edinger, E. (1990). *Anatomy of the psyche: Alchemical symbols in psychotherapy*. Open Court.
Edinger, E. (1999). *Archetype of the apocalypse*. Open Court Press.
Edinger, E. F. (1964). Trinity and quaternity. *Journal of Analytical Psychology*, *9*(2), 103.
Edinger, E.F. (1986). *The Bible and the psyche: Individuation symbolism in the Old Testament*. Inner City Books.
Edinger, E.F. (1987). *The Christian archetype: A Jungian commentary on the life of Christ*. Inner City Books.
Efthimiadis-Keith, H. (2010). Genesis 2:18-25 from a Jungian and Feminist-Deconstructionist Point of View. *Old Testament Essays*, *23*(1), 44–65.

Ehrman, B.D. (2012). *Forgery and counterforgery: The use of literary deceit in early Christian polemics*. Oxford University Press.
Eichrodt, W. (1967). *Theology of the old testament*. John Knox Press.
Eliade, M. (1961). *The sacred and the profane*. Harper Torchbooks.
Eliade, M. (1975). *Myths, dreams, and mysteries; The encounter between contemporary faiths and archaic realities*. Harper and Row.
Eliade, M. (1991). *The myth of the eternal return or, cosmos and history* (W. R. Trask, Trans.). Princeton University Press. (Original work published 1949).
Ellens, J.H. (1997). The Bible and psychology, an interdisciplinary pilgrimage. *Pastoral Psychology, 45*, 193–208).
Ellens, J.H. (2007). *The destructive power of religion*. Praeger.
Ellens, J.H. & Rollins, W.G. (Eds.) (2004). *Psychology and the Bible*. Praeger.
Ellerbe, H. (1995). *The dark side of Christian history*. Morningstar and Lark.
Elwin, V. (1943). The vagina dentata legend. *British Journal of Medical Psychology, 19*, 439–453.
Erikson, E. (1958). *Young man Luther*. W.W. Norton.
Feinberg, J.S. (2005). *No one like him: The doctrine of God*. Crossway.
Feiner, A. H., & Levenson, E. A. (1968). The compassionate sacrifice: An explanation of a metaphor. *Psychoanalytic Review, 55*(4), 552–573.
Ferenczi, S. (1933). Confusion of tongues between adults and the child. In M. Balint (Ed.), *Final Contributions to the Problems and Methods of Psycho-Analysis* (pp. 156–167). Karnac Books.
Ferguson, J. (1978). *War and peace in the world's religions*. Oxford University Press.
Festinger, L., Riecken, H., & Schacter, S. (1956). *When prophecy fails: A social and psychological study of a modern group that predicted the destruction of the world*. University of Minnesota Press.
Feuerbach, L. (2008/1881). *The essence of Christianity*. Dover Publications.
Finkelstein, I., & Silberman, N.A. (2002). *The Bible unearthed*. Touchstone.
Frazer, J.G. (1919). *The golden bough*. (3rd ed., part 2). Macmillan.
Freud, S. (1909). A case of obsessional neurosis. *Standard Edition, 10*, 233–234.
Freud, S. (1913). Totem and Taboo. *Standard Edition* 13, p. 88.
Freud, S. (1923). A neurosis of demonical possession in the seventeenth century (J. Riviere, Trans.). In *Collected papers* (vol. 4, pp. 436–472). Basic Books.
Freudmann, L.C. (1994). *Antisemitism in the New Testament*. University Press of America.
Fromm, E. (1950). *Psychoanalysis and religion*. Yale University Press.
Fromm, E. (1955). *The dogma of Christ and other essays on religion, psychology and culture*. Hogarth Press.
Fromm, E. (1996). *You shall be as gods*. Fawcett Premier Books.
Funk, R.W. (1997). *Honest to Jesus: Jesus for a new millennium*. HarperSanFrancisco.
Gallagher, R. E. (2009). A case of demonic possession—and its many counterfeits. *The Dunwoodie Review, 32*, 274–284.
Gane, R. E. (2022). Sacrifice and the old testament. In B. N. Wolfe et al. (Eds.), *St Andrews Encyclopaedia of Theology*. https://www.saet.ac.uk/Christianity/SacrificeandtheOldTestament
Garber, D.G. (2004). Traumatizing Ezekiel: The exilic prophet. In: Ellens, J.H. & Rollins, W.G. (Eds.). *Psychology and the Bible*. Praeger.

Garbini, G. (1988). *History and ideology in ancient Israel*. Crossroad Publishing.
Garfinkel, S. (1989). Another model for Ezekiel's abnormalities. *Journal of the Ancient Near Eastern Society of Columbia University, 19*, 39–50.
Geschwind, N. (1983). Behavioural changes in epilepsy. *Epilepsia 24*(1), S23–S30.
Ghent, E. (1990). Masochism, submission, surrender—Masochism as a perversion of surrender. *Contemporary Psychoanalysis, 26*, 108–136.
Gimbutas, M. (1991). *The civilization of the goddess: The world of old Europe*. Harper.
Gimbutas, M. (2005). *The living goddesses*. University of California Press.
Gohr, M. (2013). Do I Have Something in My Teeth? Vagina Dentata and its Manifestations within Popular Culture. In: B. Fahs, M. Duty, & S. Stage (Eds.), *The Moral Panics of Sexuality*. Palgrave Macmillan.
Goldbrunner, J. (1964). *Individuation: A study of the depth psychology of Carl Gustav Jung*. University of Notre Dame Press.
Goldhagen, D. (2003). *Moral duty: The role of the Catholic Church in the Holocaust and its unfulfilled duty of repair*. Vintage Books.
Gordon, R. (1987). Masochism: the shadow side of the archetypal need to worship. *The Journal of Analytical Psychology, 32*(3), 227–240.
Greven, P.J. (1992). *Spare the child: The religious roots of punishment and the psychological impact of physical abuse*. Vintage Books.
Gross, R.M. (1996). *Feminism and religion*. Beacon Press.
Hagner, D. A. (2016). How "New" is the New Testament? Continuity and Discontinuity Between the Old Testament (Formative Judaism) and the New Testament (Early Christianity). *Asian Journal of Pentecostal Studies, 19*(2), 99–107.
Haley, J. (1969). *The power tactics of Jesus Christ*. Avon Books.
Halperin, D.J. (1993). *Seeking Ezekiel: Test and psychology*. Penn State University Press.
Harpur, T. (2004). *The pagan Christ*. Thomas Allen Publishers.
Heilman, S., & Friedman, M. (2012). *The Rebbe: The life and afterlife of Menachem Mendel Schneerson*. Princeton University Press.
Heschel, A.J. (1962). *The prophets*. Jewish Publication Society of America.
Heschel, R.M. (1955). *God in search of man: A philosophy of Judaism*. Farrar, Straus, and Giroux.
Hick, J. (Ed.) (1977). *The myth of God incarnate*. SCM Press.
Hick, J. (2010). *Evil and the God of love*. Springer Publications.
Hopkins, B. (1989). Jesus and object-use: A Winnicottian account of the resurrection myth. *International Review of Psycho-Analysis, 16*, 93–100.
Horney, K. (1973). *Feminine psychology*. W.W. Norton.
Horney, K. (2000). *New ways in psychoanalysis*. W.W. Norton.
Hostie, R. (1957). *Religion and the psychology of C.G. Jung*. Sheed & Ward.
Hubert, H., & Mauss, M. (1964). *Sacrifice: Its nature and function*. University of Chicago Press.
Ivey, G. (1993). Psychodynamic aspects of demonic possession and Satanic worship. *South African Journal of Psychology, 23*(4), 186–194.
Jackson, M.C., & Fulford, K.W.M. (1997). Spiritual experience and sychopathology. *Philosophy, Psychiatry &Psychology 4(*1), 42–65.
Jaffe, D. S. (1968). The masculine envy of woman's procreative function. *Journal of the American Psychoanalytic Association, 16*(3), 521–548.

Jay, N. B. (1985). Sacrifice as remedy for having been born of woman. In C.W. Atkinson, C.H. Buchanan & M.R. Miles (Eds.), *Immaculate and powerful: the female in sacred image and social reality* (pp. 283–309). Beacon Press.

Jaynes, J. (1976). *The origin of consciousness in the breakdown of the bicameral mind.* Houghton Mifflin.

Juergensmeyer, M. (2001). *Terror in the mind of God.* University of California Press.

Jung, C.G. (1963). *Memories, dreams, reflections.* Vintage Books.

Jung, C.G. (1975). *Letters* (vol. 2. G. Adler & A. Jaffe (Eds.). Trans. R.F.C. Hull). Princeton University Press.

Jung, C.G. (1976). *The visions seminars* (vol. 1). Spring Publications.

Jung, C. G. (1998). *Jung's seminar on Nietzsche's Zarathustra.* Ed. & Abridged by J. L. Jarrett. Princeton University Press.

Kamat, S., & Tharakan, K. (2021). The sacred and the profane: Menstrual flow and religious values. *Journal of Human Values, 27*(30), 261–268.

Kille, D.A. (2001). *Psychological biblical criticism.* Augsburg Fortress Press.

Kimball, C. (2002). *When religion becomes evil.* Harper Collins.

Kirkpatrick, L. A. (2005). *Attachment, evolution, and the psychology of religion.* Guilford Press.

Klein, L. K. (2018). *Pure: Inside the Evangelical movement that shamed a generation of young women and how I broke free.* Simon and Schuster.

Klein, M. (1935). A Contribution to the Psychogenesis of Manic-depressive States. *International Journal of Psycho-Analysis, 16*, 145–174.

Kluger, R. S. (1967). *Satan in the Old Testament.* Northwestern University Press.

Kluger, R. S. (1974). *Psyche and Bible.* Spring Publications.

Kohut, H. (1972). Thoughts on narcissism and narcissistic rage. *Psychoanalytic Studies of the Child, 27*, 369–399.

Kohut, H. (1978). Creativeness, charisma, group psychology: Reflections on the self-analysis of Freud. In P. H. Ornstein (Ed.), *The search for the self: Selected writings of Heinz Kohut: 1950–1978* (pp. 793–843). Karnac Books.

Kohut, H. (1997). *The restoration of the self.* University of Chicago Press.

Kohut, H. & Wolf, E. (1978). The Disorders of the self and their treatment (An Outline). *International Journal of Psycho-Analysis, 59*, 413–425.

Kugel, J.L. (1997). *The Bible as it was.* Belknap Press of Harvard University Press.

Kuhn, A.B. (1940). *The lost light: An interpretation of ancient scriptures.* The Academy Press.

Landsborough, D. (1987). St. Paul and temporal lobe epilepsy. *Journal of Neurology, Neurosurgery, and Psychiatry, 50*, 659–664.

Lederer, W. (1968). *The fear of women.* Harcourt Brace Jovanovich.

Lerner, G. (1986). *The creation of patriarchy.* Oxford University Press.

Lewis, C.S. (2015a). *A grief observed.* HarperOne.

Lewis, C.S. (2015b). *The problem of pain.* HarperOne.

Lüdeman, G. (1996). *The unholy in Holy Scripture: The dark side of the Bible.* John Knox Press.

Lupton, M. J. (1989). Claude dagmar daly: Notes on the menstruation complex. *American Imago, 46*(1), 1–20.

Luyten, P., Corveleyn, J., & Fontaine, J. R. J. (1998). The relationship between religiosity and mental health: distinguishing between guilt and shame. *Mental Health. Religion & Culture, 1*(8), 165–184.

Maccoby, H. (1998). *The mythmaker: Paul and the invention of Christianity*. Barnes & Noble Books.

Markus, R. (2000). Surrealism's Praying Mantis and Castrating Woman. *Woman's Art Journal, 21*(1), 33–39.

Marmodoro, A. & Hill, J. (Eds.) (2011). *The metaphysics of the incarnation*. Oxford University Press.

Mayers, K. S., Heller, D. K., & Heller, J. A. (2003). Damaged sexual self-esteem: A kind of disability. *Sexuality and Disability, 21*(4), 269–282.

McGinn, B. (1994). *Antichrist: Two thousand years of the human fascination with evil*. HarperCollins.

McGrath, A. E. (2022). The doctrine of the trinity: Intellectual construct or ontological reality? Reflections from the philosophy of science. *International Journal of Systematic Theology, 26*(1), 70–90.

McWhinnie, L. (2017). Gender and the Trinity: An Analysis of Feminist, Traditional and Alternative Approaches. *Churchman, 131*(1), 39–47.

Melcher, S. J. (2003). The problem of anti-Judaism in Christian feminist biblical interpretation: some pragmatic suggestions. *Cross Currents, 53*(1), 22–31.

Meloy, J. R. (1986). Narcissistic psychopathology and the clergy. *Pastoral Psychology, 35*, 50–55.

Mercer, J. (2013). Deliverance, demonic possession, and mental illness: some considerations for mental health professionals. *Mental Health, Religion & Culture, 16*(6), 595–611.

Merkur, D. (2004). Reading the prophecies of Jeremiah through a psychoanalytic lens. In J. H. Ellens & W.G. Rollins (Eds.), *Psychology and the Bible* (pp. 141–184). Praeger.

Mettinger, T.N.D. (2013). *The riddle of resurrection: "Dying and rising gods" in the Ancient Near East*. Eisenbrauns.

Metzger, J.A. (2009). Where has Yahweh gone? Reclaiming unsavory images of God in New Testament studies. *Horizons in biblical theology, 31*, 51–76.

Miles, J. (1995). *God, a biography*. Knopf.

Miles, J. (2001). *Christ, a crisis in the life of God*. Knopf.

Miller, J.W. (1997). *Jesus at thirty: A psychological and historical portrait*. Augsburg/Fortress.

Mills, J. (2017). *Inventing God: Psychology of belief and the rise of secular spirituality*. Routledge.

Milner, M. (1969). *The hands of the living God*. International Universities Press.

Minton, S.A., & Minton, M.R. (1969). *Venomous reptiles*. Charles Scribner.

Mizruchi, S. L. (1998). *The science of sacrifice: American literature and modern social theory*. Princeton University Press.

Montgomery, R. E. (1974). A cross-cultural study of menstruation, menstrual taboos, and related social variables. *Ethos. 2*, (2), 137–170.

Neumann, E. (1954). *The origins and history of consciousness*. Princeton University Press.

Neumann, E. (1983). *The Great Mother*. Princeton University Press.

Noonan, B. J. (2021). On the efficacy of the atoning sacrifices: A Biblical theology of sacrifice from Leviticus. *Bulletin for Biblical Research, 31*(3), 285–318.

Oates, L. (1997). *Prophetic charisma: The psychology of revolutionary religious personalities*. Syracuse University Press.

Oates, L. (2010). *The charismatic personality*. Australian Academic Press.
Olatunji, B. O., Abramowitz, J. S., Williams, N. L., Connolly, K. M., & Lohr, J. M. (2007). Scrupulosity and obsessive-compulsive symptoms: Confirmatory factor analysis and validity of the Penn Inventory of Scrupulosity. *Journal of Anxiety Disorders*, *21*(6), 771–787.
Ostow, M. (1996). *Myth and madness: The psychodynamics of antisemitism*. Transaction Publishers.
Otero, S. (1996). "Fearing our mothers": An overview of the psychoanalytic theories concerning the vagina dentata motif. *The American Journal of Psychoanalysis*, *56*(3), 269–288.
Pagels, E. (1996). *The origin of Satan*. Vintage Books.
Patai, R. (1990). *The Hebrew goddess*. Wayne State University Press.
Penchansky, D. (1999). *What rough beast? Images of God in the Hebrew Bible*. John Knox Press.
Penchansky, D. (2005). *Twilight of the gods: Polytheism in the Hebrew Bible*. John Knox Press.
Perera, S. B. (1986). *The scapegoat complex: Toward a mythology of shadow and guilt*. Inner City Press.
Perry, J.W. (2011). *The self in psychotic process*. Literary Licensing.
Phipps, W.E. (1980). The menstrual taboo in the Judeo-Christian tradition. *Journal of Religion and Health*, *19*(4), 298–303.
Quinn, P.L. (1986). Christian atonement and Kantian justification. *Faith and Philosophy* *3*, 440–462.
Rae, S. (2018). *Moral choices: An introduction to ethics*. Zondervan Academic.
Rahner, K. (1966). *Theological investigations, vol. 5*. Darton, Longman & Todd.
Raitt, J. (1980). The vagina dentata and the immaculatus uterus divini fontis. *Journal of the American Academy of Religion*, *48*(3), 415–431.
Ranke-Heinemann, U. (1994). *Putting away childish things*. HarperSanFrancisco.
Reich, T. (1941). *Masochism in modern man*. Grove Press.
Riley, G.J. (1999). Devil. In K. Van der Toorn, B. Becking & P.W. Van der Horst (Eds.), *Dictionary of Deities and Demons in the Bible* (pp. 244–249). Brill.
Rizzuto, A.M. (1979). *The birth of the living God*. University of Chicago Press.
Robinson, H. W. (1948). *Two Hebrew Prophets*. Lutterworth Press.
Rollins, W.G. (1983). *Jung and the Bible*. John Knox Press.
Rollins, W.G. (1999). *Soul and psyche: The Bible in psychological perspective*. Fortress Press.
Rollins, W.G., & Kille, D.A. (Eds.) (2007). *Psychological insights into the Bible*. Eermans Publishing.
Ross, L. D., Lelkes, Y., & Russell, A. G. (2012). How Christians reconcile their personal political views and the teachings of their faith: Projection as a means of dissonance reduction. *Proceedings of the National Academy of Sciences of the United States of America*, *109*(10), 3616–3622.
Round table discussion: Anti-Judaism and Postcolonial Biblical Interpretation. (2004). *Journal of Feminist Studies in Religion* *20*(1), 91–132.
Rubenstein, R. (1972). *My brother Paul*. Harper and Row.
Ruether, R. (1974). *Faith and fratricide*. Seabury.
Ruether, R. (1981). *To change the world: Christology and cultural criticism*. SCM Press.
Ruether, R. (1993). *Sexism and God-talk: Towards a feminist theology*. Beacon Press.

Ruether, R. R. (2014). Sexism and misogyny in the Christian tradition: liberating alternatives. *Buddhist-Christian Studies*, *34*, 83–94.
Russell, B. (1967). *Why I am not a Christian*. Touchstone.
Sanford, J. A. (1981). *The man who wrestled with God: Light from the Old Testament on the psychology of individuation*. Paulist Press.
Schaer, H. (1950). *Religion and the cure of souls in Jung's psychology*. Pantheon Books.
Schept, S. (2021) Lilith: A rabbinic projection of the demonic female. *Psychological Perspectives*, *64*(2), 189–200.
Scholem, G. (1973). *Sabbatai Sevi, the Mystical Messiah*. Princeton University Press.
Schonfield, H. J. (2012). *Those incredible Christians*. CreateSpace Independent Publishing.
Schultz, M. (1986). The blood libel. *Journal of Psychohistory 14*, 1–24.
Schwartz, R. (1997). *The curse of Cain: The violent history of monotheism*.
Schweitzer, A. (1981). *The quest of the historical Jesus*. SCM Press.
Seth, N., (2002). Hindu avatara and Christian incarnation: A comparison. *Philosophy East and West, Vol. 52*(1), 98–125.
Shaw, G. (1983). *The cost of authority: Manipulation and freedom in the New Testament*. Fortress.
Shlain, L. (1998). *The alphabet versus the goddess*. Viking Penguin.
Smith, M.S. (2004). *The Memoirs of God: History, memory and the experience of the divine in ancient Israel*. Fortress.
Smith, W. R. (1972). *The religion of the Semites: The fundamental institutions*. Schocken Books.
Spanos, N.P. (1996). Historical manifestations of demonic possession. In *Multiple identities & false memories: A sociocognitive perspective* (pp. 157–170). American Psychological Association.
Speiser, E.A. (1962). Mesopotamian motifs in the early chapters of genesis. *Expedition Magazine 5*(1). Accessed September 19, 2023.
Spiro, M.E. (1997). *Gender ideology and psychological reality: An essay on cultural reproduction*. Yale University Press.
Stein, G. (2009). Did Ezekiel have first-rank symptoms? *The British Journal of Psychiatry*, *194*(6), 551–551.
Stein, G. (2010). The voices that Ezekiel hears. *British Journal of Psychiatry*, *196*(2), 101–101.
Stein, M. (2018). *The Bible as a dream*. Chiron.
Stolorow, R. D., & Lachmann, F. M. (1980). *Psychoanalysis of Developmental Arrests*. International Universities Press.
Stone, M. (1976). *When God was a woman*. Harvest.
Strang, V. (2004). *The meaning of water*. Berg Publishers.
Strozier, C.B. (1994). *Apocalypse: On the psychology of fundamentalism in America*. Beacon Press.
Sugar, M. (2002). Commonalities between the Isaac and Oedipus myths. *Journal of the American Academy of Psychoanalysis*, 30, 691–706.
Tacey, D. J. (2015). *Religion as metaphor*. Transaction Publishers.
Tam, E.P.C. (1997). Are Christian martyrs abuse victims, neurotics, or suicidal? Comments on the psychological study of Christian martyrdom. *Journal of Psychology and Theology*, *25*(4), 458–467.
Tarpley, H. (1993). Vagina envy in men. *Journal of the American Academy of Psychoanalysis*, *21*(3), 457–464.

Taves, A. (2011). *Religious experience reconsidered: A building-block approach to the study of religion and other special things*. Princeton University Press.
Taves, A. (2016). *Revelatory events: Three case studies of the emergence of new spiritual paths*. Princeton University Press.
Theissen, G. (1987). *Psychological aspects of Pauline theology*. (Trans. John P. Galvin). Fortress.
Thompson, S. (1997). *Motif-Index of Folk-Literature: a Classification of Narrative Elements in Folktales, Ballads, Myths, Fables, Mediaeval Romances, Exempla, Fabliaux, Jest-Books and Local Legends*. Indiana University Press.
Thompson, T. L. (2000). *The mythic past: biblical archaeology and the myth of Israel*. Basic Books.
Trible, P. (1979). Eve and Adam: Genesis 2-3 Reread. In: C.P. Christ & J. Plaskow (Eds.), *Womanspirit Rising: A Feminist Reader in Religion*. Harper.
Van Bruggen, J. (2007). The martyrdom of Paul. In G. Glas, M.H. Spero, P.J. Verhagen, & H.M. van Praag (Eds.), *Hearing visions and seeing voices*. Springer.
Von Franz, M.-L. (1980). *Projection and re-collection in Jungian thought: Reflections of the soul*. Open Court Publishing.
Von Kellenbach, K. (2020). Guilt and the transformation of Christian-Jewish relations. *Studies in Christian-Jewish relations, 15*(1), 1–21.
Walker, B. (1983). *The woman's encyclopedia of myths and secrets*. Harper & Row Publishers.
Weaver, (1999). *The historical Jesus in the twentieth century 1900-1950*. Trinity Press.
Weber, M., & Eisenstadt, S.N. (1968). *On charisma and institution building*. University of Chicago Press.
Weil, S. (1951). *Waiting for God*. G.P. Putnam's Sons.
White, V. (1960). *Soul and psyche: An Enquiry into the relationship of psychotherapy and religion*. Collins Publications.
Wilson, E.O. (2015). *The meaning of human existence*. Liveright Publishing.
Winer, J. A., Jobe, T., & Ferrono, C. (1984). Toward a psychoanalytic theory of the charismatic relationship. *Annuals of Psychoanalysis, 12*, 155–175.
Wink, W. (1998). *The powers that be: A theology for the new millennium*. Doubleday.
Winnicott, D.W. (1969). The use of an object. *International Journal of Psychoanalysis, 50*(4), 711–716.
Winnicott, D.W. (1975). *Through Paediatrics to Psychoanalysis*. Hogarth Press.
Winnicott, D. W. (1982). The development of the capacity for concern. In *The Maturational Processes and the Facilitating Environment* (pp. 73–82). International Universities Press.
Winnicott, D.W. (1986). *Home is where we start from: Essays by a psychoanalyst*. W.W. Norton.
Wright, J.R. (2018). *Reimagining God and religion: Essays for the psychologically minded*. Chiron.
Wroe, A. (2000). *Pontius Pilate: The biography of an invented man*. Random House.
Young, A.J. (2009). In likeness and unity: debunking the creation order fallacy. *Priscilla Papers, 23*(2), 12–15.
Zhong, C.-B., & Liljenquist, K. (2006). Washing Away Your Sins: Threatened Morality and Physical Cleansing. *Science, 313*(5792), 1451–1452.

Index

Pages followed by "n" refer to notes.

Aaron 134
Abelard, Peter 160, 162n8
Aberbach, D. 166
Abraham 78–81
abuse of children 79–81
Acland, A. F. 112
The Acts of Paul 74–75
Adam and Eve *see* Garden of Eden
Adler, Alfred 128
Ahab 41, 134
Akkadian Epic of Gilgamesh 55
Alexander the Great 59
Altschuler, Eric 149
Amalekites 26
Ambrose, Saint 31, 107–108
Amos 3: 6 43
Amos 4: 7–12 43
Anabaptists 114
angels 34–35
Anselm: atonement for 159; *Cur Deus Homo* 159; satisfaction theory 159
Answer to Job (Jung) 43
anthropomorphic metaphors 15
anti-abortion violence 105–106
anti-Judaism 117–121
anti-Semitism 118, 120, 124n22
apocalypse/apocalyptic fantasies 30, 58–60, 63, 116
Apocalypto 99
apologists 12
Aquinas, Thomas 83–84, 159; martyrdom for 75; women for 85
archeology 51
archetypal evil 36
archetypal images 39
Arius 176

asceticism and masochism 75–76
assimilation through reflection 40
Athanasius 176
atonement 158–161; satisfaction theory 159–160; substitutionary 161; vicarious 160
Attis: death and resurrection 186
Augustine, Saint 83–84, 177; Devil for 35; Garden of Eden story and 63–64; just war 31, 107–108; sin for 154–155, 159
authoritarianism 138
authority of the Bible 13–16
autonomous complex 143
avatar(s): in Hindu tradition 172; Jesus as 172
Azazel 32

Babylonian Exile 23n3, 34, 46, 50, 59, 67, 121, 132, 150
Bakan, David 89; *The Duality of Human Existence* 89; on infanticide 77–79
Balaam's ass 19, 23n5
Bataille, Georges 101
Becker, Ernest 186
Becking, Bob 51
bereavement 185
Bergmann, Martin 77–78, 81
Bettelheim, Bruno 89
Bible 1, 6–17, 24–25; authority of 13–16; authors of 11–12; demonic possession 151; as divinely inspired 2; historical importance 38; as inerrant 17; infanticide in 77–79; interpretations 1–2, 8–12, 38; murderous behavior 29; psychological-critical approach to 11; psychological lens 38–40;

psychological *vs.* theological approaches to 12–13; reader-response criticism 11; violence 3–4
Black Death 119
blasphemy 134
blood: menstrual 92, 95–98; sacrifice and ritual 98–103
Blumenthal, D. R. 27
Bonaventure 177
book: of Acts 142; of Daniel 115, 170; of Deuteronomy 52; of Enoch 34; of Hebrews 78; of Job 77; of Joshua 51; of Judges 78; of Lamentations 74, 79; of Leviticus 40, 92
Bronze Age 85
Broome, Edwin 148
Brueggemann, W. 27
Buber, Martin 4n1
Buddha 181
Buddhism 20
Bultmann, Rudolf 16, 57, 68n2

Callan, Terrance 137
Calvin, John 84, 159
Campbell, Joseph 52–54, 62–63
Capps, Donald 89
Carlin, Nathan 89
Castelein, John 112
catatonia 148
charisma 164–167, 187n2
Charlemagne 108
child/children: abuse 79–81; sacrifice/sacrificing 77–79
Christian Identity 30, 37n4, 106
Christianity 2; Constantine's sponsorship 17; narcissism in 136–139; supremacy 110–111; *see also* Bible; Gospel(s); Jesus
Chrysostom, St. John 35, 111
Church: as authoritative guide 16; councils 7, 17; doctrine and dogma 16–17; Ranke-Heinemann on 16; teachings 7
circumcision 77, 110
cleansing *see* ritual purity
Clement of Alexandria 85
cognitive dissonance 114–117
consciousness: divine 181–182; unconscious and 182
conspiracy theories 33
Constantine 17
contagious effect 92–93

continuity after death 186–187
Cook, Michael 118
Corbett, Lionel 21, 41, 112
Corinthians 137
Council of Chalcedon 180
Council of Elvira 95
Council of Mâcon 85
Council of Nicaea 170, 172, 175
Council of Trent 64
Couvade syndrome 89
Creed, Barbara 90
Creed of Chalcedon 170
Cross 127
Crossan, John 184
crucifixion 162n8; critics on 67; destructiveness of 185
Cupitt, Don 19–20
Cur Deus Homo (Anselm) 159
Cyrus 133

Daly, Claude 124n17
Daschke, Dereck 150
David, King 51
death: continuity after 186–187
defilement 91–95
deliverance 58, 151; *see also* exorcisms
demonic possession 151–152; belief in 152; women and 151
destructive power 105–108
Deuteronomy 27–28 41
Deuteronomy 23: 3 95
Devil 34–36; Jung on 36; as a source of evil 27
de Vos, G. A. 101
diet and dietary laws 93–94
divine impregnation 54–55
divinity 181
doctrines and dogmas 3, 7; Jung's symbolic approach to 8
Douglas, Mary 93–94
Dreifuss, G. 80
The Duality of Human Existence (Bakan) 89
Dundes, Alan 90, 119
Dunn, James 174
Durkheim, Emile 101

Edinger, Edward F. 39, 54, 59, 66, 102, 147–148, 180
ego 182
Ehrman, Bart 52–53
Eichrodt, W. 27
Eliade, Mircea 66, 101

Elijah 46
Elisha 46, 136
Ellens, J. Harold 6–7, 30, 39, 121–122
Elwin, Verrier 90
English Civil War of 1642 108
Enuma Elish 31
Epistle to the Hebrews 74
The Essence of Christianity (Feuerbach) 17
Eve *see* Garden of Eden
Evil and the God of Love (Hick) 36
Exodus 51
Exodus 15: 3 42
exorcisms 35, 104, 151–152
Ezekiel 15, 24, 35, 41, 92, 134, 140; 7: 7–8 121; mental state or illness 144, 147–150

fascism 129
Fear and Trembling (Kierkegaard) 80
fear of women *see* male fear of women
Ferenczi, S. 130
Feuerbach, Ludwig 17–19, 62; *The Essence of Christianity* 17; *Lectures on the Essence of Religion* 19; transcendence of God for 18
Filicide 48n1
First Nation groups 89–90
First Temple period 34
First World War 185
flood myths 24–25
Francis, Pope 34
Franciscans 108
Frankl, Victor 37
Frazer, James 97, 122n4, 186
free will defense 36
Freud, Sigmund 18–19, 22, 32–33, 46, 77, 88, 120, 122n1, 129, 149, 152, 188n12; "Medusa's Head" 88; phallocentric theory 88
Fromm, Erich 65–66, 128, 158
fulfillment prophecy 45
fundamentalism 158

Galatians 3: 28 82
Garber, David 140, 150
Garbini, Giovanni 50–51
Garden of Eden 55, 63–67, 97–98, 121, 154, 159, 182; Augustine on 63–64; Edinger on 66; Fromm on 65–66; Jung on 66–67; Kluger on 66; male dominance 87; narcissistic element 65–66; Paul and 63–64, 71, 82; serpent 64–67; Stone on 65; women and 82, 84, 97
Genesis: 2–3 65; 6: 1–4 34; 2: 18 61; 3: 16 98; creation story 55, 62; Stone on 65
Geschwind, N. 142, 149
Geschwind syndrome 142
Ghent, Emmanuel 76
glossolalia 111–112
Gnostics 17, 47, 63
God 14; anger 27; divine impregnation by 54–55; Feuerbach on 17–19, 62; harmful behavior 27; Orthodox Jews and 14; power of 125–128; as *Summum Bonum* 44
Gohr, Michelle 90
Goldbrunner, Joseph 4n1
The Golden Bough (Frazer) 97
Goldhagen, Daniel 124n22
Gordon, R. 76
Gospel(s): of John 35, 117–118, 164, 168–170, 172, 184; of Mark 138, 168, 170; of Matthew 83, 118; myths/mythologies 62–63; resurrection 183–185; satisfying agendas of Christian groups 17; Synoptic 168–170, 174
Greek Church Fathers 155
Greek myth 54–55
grief: fundamentalism as way of coping with 158
guilt and shame 153, 156–158, 161n6; childhood and 156; parental judgment 156; sexuality/sexual feelings 156–157; transmission of 155

Haley, Jay 74
Halperin, David 149
Harpur, T. 55
hate/hatred 112–113
Hebrew Bible 14; apocalypse promises 59; contemporary scholars 14, 51; disasters and 121; hermeneutic approaches 52; infanticide in 79; misreading and mistranslation 45–47; moral code 120; mythic imagery 55, 57; narcissism 132–136; prophecies 46; prophets 142–150; resurrection 183; ritual purity 91–98; Satan 34; scapegoat complex 31–32; sin 155–156; *see also* Yhwh
Hellenistic period 34
Hellenization 59

Index

Heschel, Abraham 140, 144–146, 152n3–152n4
Hick, John 36; *Evil and the God of Love* 36; Incarnation for 180–181
Hindu/Hinduism 172
Hitler, Adolf 165
Holy Scriptures 1
holy war 28, 107–108
homoousios 178–179
Homo Sapiens 108–109
homosexuality 82
Honest to God (Robinson) 57
Hopkins, Brooke 185–186
Horney, Karen 73, 88
Hosea 5: 3–7 92
Hosea 13: 16 48n1
Hostie, Raymond 4n1

idealization 72–73, 164–167
identity: resurrected individual 184; trinity 176
idols, worship of 15
image of God 13, 40–45; anthropomorphic 15; dark side 13, 27; human psychology 17–19, 40–42; loving 27; projection of human psychology 17–19
Incarnation 172, 180–182; compositional view 182; Hick on 180–181; Jung on 182; psychological approaches to 182
Index of Forbidden Books 130
individuation: archetypal phase 167; unconscious 182
infanticide 77–79
Inquisition 45
intermarriage 95
interpretations of Bible 1–3, 38; deceit and self-deception 45–47; fallacious or illusory 16; literal reading and 8; value and limitations 8–12
intolerance 138
invasion of Canaan 50–51, 107
Isaac 77–81, 122n5
Isaiah 35; 52–53 32; 34: 5–6 3; 42: 13 42; 45: 7 43; 7: 14 45; 53: 3 45–46; 53: 8 115; 6: 1–10 144; as prophet of salvation 144; visionary experience 143
Ishtar: death and resurrection 186
Islam 115
Israel and Israelites 26–28, 30–32, 34, 41–42, 46, 49n4, 50–52, 59, 67, 77, 81, 87, 92–95, 102–103, 107, 110, 114, 116–117, 121–122, 131–134, 136, 144–145, 147, 149–150, 164, 173
Ivey, Gavin 152

Jaffe, Daniel 89
James, William 146
Jay, Nancy 102–103
Jaynes, Julian 143
Jephthah 78, 136
Jeremiah 42, 77, 128, 132, 143–144, 146–147, 152n5; anguish and depression 146; prophecies 147
Jerome, Saint 96
Jerusalem 31–32, 51–52, 58–59, 67, 77, 81, 91, 96, 99, 103, 106, 108, 110, 114, 116–117, 132–133, 149–150, 171
Jesus 14; as an innocent scapegoat 32; as the avatar of god 172; biblical portrayal 163–187; casting out of demons or evil spirits 151; charisma 164–167; Devil and 35; human nature 181; image in the Gospel stories 168–172; Incarnation 180–182; kindness 44–45; Kingdom 7; as a mana personality 167; as a moral exemplar 185; mythic elements in story of 62–63; oral transmission 174; Parable of the Wicked Tenants 117; Paul's image of 172–174; postmortem appearances 185; resurrection *see* resurrection; Second Coming 29, 35, 58, 68, 114, 117, 144, 184; trinity 174–180
Jews: Acts 118; death of Jesus and 116–119; Gospel of John 117–118; Gospel of Matthew 118; Matthew 27: 25 117; paranoid fantasies 119; passion narratives 117; *see also* anti-Judaism; Hebrew Bible; Judaism; Yhwh
Job 43, 77
John 14: 28 173
Josephus 118
Joshua 25
Joshua 7 155
Judaism 2, 110–111; oppression of women 120; sin in 155–156; *see also* anti-Judaism; Hebrew Bible; Jews; Yhwh
Judas 35
Juergensmeyer, M. 30–31, 106

Jung, Carl 1; Devil for 36; direct experiences of sacred for 39–40; feminist critics 187n10; Garden of Eden for 66–67; incarnation for 182; psyche for 7–8; religion for 24–25; trinity for 178–180
just war 30–31, 107–108

Kahn, Masud 76
Kali (goddess) 90
Kant, Immanuel: debt incurred by sin 160; vicarious atonement for 160
Kennedy, John F. 45
kenotic (self-emptying) theory 181
Kille, Andrew 10–11, 63
King of Moab 77
Klein, Melanie 88, 129
Kleinian theory 61
Kluger, Rivka 66
Kohut, Heinz 11, 26, 33, 101, 135, 165–167, 187n5
Korah 42
Kugel, J. L. 60–61
Kuhn, Alvin 55

Lamentations 3: 38 43
Landsborough, D. 141
Last Judgment 30
Lectures on the Essence of Religion (Feuerbach) 19
Lederer, Wolfgang 87–88, 96–97
Leviticus 96
Leviticus 16: 2 91
Lewis, C. S. 36
liberal theologians 15
Lilith 61, 68n4
Luke 170
Luke 14: 26 168
Luke 19: 27 29
Luke 24: 50–53 62
Luther, Martin 35, 84; *Vindication of Married Life* 83

Macbeth effect 123n14
Maccabean revolt 59
Maccoby, Hyam 118
magical thinking 103–104; *see also* superstitions
Makuxi of Guyana 96
male fear of women 87–91; psychological factors 87–89; vagina dentata 89–91
Malleus Maleficarum 85, 91
mana personality 103, 124n19, 167

Marcion 47
Mark 10: 18 173
Mark 13: 32 181
Mark 14: 61–62 170–171
Mark 16: 16 138
martyrdom: etymological root 75; masochism and 74–75
Mary: glorification of 55; physical assumption of 7; virginity 83–84
masochism 69–76; ascetical practices 75–76; concept 69; Ghent on 76; Gordon on 76; martyrs/martyrdom 74–75; Paul and 69–73; psychodynamic aspects 73–74
maternal infanticide 79; *see also* infanticide
Matthew 170; 5:17–18 170; 10:23 170; 2: 16–18 78; 23: 15 110; 7: 1 168; 7: 6 168; 19: 19 168; 17: 9 170; 28: 19–20 176; 27: 52 183; 25: 40 187n7
McGrath, Alistair 177
"Medusa's Head" (Freud) 88
Meloni, Giorgia 187n8
Meloy, J. Reid 131
menstrual blood 92, 95–98
mental illness 140–152; demonic possession 151–152; diagnostic criteria 151; Ezekiel 140, 147–150; prophets 142–147; temporal lobe epilepsy (TLE) 141–142, 149
Merkur, D. 147
Mesopotamian myths 55
Metzger, J. A. 29–30
Micah 171
Micah 5: 4 48
Miles, Jack 67
Miller, William 115
Mills, Jon 20
miracle stories 12, 23n3, 62–63
misogyny 81–85
Monophytism 181
monotheism 48, 134, 175
Montgomery, Rita 96
moral purity 92
Moses 21, 23n3, 25, 28, 39–40, 50, 52, 55, 134, 139n6, 142
Mt. Sinai 14, 51, 132
myths/mythologies 13, 50–68; apocalyptic 58–60; failure of biblical promises 67–68; Garden of Eden 63–67; Gospel stories 62–63; interpreting 60–62; redemptive violence 31; as sacred story 53–58

narcissism 18–19, 129–138; Christianity 136–138; dynamics 130–132; Hebrew Bible 132–136; Paul's needs 137–138
nationalism 106
Natural History (Pliny) 97
Nazis 95, 119
Nero 74–75
Nestorianism 181
Neumann, E. 66, 90
New Apostolic Reformation 124n20
New Testament 13–14, 151, 164, 181; dark side of God 44; Devil in 34–35; Hebrew Bible and 47–48; Jesus' exorcisms of devils 35; moral defilement 94; mythological motifs 55; problems with credibility 52–53; Ranke-Heinemann on 16; women and 81–83
Nietzsche, F. 128; *Thus Spake Zarathustra* 153
Noah 25, 34, 42
Numbers 25 95
numinous imagery 8
Nuremberg Laws 95

Oates, Len 166–167, 187n4
object 185–186; loved 186; mother as 188n12; psychoanalytic use of 188n12; Winnicott on 185, 188n12
Old Testament 39, 47–48, 50, 143
1 Corinthians: 7: 2–3 85; 7: 12–13 94; 11:9 82
1 Thessalonians 138
On the Apparel of Women (Tertullian) 84
oral tradition 174
Orbán, Viktor 187n8
Otto, Rudolph 8
ousia 174, 178, 187n9

pagans 17
Pagels, Elaine 111
pain 36–37; *see also* suffering
Palestine 59, 110
Palestinians 106
Parable of the Wicked Tenants 117
parturition envy 89
The Passion of the Christ 99
Paul 130; ascetical attitude 75; asexual life and unmarried state 83; either-or-splits 110; eschatological anxiety 138; Garden of Eden story and 63–64, 71, 82; glossolalia 111; image of Jesus 171–174; letter to the Romans 127; martyrdom 74–75; masochism and 69–73; misogyny 82; narcissistic needs 137–138; resurrection and 183; self-criticism 71; sin and 71–73, 155, 159–160; temporal lobe epilepsy (TLE) 141–142; visionary experience on road to Damascus 141–142, 173; vituperation 71; women and 82–83
Pauline letters 181
Pelagius 155
Penchansky, David 27, 42
Peter 122n3, 171
phallocentric theory 88
Pharaoh 28, 134
Philo of Alexandria 118
Phineas 31
pigs 94
Pilate 118
Plato: *Timaeus* 178
pollution 92; source of 93
polytheism 177
post-traumatic stress disorder 150
power 125–138; human relationships 129–130; narcissism *see* narcissism; psychodynamics 128–130
projection 113; of human judgment onto God 121–122
prophets: Heschel on 144–146; mental state 142–150; moral strictures 145; visionary state 144
Protestants 57, 62
Protevangelium of James 123n11
Proverbs 3: 12 74
Psalm 106 134
Psalms 42
psychologism 1, 4n1
purity/purification: moral 92; ritual *see* ritual purity

QAnon 33, 37n5
Quakers 108
quaternity 179–180

Rahner, Karl 137
Raitt, Jill 90–91
Ranke-Heinemann, Uta 16, 83–84
reader-response criticism of Bible 11
redemptive violence 31
Reich, Theodore 73–74
religion: as a balm for suffering 36–37; human psychodynamics 25–32; Jung on 24–25; nationalism and 106; non-realist approaches to 19–20; splitting 109–111

religious beliefs 32–36; attachment theorists 33; Devil 34–36; Freud on 32–33; Kohut on 33; mental health and 33; skeptical observers on 33
resurrection 33, 183–187; belief in 185; as continuation of consciousness 184; Gospel stories 183–185; psychological approaches 185–186; skeptics on 184–185
retribution 160
Ricoeur, Paul 11, 31
Riemer, J. 80
Riley, Greg 34
ritual purity 91–98; menstrual blood 92, 95–98
Robinson, H. Wheeler 149
Robinson, John 57
Rollins, Wayne 9, 11
Roman Catholic Church 7, 17; doctrines and dogmas 172; Jung's approach to spirituality and 8; menstruation and 96; political power of 17; Second Vatican Council 130
Roman period 34
Romans 171–172
Romans 5: 12–14 154–155
Romans 12: 9–21 173
Ross, Lee 116
Rubenstein, Richard 73, 78
Ruether, Rosemary 85
Russell, Bertrand 45

sacrifice/sacrificing 98–103; children 77–79
salvation 94, 105
Sanford, J. A. 66
Sargon 1 55
satisfaction theory of atonement 159–160
Saul, King 136
scapegoat/scapegoating 31–32
Schaer, Hans 4n1
Schept, Susan 61
schizophrenia 148
Schneerson, Menachem 115
Scholem, Gershom 114
Schonfield, Hugh 174
Schultz, Magdalene 119–120
Schwartz, Regina 105
Schweitzer, Albert 163
Second Coming of Jesus Christ 29, 35, 58, 68, 114, 117, 144, 184
Second Temple period 34
Second Vatican Council 130

Self 7, 20–22, 63; dark side 36; intrapsychic images 21, 36
self-induced hypnosis 143
selfobject 72–73
serpent: Garden of Eden story 64–67; menstrual blood and 96; as a symbol of the goddess 64–65
Sevi, Sabbatai 114–115
sexual customs 86
sexual immorality 157
sexual morality 157
Shadow of the Galilean (Theissen) 174
shame *see* guilt and shame
Shaw, Graham 138
Shiva (god) 90
Shlain, Leonard 86
sin 153–161; atonement 158–161; Christian theology 154–155; guilt and shame 153, 156–158; Hebrew Bible 155–156; intrinsic 155, 161; Paul and 71–73, 155, 159–160
slavery 25, 40, 49n4, 50, 83, 105, 133
social conspiracy theories 33
Southern Baptists 97
Spanish missionaries 107
spiritual abuse 158
Spiro, Melford 87
splitting 109–111
Stein, George 148
Stein, Murray 47
Stone, Merlin 65, 86
Strang, Veronica 104
Suarez-Orozco, M. M. 101
substitutionary atonement 161
suffering 36–37
Sumerian traditions 65
Sunday schools 113
supersessionism 113, 119
superstitions 103–104; *see also* magical thinking
Synoptic Gospels 168–170, 174
systematic blindness 8

Tacey, David 55–56, 184
Talmudic interpretations 14
Tarpley, Harold 89
Taves, Ann 167
Teeth 90
Tel Dan 68n1
temporal lobe epilepsy (TLE) 141–142, 149
Ten Commandments 135
terrorism 105
Tertullian 84

Theissen, Gerd 112; *Shadow of the Galilean* 174
Theodosius 127
therapeutic myth 67
Thus Spake Zarathustra (Nietzsche) 153
Timaeus (Plato) 178
TLE *see* temporal lobe epilepsy
Torah 14
transcendent reality 1
tribalism 95, 108–109
trinity 13, 174–180; Arian heresy 175–176; Council of Constantinople on 175–176; Council of Nicaea on 175; feminists on 176–177; Jung's account 178–180; male image of God 176; metaphysical implications 177; psychological model of 177; social model 177; as a symbol 179–180
2 Enoch 35
2 Kings: 3: 27 77; 6: 24–30 79

UFO 115
unconscious 2, 4; consciousness and 182; individuation process 182; mutual redemption 182; wholeness 179
Uzzah 28, 91

vagina dentata 89–91
van Bruggen, Jacob 70–71
vicarious atonement 160
Vindication of Married Life (Luther) 83
violence 26–29; Bible and 3–4; Christian scriptures 29–31; redemptive, myth of 31; religious 105–107; retaliatory 27–28; scapegoat complex 31–32
Virgin Birth 54
visionary experiences 185
visionary rumors 185
von Franz, M.-L. 15, 21, 40

Walker, Barbara 90
warfare 105
Weber, M. 165, 167
Weil, Simone 36
White, Victor 4n1
wholeness/completeness 179–180
Wilson, E.O. 108–109
Wink, Walter 31
Winnicott 88–89, 112, 129, 185, 188n12
women: discrimination and prejudice against 81–85; male fear of 87–91; menstruation 95–98; religious suppression of 85–91; vagina dentata 89–91
Wright, Jerry 48

xenophobia 95

Yhwh: being emotionally unstable 41; command to Abraham 42; dark side 42–43; female consort 52; good and evil 34; judgments 121, 134; as mass murderer 28–29; narcissistic vulnerability 41, 132–136; negative portrayals 27; as omnipotent 47; Penchansky on 42; Psalms on 42; sacrifice of firstborn 78; serpent and 65; suppression of women and worship of goddess 86–87; worship of 38; *see also* Hebrew Bible
Young, Frances 181
Yuki Indians 96

Zechariah 114, 171
Zechariah 14 114
Zeus 55
Zion 48
Zionist 106

For Product Safety Concerns and Information please contact our EU
representative GPSR@taylorandfrancis.com
Taylor & Francis Verlag GmbH, Kaufingerstraße 24, 80331 München, Germany

www.ingramcontent.com/pod-product-compliance
Lightning Source LLC
Chambersburg PA
CBHW061714300426
44115CB00014B/2681